How Vast is the Ocean

An Odyssey of Desperation and Hope

Paul Ryan

Copyright & Non-Fiction

The copyright of this work is held exclusively by the author Paul Ryan and may not be used in any way whatsoever without the author's prior written consent.

ISBN: 978-0-6453315-3-0

Acknowledgements

I owe a great deal to the help and encouragement I received from the members of our small but enthusiastic writing group – Jacky Martin, Jeremy Martin, Raynette Mitchell, and Trevour Armstron, the latter two being successful authors.

My sincere thanks to those beta readers who took the time to read the manuscript for *How Vast is the Ocean* and give valuable feedback – Steve Jackson, Karen Tarver, Liz Diggles, Cath Shaw, and Julie Parsons. Ian Hutchings used his considerable maritime experience to advise me on nautical aspects. In addition, I would like to thank Busy Bee Editing (www.busybeeediting.co.za) for their proofreading and editing of *How Vast is the Ocean*.

Paul Ryan
October 2023

Contents

Acknowledgements ii
With Hope in the Balance.. 1
Departure 22
Them Bloody Steam Trains...................................... 32
Frustration 44
Boarding 60
Leaving Ireland 81
The Troubles Start 96
Where the Butter Melts 114
Dire Straits 127
Cape Town 137
A Stretch Too Far 159
Hobart Town.. 178
The Last Leg and Hope on the Horizon.................. 192
Landed at Last... 212
Land to Call Their Own 227
Settling In.. 240
Epilogue 251
Author's Notes... 260
Voyage of Erin go Bragh from Queenstown............ 264
Track of the Erin go Bragh, Based on the Ship's Log ... 266

With Hope in the Balance

It was an evening in early December 1861 when Annie Ryan got up from a chair by the fire and shuffled on her arthritic knees to answer the knock on the door of her cottage in Kilclonfert, King's County. *Who in tarnation could that be, calling at this time of day?* she thought as she moved across to the door.

Now, Annie was as devout a Catholic as any seventy-one-year-old Irish woman could be, so there was a mixture of shock and wonder when she opened the door to find a black-clad priest on her doorstep in the gathering gloom. But this wasn't Father Murphy, her parish priest. It was a much better-attired and younger priest.

God in heaven, has someone died? was her first thought.

Then Annie recognised him as the priest who had addressed the congregation towards the end of mass at Saints Peter and Paul church two Sundays ago. His black overcoat was matched with a black, square biretta sitting firmly on his head with its three peaks and a tuft at the top. She noted that this priest's outfit was not in the shabby state of their local parish priest. His black boots had a shine only partially covered by mud from the street. He was somewhere in his late twenties and had a broad smile on his clean-shaven face that exuded confidence, while his posture displayed a certain vitality.

"Would I be addressing Mrs Ryan?" asked the priest.

"That you would, Father. Would you care to come inside out of this evening chill?"

"With pleasure, Mrs Ryan, but first, I should introduce myself. My name is Father Patrick Dunne," exclaimed the priest as he bent and came through the door.

As he removed his woollen overcoat, it could be seen that his black soutane had a glossy sheen and no evidence of wear, though it was evident that he had some garment under it to keep out the cold, making him appear bulkier than his natural slim self. The room was lit only by a candle on a rough wooden table and the glow of a slow-burning, smoky peat fire. As his eyes adjusted to the dim light with the smell and haze of peat smoke hanging in the air, Father Dunne noted the meagre state of the cottage and of the room's occupants. At the table, sitting on a straight wooden chair before the fire in the hearth, was a small and underweight woman with a large woollen shawl over her head and shoulders, enveloping her like a rug. There were also two older girls sitting at the table, darning some socks and stitching patches on already patched clothing, while on the stone floor, a young girl was playing with a rag doll.

As Father Dunne entered the dimly lit room, the woman at the table rose as did the two elder girls.

"You're very welcome, indeed, Father," said Annie, with a look on her face showing that she was somewhat in awe of this fancy-looking priest visiting them in their humble dwelling. "This here is my daughter-in-law, Jane Ryan; she being married to my son Edward, or Teddy as we likes to call him. He should be here soon from his work."

The priest nodded in Jane's direction, "I am pleased to meet you, Mrs Ryan, for it's you and your husband I've come to talk to."

"Then, these are Jane and Teddy's daughters, Anne and Maria," continued Annie, indicating the two older teenage women at the table. "And the young one on the floor is Teresa or Tessie. Please come and take a chair by the fire, and may I get you some hot tea to warm yourself?"

Father Dunne acknowledged the girls as he sat down and smiled at Annie. "That would be wonderful; thank you, Mrs Ryan."

At that moment, the door opened, letting in an icy gust of wind, along with a man of average height. His face, with stubble-covered cheeks and chin, showed the effects of hard work in the open for much of his fifty-one years. He looked like he could do with a good feed. An old, scruffy pair of thick flannel trousers and a rather threadbare Ulster overcoat hung loosely on his thin frame. On his head was a battered high-crowned hat while a scarf was wrapped tightly round his neck against the cold. Over his shoulder was a bag of potatoes, or praties as they were known, rejects from the farm that would have to suffice for the family's meals for a day or two.

"Ah, there you are, Teddy," exclaimed Annie. "This here is Father Dunne. You remember who talked to us at mass about there being a chance to go to Australia; when was it? Yes, two weeks ago. He came to pay us a visit."

Teddy surveyed the scene of the well-dressed priest seated at the table with Jane, his daughters, and Annie, busy preparing tea at the fireplace.

"You're very welcome, I'm sure, Father," he said respectfully. He would have liked to have asked the priest why he was calling on them, but having such an eminent person in the house made him tongue-tied.

Jane looked up as Teddy approached them all, giving him a weary smile. *He looks bone tired after a hard day, again, and all that work for a pittance, then having to walk home in the cold,* she thought.

Jane had her own burdens, being heavy with their eighth child, and her swollen belly contrasted with her slight frame and narrow face that also showed all of her forty years, the last twenty of which had seen her caring for her husband and children.

Teddy approached his wife, put his hands on her shoulders and kissed her head. Then, he looked expectantly at the priest.

Father Dunne had risen as Teddy came forward, and now he addressed him. "I am pleased to meet you, Teddy. As I said to your kind mother, I've come to talk with you and Jane."

The priest sat back at the table while Annie made some tea. "So, how are you all doing, Edward? I can see life is difficult for you. How did you survive the famine?"

"Well, to be sure, it's been hard, Father, there's no denying that, what with so many mouths to feed. I'd been a crofter since Jane and I were married some twenty-two years ago. But the famine meant we owed so much rent and had no means of paying. Then with the lean years that followed, it was difficult to grow enough to feed ourselves and buy some provisions for the family most years, with little left over to pay the monthly rent, let alone that which was owed from past years. Ole Baron Greene was patient and didn't evict us during them hard years, but when we couldn't meet what he was askin', last year, he told us we had to go, and he'd get somebody who could pay."

"At least you have a roof over your heads," volunteered Annie. "And glad I am that the Lord has spared me to be around to care for these homeless kin, though my husband has been dead and buried these last four years."

Teddy smiled at his mother and continued, "Both myself and my second son have some labouring work on the estate up the road while the eldest son works on the county roads. But the wages are poor, and if the crops fail, as they have this year, Andrew and I could well be out of work. So, what's to be done then? We've little enough money to buy food, and the chances of getting another crofter tenancy are as likely as hell freezing over."

"Ah, Edward, that's a sad tale you're telling. God bless you for trying as you did and caring for your wife and little ones. But I haven't come here to commiserate with you. I've come with a proposal that may give you a chance at a new and better life."

"You'd be talkin' about this goin' on some ship to Australia, would you, Father?" said Jane sceptically as she moved to make herself more comfortable, wrapping her shawl tighter around her small frame. Despite the fire, the room had a damp chill, with draughts coming through cracks in poorly aligned doors and windows.

"Indeed, I am," replied the priest as he accepted a mug of hot tea from Annie and held it cupped in his hands to take in the warmth. "I saw that you, Edward and Jane, had put your names down to be considered. So, I've come to tell you that you, as a family, are being offered a passage on a ship to Queensland in Australia."

It took a while for Edward and Jane to fully register what Father Dunne was proposing. It was Teddy who broke the silence.

"Are you serious, Father? A passage to Australia for me, Jane and the children? It is awful hard to take in, Father. You haven't just come from O'Rafferty's Pub, have you? He's got a mighty strong poteen that could addle anyone's brain with just a glass."

"No, Edward. It's the truth. There's a Bishop James Quinn in Brisbane, in the new colony of Queensland. He's a Dublin man, but we won't hold that against him. In fact, as a young priest, he helped many suffering the cholera after the Great Famine. Then he was the chaplain to the Sisters of Mercy when their house was founded, and he supported them when they went to help the soldiers with Florence Nightingale at Scutari in the Crimea. Because of all this work, the powers that be made Father Quinn a bishop two years ago and sent him off to the colony of Queensland that had only been formed that year.

"Now, once he arrived, he saw how there was a great need for people to do all sorts of work. At the same time, the Government of Queensland was in dire need of settlers to farm the land. Bishop Quinn knows how desperate times have been for so many in Ireland, with many on the point of starvation. He has been determined to help these fellow Irish and is organising to transport Irish families and others who wish to emigrate. So, Edward and Jane, would you like to sail on one of the first of these ships and become a farmer out there in this new colony?"

"Well now," said Jane, "that's very welcome and good news, Father. But how are we expected to pay for this passage out to this Brisbane in Australia? We haven't enough to buy decent clothes for the children or eat a good meal."

"Jane, Bishop Quinn has set up an organisation called the Queensland Immigration Society to help bring bog-poor Irish out to a better home. Many Irish in Queensland have also helped by contributing money to the Society. And I'm helping to organise as many such Irish from around the Tullamore area to accept this passage.

"Many families have been evicted from the Geashill estate not far from here, and there''s many worse off than yourselves, plus there are others in towns like Tullamore who are anxious for a better life."

Teddy looked at the father, who then explained that the Government of Queensland, which was on the east coast of Australia, north of Sydney, was anxious to get farmers to move to the colony and start farming. Too much of the land was being taken up by pastoralists. So, they were offering what were called land orders to the value of eighteen pounds for any person coming to Queensland or to the persons who would assist immigrant farmers to come, such as this Queensland Immigration Society. With this money, the Society would be able to purchase the passage for people like themselves in Ireland.

"Bishop Quinn knows that you and the others being asked to go on this trip are but poor crofters or lucky to have a labouring job, with hardly a penny to spare, and that is why he set up this Immigration Society," explained Father Dunne. "Though if you can afford to contribute, we're asking that you put in something, like six or eight pounds towards your fares; and I should tell you that it is not only the poor Irish who can be benefited by the Society but anyone from the British Isles, whether they be Catholic or not."

"Well, we might be able to come up with a few pounds towards the trip, Father. Perhaps John will agree to part with some of his wages going towards it," said Teddy.

"And when would we be expecting to start on this voyage to the other side of the world?" asked Jane.

"The first ship is being arranged, and they plan for it to leave early next year. When I know for sure, I shall let you know."

"How do we get from here to where the ship is sailing? And where would that be, Father?"

"I believe the ship will sail from Queenstown[1], near Cork."

"That is over a hundred miles from here, husband, and who will pay for us all to get to Cork when we no longer have a cart with a horse? You always were a dreamer, Teddy, but now we need to be practical. I'm not against going to start up in some distant foreign land, where there's probably still savages likely to try and spear us all, but we need to think how we'll do it and what it means."

Father Dunne answered in a low voice, "You're right to be concerned about the particulars, Jane. The details will be worked out by the diocese here and myself, but it seems to me the best way to get to Cork is to get on a train belonging to the Great Southern and Western Railway at Tullamore, and that will take you quickly down to Cork. I am sure we can organise transport for you and others from here to meet the train, which is only seven miles from Kilclonfert."

Jane objected strenuously, "There is no way you are getting me on that steam thing on rails. It travels too fast, is unsafe, and you get covered in coal soot and smoke

---

[1] Known as Queenstown from 1849 to 1920 it was otherwise called Cobh.

while sitting in them open carriages us poor folk have to travel in."

"Well, the alternative will be a long trip by horse and cart and having to stop and find shelter for the night along the way," said Teddy, who was not to be put off by his wife's objections.

"If that's how it must be, then I'd rather take my chances with the horse and cart. At least one can control the horse, which, like as not, they're not sure about doing with that engine thing, billowing smoke and steam and rattling along at speeds as fast as a horse can gallop, and you know what I think about galloping on horses. And, another thing, Teddy Ryan, how are we going to buy land and set up a farm when we've hardly enough to feed ourselves?"

At this, the priest intervened. "There'll be money from the land orders I told you about to help you get started. In addition, after you have been farming for two years, I understand that the Queensland Government will provide another land order to the value of twelve pounds for every adult who has settled from overseas. Two children between the age of four and fourteen count as one adult. That means you could get quite a sum of money, enough to buy land, some tools and maybe even some animals like a horse or cow."

"It all seems too good to be true. Is this Queensland Government so charitable they will pay out so much for nothing?" mused Teddy.

"No, it's true all right," replied Father Dunne. "They need farmers to settle and farm the land, and there is an awful lot of land to settle. So, do I take it you still wish to be included amongst these immigrants, Jane and Edward?"

Teddy looked at Jane, who nodded. "Well, despite my concerns, I know the Blessed Virgin and St. Bridgit will look after us, so, yes, Teddy, let's take the children and try our luck in this Queensland. It can hardly be worse than here now, with no land to farm and precious little to earn from our labour work."

"I agree, Father," said Edward. "I feel we have to take a chance on a new life like so many others who mainly went to America before the war broke out there."

"Very well, I shall put you and your family down as passengers on this first ship. When more information is at hand, I will let you know. Now, I must leave you as I have others to whom I must break the same news."

After the priest had left, Teddy sat down wearily and looked at Jane, his eyes saying what his heart and mind felt. *How were they going to manage if life continued as it was, and with another child on the way?* He and Jane had been through much together, and it was usually Jane who was the sensible, no-nonsense one with a sharp tongue. Teddy was more of a dreamer and easy-going, although his stubbornness had helped him endure much hardship and still provide for and love his family. A strong bond and affection existed between Teddy and Jane, although their present plight was putting that to the test.

He did not want this existence for his family, sharing this small house with his mother in the village of Kilclonfert in Kings County. Life had been somewhat easier as a crofter leasing land from Baron Greene, not far from Kilclonfert. There they had some forty acres and, in good years, were able to grow praties, corn and oats, plus they kept a few pigs and a couple of cows.

They sold some of the oats, corn and pork to get provisions such as flour, tea and sugar, plus some clothes. The Irish loved their tea, even those in the poorer rural areas, and there always had to be a good amount of sugar to go into the cup. A good cuppa tea was often the solution to many a problem or bad news. This was something that had changed in the years since the end of the potato famine, with many rural families buying foodstuffs from stores rather than being totally subsistent on their farm produce.

The Ryans had lived in a sturdy stone and thatch crofter's house and were usually able to keep body and soul together with what they produced, but life became very hard with the onset of the Great Hunger in 1845 caused by the potato blight. For six years, they had struggled with barely enough to eat much of the time, although their oats, pigs and cows enabled them to survive the lack of praties. By 1852, despite the famine having officially ended, matters were still desperate for Teddy and his family, and he had been caught stealing praties to help feed the family. Arraigned to appear at the quarter sessions, he was lucky to find a realistic and understanding magistrate, so he was only fined a few shillings.

Teddy had obtained the lease over the land some twenty years earlier. But it was a short-term lease, the usual Irish practice, so there was always a degree of insecurity. However, particularly during and after the famine, their income was low or non-existent, and Teddy's rent was in arrears for several years. Baron Greene had been lenient, unlike many landlords who had no charity when it came to evicting the thousands of Irish families unable to pay their rents during the famine. One of the most notorious of these was Major Mahon in County Roscommon. Then in more recent years, the new Baron Digby on Geashill Estate, just down the road from Kilclonfert, had set about evicting rent-delinquent crofters.

Teddy managed to keep his land during the famine and somewhat improved the farm's income from 1853. However, the famine had drained their resources, and there had been several years of poor weather – very wet in 1852 and 1853 and then arid conditions throughout 1857. Crops failed, yields were poor, and income was scarce; with not enough to pay off the arrears in rent, let alone the current rent. Then in 1859, the potato blight returned, and the Ryan family's situation became more desperate. By 1860, with the blight continuing, Baron Greene's patience expired with his need to obtain income. Teddy and his family were evicted from the farm and home where they had lived for over twenty years. It was a bitter pill to swallow.

They had been fortunate that they had been able to move in with Teddy's mother, who was now seventy years old and living on her own in Kilclonfert. They were cramped in the small stone and thatched house, but at least they had a roof over their heads. Teddy had been able to sell their cows and pigs, giving them a few pounds. He and Andrew had then found work as labourers on nearby estates.

John had earlier got himself a job working on the county roads to help with the family's income. By 1800, Ireland had a very good network of roads, focusing mainly on market towns. Although he had been working as a labourer, John found the job suited him and he gained considerable experience in the maintenance of the roads and repairing of bridges. Most roads were macadamized, using crushed stone of various sizes laid on a slight convex surface to facilitate drainage.

The last months of 1861 were hard, with the winter cold coming early. Labouring work in the estates was not constant, so the family income often relied on John's more stable income from his road and bridge work. Then, at Sunday mass in late November, this well-dressed priest had addressed them at the end of the mass. He had explained that the Catholic diocese in a place called Brisbane in Australia was organising for Irish people to migrate to Queensland, where Brisbane was located. He said his name was Father Dunne and that the bishop of Brisbane, a good Irishman by the name of Quinn, had asked him to arrange for a ship to carry the migrants and to offer passages on the ship.

There was much talk among the parishioners after mass, with many saying they thought it would be a great opportunity, although some suggested that Father Dunne had a touch of the Blarney and that there had to be a catch somewhere. There were many questions, but the parishioners had been told that if they were interested, they could give their names and addresses to the parish priest, and Father Dunne or someone else would be in touch.

Teddy had talked it over with Jane and the older children when they returned home. Then he had put their names down, partly to be in the running to get on the migrant ship and partly to find out more about the voyage out and what to expect in Queensland, although, like so much in his life in recent years, he hadn't held out much hope that they would be selected.

Now, after Father Dunne's visit, he posed the question to Jane. "So, what do you really feel about moving to Australia, my love? I know it will be a big change, and there are many things I am not certain about, but the offer seems like a good one. Wouldn't it be grand, Jane, to leave this sorry existence here and start anew with our land to farm, which is more than we could ever hope for here?"

"It does sound like a grand scheme, Teddy, and I can see you have a mind to go, but just stop and think for a minute. It is a mighty long way to be sailing in a ship to the other side of the world and us with the young children to care for and another on the way, although the older ones can no doubt help with the care."

Jane turned and directed her two older daughters to start preparing their meagre supper. Teddy's mother had some bacon given to her by one of her parish friends, which would be combined with a couple of turnips and some of the praties Teddy had just brought home. She turned back to Teddy.

"You're right about one thing, husband. There are many uncertainties. Like what will the land be like? Will it be any good for growing something worthwhile, and what will that something be? I pray to God that it is more than praties; And it's an English colony, so how will they treat the Irish there? We will need a house to live in, so how do we get that or build it? And all the while, there's the children, or at least the five younger ones who need to be fed and cared for."

"Yes, I hear you, Jane Ryan, and I don't have answers to your questions, and maybe even Father Dunne can't answer too many of them. But I feel we should go because staying here seems to have little to offer in the future for myself or our boys, and I'm also sick of rotten praties."

Not long after, there was a commotion at the door as the two older sons came in, arguing. "I tell you, he is trying to cheat me!" exclaimed Andrew, the more hot-headed of the two.

"That's as may be," said John, "but you can't go and upset the gamekeeper when you need the work and the money it brings."

They saw Jane and Edward sitting at their rough wooden table, and John apologised. "I'm sorry for the suaitheadh, Mother. Andrew feels the gamekeeper has cheated him out of some earnings for the fencing he did last week, and it's likely he has been, as the man is a vile, rotten, Sasanach."

"Well, you may not have to put up with the thieving bastard for much longer. Come and sit while your mother and I tell you of some news that we have had."

The boys moved to the small double bed that was part of the kitchen and living area and sat looking at their parents expectantly. "Well, how would you like to set up a new home in Australia?" Teddy said, smiling.

The jaws of both young men dropped, with Andrew exclaiming, "What did you say, Father?"

"We've just had a visit from a Father Dunne. He told us about the government in this new colony of Queensland in Australia, who are looking for farmers to settle on the land there. It seems the local Catholic diocese has some scheme to pay the passages for a boatload or two of Irish and others to go and do some farming. There's a ship leaving Queenstown early next year, and your mother and I have agreed that we would like to be on it with all of you!"

"Why, that's truly grand news, Father! I agree. I think we should go," said Andrew. "There's nought to keep us here, particularly since we lost our crofter's land, and you and I have to fend as best we can as labourers, and we can't be sure of that work if the harvests are poor. With the heavier than usual rains this summer and half the praties rotten, it will be a hard winter again. Having the opportunity to own our land in a place that is likely warmer and with less rain than here would be a grand deal, Father. And there's got to be all sorts of ways of earning extra money in a colony that is just starting out."

"So, where is this Queensland, and what sort of land would we be getting?" asked John. "Would we be crofters there as well and beholden to some almighty English landlord? After all, it is an English colony, is it not?. And what would we be growing there?"

"All I can tell you is that Queensland is on the east coast of Australia, north of Sydney. I don't know what sort of land it will be, but if they're looking for farmers to settle on it, it should be somewhat good for farming, And, from what the father says we would have a chance to own land ourselves, with money initially contributed by the government and this Immigration Society."

"It certainly sounds like a good chance to better ourselves," said John, "and not just by farming. There should be all sorts of chances for someone to earn a good living in other ways if it's a new colony. How long will the voyage take to this Queensland?"

"We go to a place called Brisbane, which seems to be the main town there, and from what I have heard from those who know someone who has gone out to Australia already, the voyage could take maybe four months," replied Teddy.

"That's a long time to be at sea, and us with the younger ones and a babe in arms," mused John.

"Aye, I am sore afraid myself," said Jane. "You hear these fearful stories of shipwrecks and drownings. It almost seems unnatural for us to be sailing on the ocean when we're better off walking on the land with our two feet."

"I can't imagine what it will be like," replied Teddy. "I've never seen the sea let alone sailed on it. There's a part of me that is scared to death of what it will be like. But God willing, and with help from both of you, we can make it. After all, I hear of all these other people who have made it, so why not us?"

****

The days passed, and December progressed, and so did the rain, which had increased again. It was a cold rain with chilly blasts of wind that snuck in through the cracks around the door of their house. Inside, the peat fire provided some warmth, though no real light, and so the family's existence was a miserable one, lived in a dim and smoky atmosphere. The thought of moving somewhere warmer was like a shining beacon beckoning them to a more comfortable harbour.

There was little joy over Christmas. Teddy and Jane once again felt frustration and guilt that they could not provide more cheer for the children, particularly the younger ones. There was no special Christmas dinner, except that John had managed to buy a chicken, which they roasted in a heavy iron Dutch oven. Andrew had also managed to get some extra bacon from the estate where he worked. Both parents didn't ask him how he came by it.

Teddy tried to bring some cheer into the household by telling Christmas stories to the younger children while Jane busied herself knitting a woollen sweater for Tessie.

It was while Teddy and Jane were sitting with Teddy's mother contemplating what the New Year might bring that there was a knock on the door, which opened to reveal a rather sodden and chilled Father Dunne.

"You're very welcome, Father. Come and sit by the fire to take the chill from your bones," said Jane.

"Tis a wet and windy day out there, indeed," volunteered the priest. "So, how are you both and how's the family?"

"As you'd be asking, Father, Jane and I have been sitting here trying to think what the New Year is going to bring us, what with the prospect of now travelling to Australia and Jane about to give birth in the next few days. That's another trial to contend with, though, hopefully, a joyful one. But what brings you here on this godforsaken day, though I;m forgetting you'd be more than likely bringing Him with you?"

"I have some more news for you about your passage out to Australia. It has been a busy time working to organise passage for all the displaced crofters and their families around Tullamore. Word has now come through that a ship has been arranged, and it is due to leave Queenstown on the 25th of January. Many others will also be travelling from hereabouts, as many as three hundred people from around the Tullamore area. So, we shall be organising a train to take us from Tullamore to Cork on the 23rd of January."

At this, Jane again voiced her opposition to taking a train.

"Now I understand your concerns, Jane, but this will be the best way to get so many people down to Queenstown on time to catch the boat. I am also organising that there be some enclosed carriages as part of the train. These will take women with small children so they are better protected from the wind, rain and smoke."

Jane seemed somewhat mollified but raised the question, "How will we get from here to Tullamore, Father? That's nigh on seven miles."

"This will have to be a group effort, but I will help as much as I can. I would be grateful if you know of people who would loan or even rent wagons. Because that is how we will all have to get to Tullamore."

Jane and Teddy absorbed what Father Dunne had told them and what it would mean for them. As usual, it was Jane who voiced her concerns first.

"This news is so hard to take in, Father. And it will all start happening in less than four weeks. My mind is in turmoil about what must be done to prepare, but also about how we will fare on such a long sea voyage and what we will find at the other end. I've heard that it can take four months to get to Brisbane and all that time at sea. That's a fearful long time, and there'll likely be storms, making life difficult or even dangerous. You hear about ships being lost at sea, and I just think it would be a tragedy. I couldn't bear having our children lost at sea and so far from home."

"Jane, I am not saying this will be an easy voyage, and it is a long time to be on board a ship, particularly with young ones. Conditions will be cramped on board, with little room around bunk beds down in the 'tween deck. Voyages at sea can be dangerous, but this is a sturdy and large ship being over eleven hundred tons, and I understand the captain is very experienced with long voyages."

"Does this ship have a name, Father?" asked Teddy.

"Aye, that it does, Edward. It's called the *Erin go Bragh*. Now isn't that a grand name for a ship on which you'll be sailing to a new and better life? It used to be called the *Florida,* and it has spent some time carrying your fellow Irish to America."

"Ah, that might be a grand name for a ship that'll be carrying a host of Irish folk. But a nice name doesn't mean it's a good ship," said Jane. "So, what do we do about feeding ourselves, Father?" continued Jane. "Do we need to bring our own food, which will be mighty hard to do for nine mouths to feed over four months?"

"As part of your passage, food will be provided on the ship, although I'm not sure how much and how good that food will be. So, I'd be taking as much food as you can to supplement what will be provided, particularly some food that will last a while, like preserves.

"Now, there are a few things I need to explain about the voyage, apart from taking what food you can. I told you the Queensland Immigration Society would be paying for your passage. These land orders that the government of Queensland is issuing are one for every statute adult. That means anyone over the age of fourteen. Then two children between the age of four and fourteen are counted as one statute adult. That means that your four youngest children will count as two adults for two fares and they will have to share ttwo bunks."

"What about the baby that's due at any moment?" asked Teddy.

"I'm afraid the baby doesn't count for a fare, so it will have to sleep with one of the adults, although you may be able to take a cot on board. It also won't eat adult food to any extent before you arrive in Queensland."

"I suppose we should be grateful that we have a passage paid for most of us. But already I'm starting to hear of difficulties, and we haven't even started out!" exclaimed Jane.

"One other thing," continued the priest. "When you get to Queensland and are making your way, the Society expects that you will repay the amount of the land order for each adult plus a donation. This is so passages can be paid on another ship for more immigrants from Ireland to come to Queensland."

"Here we go again,' exclaimed Teddy wearily as he looked across at Jane. "We are going from one situation where landlords demand rent money when we haven't enough to feed and clothe ourselves to another where we have to pay a good amount when we don't even know how we'll do with any farming we undertake. I don't know, Father. Is it really worth it and going to be better out there after making such a long and tiresome voyage?"

"Perhaps it seems a lot to be asking when you haven't even left here, but the main thing is that you all have passages out to Queensland, and there's every chance you will fare much better there than here. You will have a chance to own your own acreage, and it's a developing colony, so there'll doubtless be many opportunities to make a decent living and more. And don't go fretting too much, Edward. We're here to help you make it to a new life, not to put extra burdens on you and your family.

"I'll let you know about the final arrangements for getting down to Tullamore in the next week or so," said Father Dunne as he rose to go. "What I can tell you is that you need to bring what bedding you can as well as pots, pans, plates, dishes, knives, and spoons to serve you on board the ship, as I don't know how well set up the accommodation will be on board, although I suspect it will be very rudimentary. These are also likely to be needed when you start life in Queensland."

"This is going to be a long and difficult journey, Father. I can feel it in my bones," said Jane, with a tired expression. "Why, even getting down to Cork and Queenstown will be mighty hard, what with the young ones and all."

"Now, don't you be quitting on us now, my love. We need to be prepared for it to be hard, but may God, in His mercy and goodness, make it lighter than we expect; let's not forget what lies at the other end of the journey. It should be a grand new beginning, and we will be more the masters of our fate than what we are here."

"You're right, Teddy, and sometimes, I wish I had your dreaming visions to keep me going, but then I think of all that needs to be done in getting there and what needs to be planned and the hardships and things that could go wrong, but we will put our trust in God, Father. Sometimes that's all we can do."

"God bless you, Jane, for your faith," nodded the father. "With that and Teddy's future dreams, I am sure you will all make it and prosper."

"Prosper, Father? Now that's something that I would dearly love to do. And it's hoping that 'twill keep us going," exclaimed Teddy.

He was to find that patience would also be in heavy demand even before they boarded their ship.

****

Two days later, Jane went into labour and delivered a healthy boy with the help of a local midwife. It was not a difficult delivery. As the midwife remarked when she presented Teddy with the new babe, "Short and to the point, though, which is all to the good as she don't have a lot of strength, the poor dear. She'll take a while to regain her strength," referring to Jane, who lay grey and exhausted in their double bed. "A few good meals would help, although I know that's hard, given your circumstances."

As Teddy held this new addition to his already large family in his arms, his mind was in turmoil. On the one hand, he could not help loving and welcoming his baby son. At the same time, he was almost panicking, wondering how he would care for this babe as well as Jane and the other young ones. Then, there was the unknown, with their departure on a long voyage to a strange new land only three weeks away. "God, the angels and saints help us and care for us all," he murmured softly.

Departure

In early January, the rains abated somewhat, though the weather turned cold, with the mud freezing solid. A thin layer of snow coated everything white, providing a lightened relief from the otherwise drab winter greyness. The Ryan family set about preparing for their departure. Jane and Teddy's mother, Annie, put their heads together to think of what foodstuffs they could take on the voyage. They used their spare cash, including contributions from John and Andrew's wages, to buy bags of rolled oats, a large container of tea, and sugar.

"I'll see if I can convince ole Murphy, the butcher, to let us have some blood or white pudding in a couple of weeks. That should last a while," suggested Annie. "And I'll set about making some boxty closer to when you're going." The traditional Irish potato cakes would provide sustenance when they couldn't light a fire to cook.

Several crofter families in and around Kilclonfert and neighbouring towns were also preparing to head to Australia on the same ship in late January. They were a close-knit community of crofters, and many a time, they had acted together to support each other. Being tenant farmers, often with small plots and a landlord they didn't trust, they shared much in common. Many had now been evicted from their holdings and were seeking a decent living or at least sufficient to put food on the table and clothes on their families' backs. Some, though, were emigrating who had managed to keep their land and were still farming. As a group, they had banded together to sell whatever surplus crops they had, mainly potatoes, turnips, wheat and corn, to get a better deal from the buyers in the markets. Now, they discussed how they could support each other, particularly those who were not farming.

After Teddy and Jane first talked with Father Dunne, they met some other emigrant crofters in the local church hall to see how best they could manage their journey to Tullamore and then on board the ship taking them to Queensland. Father Dunne and the local parish priest had assisted by appealing during Sunday mass for any who could help their fellow Irish Catholics to set up a new home in Australia to kindly do so. Some families had carts and horses, while others knew relatives or friends who were prepared to lend them horses and carts and a driver for the trip to Tullamore.

Of course, when they got together, there was much talk about the trip to Australia and what it would be like in that distant land, often with a jug or two of local moonshine to aid and fortify the discussion. Flanigan from down the road had it on good authority that the voyage out there was mighty rough, the food on board was worse than hog feed, and the local militia in Australia was dead set against the Irish. He said this came from a cousin in New South Wales, who had already made the trip, although not of his own volition, after stealing one of his landlord's pigs to get a bit of bacon for his family.

Jimmy Duffy would swear on his mother's grave that he'd heard from a friend of a friend of a man who had gone out to the colony of Victoria that there was so much gold to be found that it would make a man and his family rich for life after just a year of digging. As far as he was concerned, he wasn't going farming. He was going to get to those gold fields and make his fortune, although he wasn't sure how far Victoria was from the new colony of Queensland.

"You're right there, Jimmy boy," shouted John Kelly, always a bit of a rabble-rouser.

However, Teddy was having none of this talk about searching for gold. It might be all right if you didn't have a large family to consider. In this, he was supported by two of his close neighbours and friends, Tony Molloy and John Gavan. The three had agreed that they would help each other get to Tullamore. Tony had a wagon that could be covered, and Teddy was good friends with John O'Neil, the landlord of O'Neil's Pub in Tullamore. He had a large wagon he used for transporting his beer supplies and had agreed to allow his son Patrick to collect the families and take them to the train at Tullamore. The alternative was for them to walk the seven or so miles, but that would be very hard on Jane, with baby Peter and the young ones to look after.

As January progressed and the departure date approached, the excitement in the Ryan household increased, and so did Jane's bad temper. "We've gotta have more bedding for on board this ship," she pestered Teddy.

"So, where do you think I can get that, woman? It's not like we've got the money to buy it. Do you expect me to steal it?"

"I don't know, Teddy, but you, Andrew and John have to beg, borrow or even steal it, maybe from the manor. Then we've gotta prepare the food we're taking' for the trip."

Jane seemed to have regained much of her feisty self following the birth of Peter, although she was still looking wane and malnourished. Nevertheless, despite her condition and small size, her grey eyes reflected a steely resolve, while her methodical mind considered what needed to be done.

What would they need before boarding the ship, and then what would the food be like, and how much would there be? It would be best to plan to take as much as they could on board, although it might not last long, she thought.

Looking up at Teddy, she gave her orders. "Stop your talking and carousing with the lads, Teddy Ryan, and get to work finding us some supplies," she demanded.

"Oh, stop your fretting, Jane, love. We'll get it sorted out. Don't you worry," was Teddy's comeback. He was used to Jane's bossy nature and knew she had a better head than he had for this sort of organising and planning.

"While talking and carousing with the boys, we have organised some carts to carry us to Tullamore, and a number of those still holding land, but coming with us, are putting together whatever spare crops, like praties and oats, they have so that we can share these amongst those without farms."

Jane looked at him with a frustrated expression and snorted, "Yes, well, that's all very good, but how many praties and other crops do we get? We also need to buy more tea and sugar."

****

Father Dunne paid them another visit ten days before they were due to depart. He said there were over fifty families, plus some single men and women making the trip from the Tullamore area, including some people from Tullamore itself. As it was important for everyone to be at Tullamore Station on time to catch the train on the morning of the 23rd of January, he felt it would be best if all the families and individuals making the trip met up and spent the night near Tullamore.

"I've arranged with the estate just north of Tullamore for you to camp there," he said. "So, if you could arrange to make your way down to the estate by the afternoon of Wednesday the 22^{nd,} that would be grand. Then we can be ready to board the train, which is due to leave at half past seven on the following day."

"When you say 'we,' Father, does that mean you are coming with us?" asked John, who was lounging on a chair at the table.

"That I am, John. All the way to Brisbane. You're my flock now, and I need to make sure you all make it while providing pastoral care."

****

The departure date was only two days away when they had another visit from Father Dunne. It was a blustery and wet day as the priest knocked on their door and came in with raindrops dripping all over the stone floor. He was in more of a hurry this time and didn't stop to chat for long. But his message left the family with more misgivings and feeling somewhat let down.

"This stormy weather has created problems with our ship. It was due to have left Liverpool yesterday, but storms and winds have kept it in port. However, they are planning on leaving by the 24th. That's in three days, and if all goes well, they'll be in Queenstown by the 27th. That means we could sail on the 28th or 29th of January."

"So, what does that mean for us leaving Tullamore this Thursday?" asked John, who was sitting whittling away on a piece of wood.

"I have sent a telegraph message to the railway company and reorganised our train to leave on Monday the 27th," replied the priest. "You will need to be ready to leave here on the $26^{th,}$ and we'll overnight near Tullamore to catch the train early in the morning, which should then get us to Cork by early afternoon."

Somehow, by the new eve of their departure, all was mostly in order. Patrick O'Neil would arrive with the wagon the next morning. Most of their belongings had already been placed in a pile, ready to be loaded the next day. In addition to their own supplies and belongings, there were also some from the Gavan family, who had divided themselves and their goods between the Ryan's wagon and one belonging to Tony Molloy.

It had been raining relentlessly during the day, with strong winds pushing dark grey clouds across the sky.

Now, in the soft afternoon light, after the rain and wind had eased, Teddy walked out of the town to the south. By the roadside, he stood and gazed across the undulating countryside with stone fences marking crofter boundaries. Crofter farming had been the only life he had known from childhood. It had been a hard life, but somehow, they had managed. There had been shelter and warmth and usually enough to eat.

Then came the the evictions. Their security, such as it was, had vanished overnight, and he had been plunged into despair, not knowing how he would feed and clothe Jane and the children. Thank God his mother was able to shelter them in her small house, crowded though they were. He said a silent prayer, thanking God for the opportunity to make a new start, although he sensed there would be many hardships to face before they could start afresh in Queensland.

Standing in the muddy street outside his mother's house, he thought, *There's not much we're taking to start a new life.* There were a few clothes, some pots and pans, knives and spoons, and some personal items, like Tessie's doll, Jane's missal, and a jug of whiskey that Teddy felt might be needed when the going got hard. Their bedding, Peter's cot, and some last items would be assembled in the morning. He wondered, again, if this was all a foolish venture and they were leaving his mother behind. She had refused to be considered for a passage, saying she was too old to start a new life. Besides, she was doing just fine, and when the time came, she would be buried next to her beloved husband, Billy.

Then the cold wind made him shiver, and his resolve strengthened as he thought of their current plight and what the future held here. The chances were good that life would be better in Queensland, and at least it should be warmer. *It's the right thing to do. I know Jane is for it, despite her grumbling, and with her, somehow we'll make it*, which thought gave him a deep feeling of warmth to his core. *Yes, with Jane, we will succeed and prosper in Queensland.*

And with that, he went inside to find Jane stirring stew in a pot on the fire. He came up behind her and put his arms around her. She struggled to free herself, complaining, "You'll upset dinner, Teddy. Now let me go," but her voice had a softness to it, and there was a half-smile on her face.

I love you, Jane Ryan, although you can be one of the most cantankerous women I know."

"Oh, and how many women would that be that you know, Teddy Ryan? Now get out of my way and let me get the supper on the table, or we'll all be starving before we start out tomorrow."

****

The next morning, after dawn, the family assembled the last of their belongings for the journey, including food that Jane had prepared. Patrick O'Neil arrived with the wagon later in the morning, and Teddy and the older sons loaded it with their various bundles, bags and boxes. Then, all was ready. Teddy said a last goodbye to his mother, knowing he would not see her again in this life. There were tears in his eyes as he hugged her, although she gruffly told him to get on with starting a new life, saying she had cared for herself, his father, and his siblings, so she didn't see a problem with caring for herself now.

The men wore caped Ulster coats with scarves, and Teddy had his high-crowned stovepipe hat pulled low over his ears. Like the rest of his apparel, it had seen better days. They helped the others climb onto the wagon, arranging bundles and bags to make themselves comfortable. Jane, her face pinched with cold and fatigue, wore a large woollen shawl over her head and shoulders as she sat holding baby Peter. Next to her, Tessie snuggled up with her doll, to whom she was explaining that they were going on a long trip across an ocean, which had an awful lot of water, much more than the pond down at the end of the lane. As they prepared to leave, another wagon came down the street and Mary Gavan, together with two of her small daughters got down and walked over to join Jane and the others in their cart.

Teddy hoisted himself up to sit beside Patrick O'Neil. Then, after a last loving look at his mother, he turned to face the road. "Let's go, Patrick. We have a ship to catch to Australia."

Patrick flicked his whip at the solid-looking hindquarters of the two Clydesdale horses, and they moved off along the frozen, muddy road. The two elder Ryan boys walked beside the cart as it moved at a leisurely pace.

The Ryan's wagon made its way south-west ward down the road towards Tullamore and was joined by others making the same journey. As the day progressed, grey clouds gathered to the west and by the afternoon they had hidden the sun. The wind had picked up, and a light rain fell shortly after.

It was mid-afternoon as the Ryan's wagon approached Tullamore, having been joined by many other wagons and families pushing carts, while some just carried whatever belongings they had. It was with some relief that they spied Father Dunne on the side of the road just north of the town. He was wearing his heavy black overcoat and biretta, directing wagons down a side road to a large, grassed field that was reasonably dry. Then, while there was still some light under the low clouds, the families set about making a camp for the night and preparing an evening meal.

Once they had halted, Jane left baby Peter in the care of twelve-year-old Catherine and, pulling her shawl around her, proceeded to organise a fire to be lit and dinner prepared. The family worked as a team as they had often done at home. Teddy and the two older boys erected a makeshift shelter with some spare canvas Patrick O'Brien had kindly thought to bring along.

Despite the cold rain and wind, there was a jovial atmosphere with a sense of anticipation and adventure among the campers. Teddy started lighting a fire from some dry wood he had thought to bring with them and set up a tripod and stand to heat their food while other families did the same. Jane had had the foresight to bring a good mutton stew, which she now ladled out of a large pot into another to be heated on the fire that was burning well. Then, the Ryan and Gavan families shared the shelter and the fire as they ate dinner.

As they were eating, Father Dunne appeared out of the surrounding gloom. "And how are you all fairing? Staying dry at least, and that stew smells good."

"Would you like some, Father?" asked Teddy. "Here, John and Andrew, let the father in by the fire."

"That would be wonderful, but just a small portion as I must move around to the other travellers," said the priest as he gratefully moved close to the fire and accepted a bowl of stew.

While he ate, Father Dunne explained the plan for the following day. The train to carry the emigrants was due at the Tullamore Station at seven-thirty. It was not far into Tullamore and the station, but they should all be there well before seven-thirty and gather by the railway tracks with their belongings and luggage for the trip. Father Dunne said they should all be on the move well before sunrise to achieve this.

"How long will it take us to get to Cork?" asked Jane. "It's an awful long way, and it will take a wagon maybe four days or more."

"Well, I am told that if we leave Tullamore by early morning, we should be in Cork by mid-afternoon."

"Mother of God, but how can it get there so fast!" exclaimed Jane. "This train must be going at some unnatural speed. I am sure God never intended us to travel so fast, Father."

"It certainly goes faster than a wagon," commented Andrew. "This is the age of steam, Mother, and things that were not possible before are now possible."

"Well, as I said, it ain't natural, and I would prefer to have no part of it, and I am sure I speak for Mrs Gavan here as well." At which the other woman nodded her head with a look of wonder and fear on her face.

Teddy stepped in to reassure Jane, telling her that no harm would come to her and that it was so much easier and more comfortable than four days in a wagon to Cork.

There was little shelter from the keening wind and rain. So, families gathered in the early dark beside their wagons and by their fires. For the Ryans, the hot stew went some way to ease the cold before women, girls, and young children climbed into the wagon to find some comfort and warmth to sleep. Teddy, John, Andrew and Patrick O'Neil spread canvas sheets on the cold ground close together under the wagons and wrapped themselves in blankets. It was not going to be a comfortable night's sleep, but they would manage as best they could. At the same time, there was excitement about their journey by rail to Cork on the morrow, a new experience for them all.

Them Bloody Steam Trains

Well before dawn the following day, Teddy was up and stirring the fire embers while sitting bundled in a blanket. It had been a sodden night, particularly for Teddy and the older boys, who found their bedding under the wagon soaked with rain blown in by the wind. But the rain had eased to a drizzle, and soon this cleared, enabling them to light a fire and have a hot meal. His two elder sons soon joined Teddy after disappearing to a far corner of the field to relieve themselves.

"It's as cold as a witch's tit!" exclaimed Andrew as he stamped his feet and held his hands out to the flames.

"Ah, just keep thinking of those warm mornings we're heading to," John muttered as he stamped his feet and pulled a blanket closer. "I heard tell it gets pretty hot down in Australia."

By now, there was stirring in the wagons, and the girls soon appeared, bringing a large basket with some of the provisions that Jane had prepared. These included a bag of rolled oats for porridge, black pudding, boxty, a container of tea and another of sugar. Anne and Maria were all for having some boxty, which they loved, but Teddy decreed that they would have porridge and keep the boxty for when they could not cook a meal. Besides, it would doubtless be a long day, and they didn't know when they might next get a meal.

So, Maria and Anne went off to fetch some water in a pot from a nearby stream. On their return, they added a good portion of oats and put it on the tripod to cook. Teddy filled a kettle with water for some tea. Jane came down with baby Peter. John found her a box to sit on while the family had porridge and tea. Then, while it was still dark, they had stowed everything back in the wagon and were ready to head into Tullamore and the railway station.

There was no wagon master, but there was a consensus and understanding among the families about the logistics and how the journey would be undertaken. Each wagon, its occupants, and the carts slowly made their way back to the main road.

As a rather motley convoy, they passed through Tullamore to the southwest side of the town where the station was located. The railway had arrived at Tullamore some ten years earlier as part of the Great Southern and Western Railway from Dublin to Cork, and there were regular services along the line. The station platform was a rudimentary affair. There was only a single rail track, and the station had been built up to about three feet on the town side of the track, with brickwork on the rail side, extending fifty yards along the tracks. Earth had been used to backfill against this to give a platform four yards wide. At the back, the earth sloped down to the road level. On the level platform, a small shed had been constructed to act as a station master's and ticket office.

Teddy and the boys worked together to unload their possessions. These were all gathered at the northern end of the platform, together with those from other emigrants, except for some foodstuffs and other items they might need on the trip. Father Dunne was directing operations and explained that most of the goods and chattels would be loaded onto two or three freight wagons while the passengers would travel in covered carriages, some of which would be enclosed. Teddy wondered how they could claim all their belongings at the other end but had no time to worry as he shepherded Jane and the younger children together to wait for the train.

There were nearly three hundred people gathered in groups or singly, both on the platform and in the area behind. Few, if any, had seen, let alone travelled on a train before, and there was an air of anticipation and excitement with many glances up the line to the north from where the train would come. It was a diverse mob with most of the men dressed in a similar fashion – drab coloured coats and shapeless trousers with high-crowned hats. The women wore long, mainly black or brown-coloured dresses, and most had large woollen shawls over their heads and shoulders. Many had babes in their arms or small children clutching their skirts. Father Dunne's black-clad figure could be seen moving among the groups answering questions and giving instructions.

As they waited, the sky lightened, and the dawn broke, although it was not promising with heavy clouds forming in the southwest; but there was no train. Gradually, as time passed and there was still no sign of a train, there was increased murmuring amongst the waiting crowd. Then, Father Dunne could be seen striding from the direction of the station building. He approached the platform's edge and raised his hands to silence the crowd.

"My fellow travellers," he announced. "I have been speaking with an official from the Great Southern and Western Railway, and they have received word by electric telegraph that our special train is delayed. They have had to wait for an engine, as that assigned to our train was needed elsewhere. So, it will be some time before it arrives here. I am told not before midday. So, I suggest you find what comfort and shelter you can, but be back here before noon."

There was much grumbling, and a few shouted insults about the Great Southern and Western Railway. The crowd started to disperse, with many heading towards the centre of the town. Patrick O'Neil had stayed with the wagon, looking forward to seeing the train come and go. So, Teddy asked if he thought his father would have room for them to find shelter in his pub for a few hours as it looked like it would start raining again soon. Patrick felt that should be possible, so the family climbed into the wagon and headed towards the town's main street. Fortunately, they were welcomed by John O'Neil and his wife Margaret, who took pity on Jane with baby Peter and arranged for a room for her and the younger children. It was a tight squeeze for the rest as several other families had also found shelter in the pub.

When it was time to leave the pub for the station, John O'Neil pressed a glass of whiskey into Teddy's hand. "This will help to keep you warm, my friend. Now take this with you as you may need further fortifying on this long trip," he said as he held out an earthenware jug of the same.

"Tanks, John, you're a good friend and a true Irishman."

Meanwhile, Margaret O'Neil handed Anne a bundle saying, "There's a few things to eat and some milk for Tessie." Jane smiled wearily, thanked Margaret, and prepared to head out into the rain with baby Peter.

Patrick was waiting with the covered wagon, and they climbed in with a few others who had been sheltering in the pub. At the station, there was still no sign of the train, but Patrick told them he was to stay until they boarded the train, so at least they had shelter from the now incessant rain and chilly wind.

An hour passed, and then word was passed around that the train could be seen approaching. Men, women, and children moved closer to the rail line and could now see the smoke from the engine. At this point, a few townspeople from Tullamore had also gathered to observe the emigrants leave.

As the train drew closer, it slowed and steam billowed from what seemed like numerous outlets on the engine, which also sounded its whistle. At this, the crowd fell back from the line and watched, some in awe, as the engine pulled a series of wooden carriages past. Several of the carriages were enclosed with doors and windows opening to compartments. Behind these were others that were like freight wagons with wooden sides all around to waist height, then with a roof supported by several posts around the perimeter of the carriage.

Father Dunne climbed onto one of the open carriages as the train stopped with more steam now almost obliterating the black-painted engine from sight. He directed that women and children should occupy the enclosed carriages and the men the open ones. He also directed that most of the luggage, particularly the heavier and more bulky items, be loaded onto the three open freight wagons at the rear of the train after the train had moved forward to allow access to some of the rear open carriages and the wagons from the platform. Other items could be placed on the roof of the closed carriages, around which ran a metal railing to hold the luggage in place.

Teddy sent Andrew to help with the baggage loading to ensure that their belongings were put on board. Patrick had given them the canvas sheet, and Teddy instructed the sons to ensure that as much of their belongings as possible were securely covered. Then, he took Jane by the elbow and told his daughters to follow him as he made his way to one of the closed carriages.

It took some time, but eventually, they boarded and found rows of wooden bench seats on each end of a compartment. While directing the older girls to fend for themselves, Teddy placed Jane with baby Peter and Tessie on seats in the compartment, where Anne, Maria, Catherine, and young William joined them. A few other women, one with a small child, also entered the compartment. Tessie seemed more intrigued by the experience than fearful.

Jane clutched Teddy's arm. "Teddy, I'm sore afraid of all this. Can't you stay here with us?"

Teddy was torn at seeing Jane so distressed and tried to comfort and reassure her. But he felt he could not take a seat from a woman or child. As he looked around the compartment, he saw fear on several women's faces and a young child crying in distress at the unknown.

"All will be well, Jane, my love, and I shall see you at Cork, if not along the way."

He left them with a final word to the older girls and William to care for their mother. Then he walked along the platform to the rear of the train. As he did so, with much puffing of smoke and steam, the train moved forward so the men could load the luggage. Teddy climbed aboard one of the open carriages through a gate on the side and found seats for himself and the older sons. There were wooden benches that stretched the width of the carriage with a narrow aisle down the middle. They were wet from the rain and sprinkled with black soot, but this could not be helped, so Teddy used his hand to remove most of the water and soot before sitting.

A short time later, Andrew and John joined Teddy, stuffing a bag with food and personal items under the seat in front. The three of them looked at each other with a grim smile, with John expressing their feelings. "Well, Dad, this is it. Let's hope this Queensland will be as grand as we're told, although it must surely be better than this here accursed rain."

The train jerked forward and began moving slowly at first, with much huffing and puffing from the engine and a sharp blast on the whistle. The townsfolk waved goodbye and yelled good wishes for a safe journey while Andrew, now enjoying himself, stated, "This is going to be one hell of a ride."

As the train gathered pace, the men and boys in Teddy's carriage all seemed to gain a sense of exhilaration, although this was somewhat spoiled by coal smoke from the engine, with its pungent smell wafting across the carriage from time to time. As the speed increased to nearly twenty-five miles per hour, so did the wind chill and the rain, for it was a cold, wet and blustery day. The men pulled their Ulster cape overcoats and scarves tighter around themselves, with many holding onto their hats. There were no bogeys under the carriages, just axles with wheels, so as the speed increased, the carriage began to sway, making life for the passengers more uncomfortable.

It was the same for Jane, the girls and seven-year-old William in the closed carriage, although, with so many passengers in each carriage, they acted as buffers for each other. Jane was not happy, though at least she and the girls were dry. Some in the carriage weren't so lucky, having rainwater dripping onto them from a leak in the roof. The situation wasn't conducive to easily breast-feeding baby Peter, who was, once again, vocally demanding sustenance. Jane decided she needed help and asked Tessie to change places with sixteen-year-old Anne. Then, with Anne's help, Jane arranged herself and her clothing to give Peter access to her breast while endeavouring to maintain some modesty. But she thought, needs must, and Peter needed feeding despite their uncomfortable conditions.

As the train headed southeast from Tullamore to join the main line from Dublin to Cork, Teddy and several other men tied their scarves over their high crown hats to keep them in place. Watching the countryside as the train sped through the rain, Teddy found it an exhilarating, though slightly unnerving, experience to travel in relative comfort, except for the wind and rain.

About half an hour into the journey, the train slowed as it joined the main line from Dublin to Cork just outside Portarlington. It then increased speed until half an hour later, Teddy saw they were entering a town. A couple of men volunteered that this was Portlaoise.

He watched as they slowly made their way through the town centre, with the train's whistle sounding repeatedly to move any curious townspeople away from the track. The rain had eased considerably at this point, and Teddy could see something of the town and houses. He couldn't help feeling somewhat important as he looked down at the staring onlookers. This was a grand start to their journey to Australia. He looked across to where John and Andrew were sitting, and they grinned back, obviously glad to be part of the adventure.

Soon after the train left Portlaoise, the rain became heavier and with no protection on the sides, it blew into the edge of the carriage. Men and boys did all they could to stay dry, but most resigned themselves to the fact that they would get wet, which was not an uncommon experience in Ireland, particularly for those working on the farms. The only saving grace was that the wind and rain kept much of the smoke and soot from covering the occupants of these open carriages.

Their journey continued through the grey and dismal afternoon, with the rain being relentless. They passed by numerous farms, most now lying fallow for the winter. Teddy must have dozed and then awoke with rain hitting him in the face. As the train changed direction and headed south, this brought the rain more directly into the carriage on the right side where Teddy was seated. Shortly after that, the train slowed and entered another town. The consensus among the men was that this was Thurles.

The train stopped near the Thurles Station for the engine to fill its water tank. Several passengers, including Teddy and his sons, took advantage of the stop and jumped down beside the tracks to stretch their legs and revive their circulation after sitting cramped for some time and to empty their bladders. Teddy walked along to Jane's carriage and climbed in, seeking his wife in the dim light. Jane smiled, though Teddy could see she was putting a brave face on things.

"How's it going, my love?" he asked softly, for he could see that baby Peter was asleep.

"We're managing, Teddy. Though it's mighty cramped in here, then, that is helping to keep us warm."

"Maybe you and the girls should get off and relieve yourselves as I don't know when we might stop again or where you could do it. I can see to Peter."

Grateful for a break, Jane made her way to the door, then handed Peter to Teddy while he used one hand to help her and his daughters off the train. After a few minutes, they came back.

Tessie, her ruddy, round face creased in a frown, looked up at Teddy and asked, "When can we get off the train, Daddy? I don't like being bounced from side to side, and that smoke is really smelly."

"We are going to be a while yet on the train, Tessie, but not long after the sun goes down, we should be in Cork, and you can get off. Then, tomorrow we shall see the big ship we will sail on to Australia."

"And that's going to take a long time, isn't it, Daddy? I mean it will take a long time to go to Australia. More than one night, I think, maybe even more than two nights."

Teddy smiled at his young daughter. "Aye, to be sure, it will take many nights to get to Australia, Tessie. But we will have beds we can sleep on. It is going to be a really exciting adventure."

The train's whistle signalled that they were about to leave, and all climbed back on board. Teddy helped Jane and handed over Peter, who was now stirring and whingeing in the cold and light rain.

The train moved off again, and Teddy made himself as comfortable as he could, anticipating it would be a while before they would stop again. After Thurles, the line headed southwest, so the wind and rain weren't so bad. As the afternoon progressed, they continued their journey at a speed they had not experienced before and with dusk approaching, Teddy and his sons gazed out with mixed feelings on the rural landscape they would not see again.

Teddy had spent all his life on farms like those they were passing, but it had been a hard life for little gain. As

Teddy looked at the passing farms, he saw and felt little hope for a future from the land here. And what future was there for his sons? Certainly not on the land as farmers, although John had much experience working on building and maintaining roads and bridges, which could provide him with some income.

About an hour after the sun had set, the train slowed again and entered a small town that Teddy saw from the sign on the station was Charleville. The train stopped, this time to replenish the coal supply, and the passengers again took advantage to stretch their legs and relieve themselves. The rain had eased to a drizzle, although a brisk cold wind blew from the southwest. At the same time, the engineer set about putting new candles into the large lamp with reflectors on the front of the train.

After relieving himself on the edge of the track, Teddy made his way to Jane's carriage to see if all was well. He opened the door and gazed in. Through the dim light of a lantern on the wall, he made out Jane, his daughters, and William. Some seemed asleep, but he could see that Jane was awake. She put her finger to her lips to indicate he should be quiet, and he could see Peter sleeping in Anne's arms. So, he left her and slowly walked back to his carriage.

The wind and drizzle made for a miserable evening, and Teddy stood and stamped his feet like many other men. There were a few derogatory comments made about the weather and their condition. "It ain't a good night for taking a train ride, that's for sure," grumbled one man as he rubbed his hands together for warmth.

When it was time to reboard the carriage and continue the journey, they hauled themselves back inside the open carriage. Despite the wind coming through the open sides, the smell of wet wool warmed by body heat was much in evidence.

The train was now heading south, and the wind had increased with intermittent heavy falls of rain that again came into Teddy's carriage, soon soaking those on the right or west side. The darkness enveloped them, and the rain intensified as they sped towards their destination, making it hard to see anything beyond their carriage. Teddy would be glad when they could stop and find warmth and shelter, although it would be getting late by the time they reached Cork, much later than they had originally expected to arrive.

Someone produced a jug of whiskey, which was passed around and helped to combat the cold and wet. It also loosened tongues, and several discussions or arguments soon occurred.

One gent remarked, "I have it on good authority that our ship, the *Erin go Bragh*, used to be in the slave trade before being fixed up to carry people like us."

"You're full of shite, you old windbag, Patrick Molloy. The only authority you know is that wife of yours. So don't go telling stories about something you know naught about," came a retort.

"No, I heard she has been on the run several times from here to America, and a good fast clipper she's supposed to be," piped up James Kelly. "Perhaps we're lucky to have such a good ship to take us to Australia, as some of these migrant ships aren't much better than slave ships."

"Well, whatever the ship or its conditions, this is going to be a fearful long journey through all sorts of weather and likely some powerful, wild storms. I tell you, we'll all be lucky to be alive to see the shores of Queensland," announced James Deeran, who generally had a rather pessimistic outlook on life.

That was too much for Ted Dempsey, one of the older men in the carriage. "You eejit, what sort of hooligan are you to be sprouting such trash when you don't know what the hell you're talking about, and all you're going to do is put a damper on things. So, shut your gob if you don't have anything worthwhile to say."

And so, the 'discussions' continued as only Irish discussions can, particularly while downing a good portion of a jug of 'holy water'. Then, not long after leaving Charleville, the train slowed as they passed through another town, this one somewhat larger, and Teddy saw from the signs on the station that it was Mallow.

An hour or so later, they slowed again, and he could see they were entering a large town. This must be Cork, they speculated. A cheer rose from the now somewhat inebriated occupants of Teddy's carriage, some of whom were not feeling the cold wind or rain as keenly as before.

Frustration

The rain had eased to a drizzle as the train made its way alongside the Cork station, where gas lamps shed a yellow light over the covered platform revealing a couple of railway employees waiting for the train. After it came to a halt, Teddy rose stiffly and made his way onto the platform, gathering his sons and their baggage as he proceeded to Jane's carriage. Anne, Maria and Catherine were already on the platform and helping unload some bags while Jane waited with Peter in her arms. She looked all done in, although she managed a brief smile for Teddy.

He helped her down and asked, "Have you eaten anything, my love?" When Jane shook her head, he suggested they each have some of the boxty Jane had brought. "It'll keep our strength up while we go to find some place to stay."

As they stood there, eating their boxty and wondering what to do next, Father Dunne stood on the steps of one of the closed carriages and called for silence. "My fellow travellers, thanks be to God that we have arrived in Cork. Some of you are soaked through, about which I am truly sorry. Now, I have here with me Mr. McCabe, who is from Messrs Baines, the agent for the Black Ball Shipping Line, who is providing our ship, the *Erin go Bragh*. Mr McCabe has some news for us regarding our ship."

A little man with a bowler hat, an overcoat and a toothbrush moustache climbed up on the step. "Ladies and gentlemen. The *Erin go Bragh* should have been leaving from Queenstown in two days on the 25th of January. However, there have been some fearfully strong storms and winds in the Irish Sea, which has meant that the ship's departure from Liverpool, seems to have been delayed. It should have arrived in Queenstown yesterday, but it hasn't. And I don't know when it is going to arrive.

"In the meantime, we have to get all of you accommodated somehow, which will be difficult given how late it is now. So, I have arranged for most of you to find shelter and somewhere to sleep in the church hall at St Augustine's and the Priory at St Francis, at least for tonight. Then, tomorrow, we can try to arrange other more suitable accommodation. There are also several hotels and boarding houses in which you may be able to find a bed. Mid-morning, tomorrow, I ask that at least one member from each family and all the individual passengers come to St Augustine's church, where I can inform you of the latest situation concerning the *Erin go Bragh* and what other arrangements for accommodations are being made. I don't want you to fret about how you will pay for food and lodgings, particularly if we have to wait a few days for the ship to arrive. As agents for the Black Ball Shipping Line, Messrs. Baines will give each passenger one shilling and sixpence per day to help you out. In fact, we have to do that according to the regulations."

There was an audible sigh of relief from many passengers that they would at least have the means to obtain lodgings and food. Then one of the men asked, "What will we do with all our belongings? We can't cart them all over town while we seek somewhere to stay. I'm talking about bedding, pots, pans, and tools."

Mr McCabe was ready with an answer. "If you offload all those goods, I have some wagons that will take them to a warehouse in Queenstown. Make sure to keep with you anything you might need while staying for a few days here in Cork."

Teddy turned to Jane and suggested they best seek shelter at the Priory or church hall. Mr McCabe had asked his associates to help sort out accommodation, and five of these men and Mr McCabe were organising passengers into groups according to where they might go. Teddy joined a group choosing St Francis's Priory, thinking it might be better than the church hall. He eventually managed to secure places for his family. The man he talked to was very sympathetic when Teddy explained that he had a wife and eight children, one of whom was only a month old.

"I can't promise that it will be anything grand, but at least you and your family will have a roof over your heads, and the friars will surely provide you with nourishing food. Just get your family and your belongings together and meet me at the entrance to the station down there," he said and pointed to the end of the platform where Teddy could see people passing through some gates.

It was about a mile to the Priory, along the cobbled streets of Cork, down and across the River Lee, then through more poorly lit streets.

Shortly after leaving the station, the life of a busy port town was in evidence, with many public houses producing a fair scattering of drunken sailors. Several leered at Teddy's daughters till he told them to get lost, backed by the weight of John and Andrew at his side.

Tessie pulled on her mother's skirt and asked, "Mother, what are those ladies doing standing outside in the cold and rain?" as they passed a lane with some of Cork's ladies of the night.

"Oh, they're probably waiting for their fathers to come and take them home," replied Jane as she ushered Tessie down the street.

Further on, as they came down to Farren's Quay along the river, there were fine three or four-storey houses belonging to wealthy merchants. But it was not a night for dawdling, with the rain and wind making the journey both uncomfortable and, for some like Jane carrying Peter, somewhat hazardous on the slippery cobbles.

The Priory was a large three-storey brick building beside an impressive brick church. The Franciscans had originally established themselves on the site in the 12th century, and these buildings resulted from several rebuilding efforts. There must have been about sixty of the passengers seeking accommodation with the Franciscan Friars, who did not seem fazed by the arrival of so many seeking shelter and food.

Inside the main entrance was a large hallway lit by gas lamps, where most passengers had made their way. A large painting of the order's founder, St Francis of Assisi, dominated one wall.

The Prior was a well-built middle-aged man, dressed in the traditional Franciscan brown hooded habit with a white cord around his waist and sandals on his feet, despite the cold. He explained to the assembled passengers that some rooms were available for women with infants and small children. The others would need to rest in the refectory and the chapter house.

"As it's such a cold and miserable night, the friars have prepared some soup and soda bread for you. This will, hopefully, get some warmth back into your bones. It will be served in the refectory before those sleeping there get settled."

Teddy approached the Prior and expressed his gratitude, to which the Prior replied, "Tis nothing, my son. We're used to housing and feeding many of the poor of this city and from elsewhere, particularly in the troubled times we've had in the recent past."

After Teddy asked John and Andrew to find spaces for themselves, the older girls and himself, he saw Jane and the younger children to a small, sparsely appointed room with only one bed, a crucifix on the wall, and a small cabinet. It would have to do for Jane, Peter, Catherine, William and Tessie. Jane was so tired that she wanted to fall on the bed and sleep, but Teddy persuaded her to have something to eat.

"You've hardly had anything all day, and you need your strength to care for and feed Peter. Now is not the time to be neglecting yourself and sickening, just before we board our ship."

"You're right, Teddy. You might be the silent type, but you have a good head on your shoulders."

"We're going to have to make the best of some hard times over the next few months, so let's take what comfort when we can get it."

With that, he went in search of his sons to see what they had managed to arrange for their sleeping accommodation. It turned out to be some spaces in the refectory. This was a large, high-ceilinged room with dark wooden beams, tall windows at one end and a good fire blazing in a hearth at the other. They would share with several other passengers and a few local men who had fallen on hard times.

With some good hearty hot broth in his stomach, Teddy settled down for the night and listened to the wind howling outside while rain drummed on the windows as he pulled his blankets around him. Snores from several of the men could already be heard. The hall had lingering smells from their meal, but the dominant odour was of damp wool and stale sweat, although this didn't deter him from dropping into a deep sleep almost as soon as he was settled.

****

The next morning the friars provided oatmeal porridge with milk for breakfast and hot tea. Then Teddy suggested that Jane stay in the Priory and rest while he went with John and Andrew to St Augustine's to hear what Mr McCabe had to say. Anne had taken Peter, and Jane was only too willing to comply with Teddy's suggestion. Before he left, Jane gave Teddy a few shillings and asked if he could find milk for the young children and perhaps some other food to help them out here and on the voyage.

Teddy had asked directions to St Augustine's from one of the friars, and it was close by - just around a few corners. In the daylight, he could now get more of an impression of

Cork, a city with eighty thousand inhabitants. This was all a new experience for Teddy and his boys, having never seen such a large city, so much larger than Tullamore. The streets were all paved with cobblestones, and some were as wide as three streets in Tullamore. One street had a strip in the centre with trees, would you believe it! This must have been in a better part of the town as there were many stone houses of two, three or even four storeys. Down other streets were one or two-storey houses painted blue, yellow, or white. The city had a busy air, with people hurrying along the sidewalks. Yes, there were actually sidewalks, so people didn't have to walk in the street while dodging horses and carriages.

He arrived at St Augustine's and joined the passengers waiting at the front of the large stone church. They milled around, anxious for word on their voyage, many spilling out onto the street, causing curious looks from some passers-by and nasty comments to 'git out of the way' from a few carriage drivers. Finally, after nearly an hour, the diminutive Mr McCabe climbed up the church steps and put his arms out to get silence.

"Ladies and gentlemen, I have heard from my office in Liverpool that the *Erin go Bragh* left Liverpool last Friday, the 24th. However, the storms and wind have been so bad and contrary that she was forced to rely on a powerful steam tug, the *Retriever*, from the new Liverpool Steam Tug Company, to tow her at least to Wexford. Unfortunately, so severe have been the gales they encountered that the tug ran short of coal twice and was obliged to put back into Holyhead in Wales. At the moment, I have not had word that they have yet again attempted to make the crossing to Ireland."

There were audible groans from many in the crowd, and one man shouted. "So, what's to become of us, and when are we going to sail?"

"As long as these strong gales continue, the ship will find it difficult to get to Cork; and I don't know when the gales will ease. Even if they ease tomorrow, the ship will take a few days to arrive. So, I have authorised my men here to issue each of you with money to pay for accommodation and food. That is one shilling and sixpence a day[2] for each adult or each two children between four and fourteen years old. You can collect enough for four days now, and if necessary, there will be more payments made when I have further news or in four days. And don't try a fast one, as each of my men has a list of passengers.

"I also have some more information on accommodation. My men have a list of boarding houses and hostels that can take some of you, including some families. So, please see my agents here to get that information. To have some order could you all form into queues. Don't worry; you will all get your money and information. Lastly, could you gather here again on Saturday, the 1st of February, when I hope to have more news for you."

There was an immediate rush towards the six agents standing on the lower steps, where queues started slowly forming. Teddy joined a queue and patiently waited as they slowly made their way forward. The other passengers showed a mixture of frustration and resignation to the fate of waiting.

"At least we will have enough money to stay somewhere if we can find a place and somewhere to eat," murmured John. "Cork mightn't be a bad place to explore for a couple of days, although if it's any longer, it will be hard."

---

[2] As per the Passengers' Act, 1855, *If the ship does not sail before three p.m. of the day of embarkation named in the contract, the passengers ... can recover rom the owner, charterer or master, subsistence money after the rate of 1s, 6d per day for each statute adult.*

When Teddy reached him, the agent was a large, portly gent with a florid face and brown derby hat. Teddy gave his name and explained that he had a wife and eight children.

"And how old is your youngest child?" enquired the agent.

"He's just a month old. Then the next oldest is five."

"Well, we don't count the baby for this payment; and it wouldn't have its own bed or need much in the way of food now, would it? And how many of your children are between four and fourteen?"

"Well, there's Tessie, who's five and William who's seven. Then Maria is twelve, and Catherine is thirteen."

"Let's see now," said the agent, who licked his pencil and scribbled on a sheet of paper. "That's one shilling and sixpence by four days is six shillings. Then, there's five of you adults and four children." He wrote in a large ledger Teddy's name and family details as he said this. "Altogether, you get two pounds, two shillings. The children between four and fourteen only get half. Can you sign your name or put your mark here," he said as he indicated where Teddy was to sign.

Teddy wasn't going to argue as two pounds would be a goodly sum. It was more than he could earn as a labourer over four days.

"What about accommodation?" asked John. "Do you perhaps have a list of places we could stay outside the St Francis Priory, where we are now?"

The gent with the derby hat pulled a sheet of paper from the back of the ledger. "Here, take a gander at that. There's some boarding houses and hotels, but I would be quick off the mark as others will also be after room and board."

Teddy looked at the list and said to his two older sons. "Andrew, you take this place on Straid Tuckey and this one on Straid Grafton. John, you try these boarding houses on Straid Phaedair and Little Cross Street, and I will ask along Main Street. We'll ask any local how to get to these streets. Just see if any can accommodate all of us, or even if we have to split up, you can both fend for yourselves, maybe with William. Let's meet back at St Francis' Priory."

They set off, pulling their coats up and their hats down, with the rain a constant drizzle now and the wind whistling around the houses and up the streets from the southwest. An hour later, all three had reassembled back at the Priory in the warmth of the refectory with Jane. Andrew had found a boarding house with one room spare, but not big enough for them all. John had discovered all his establishments full.

"Well, I managed to get a half-decent room at this hotel on Main Street just ahead of another man and his wife. But I had to pay four night's board in advance to keep it," said Teddy. "That room can take you, Jane, and the girls with Peter, while I will go with the boys to the place Andrew found. I think both of those sound better than staying on here."

"What about food, Teddy?" asked Jane. "How will we manage that?"

"I think we'd best gather to eat at the hotel where you're staying, love; maybe we'll find somewhere better over the next day or two. Goodness knows how long we will be stuck here before our ship arrives, but I fear it will be more than a few days."

The family set about transferring their baggage to the boarding house and hotel. Jane waited with Peter and Anne until Teddy organised her room at the hotel, then he helped her move there through the rain, which had intensified as the afternoon wore on and evening approached. By the time they had arrived Jane and the girls' clothes were wet through. Jane dismissed Teddy with thanks and proceeded with her daughters to get their wet clothes off and put on some dry ones.

****

Over the next three days, the wild weather showed no sign of letting up, and as a result, their spirits sank, wondering when the *Erin go Bragh* would be able to make it across to Queenstown. The older sons took William and explored Cork when the rain eased. Teddy spent much of his time with Jane, while the older daughters helped with Peter and did some of their own exploring, taking Tessie with them as she refused to be left behind. During their explorations, John and Andrew found a more amenable and cheaper eating establishment, where they negotiated a deal for dinners for the whole family. And so, January eased into February with the Ryan family and other passengers eager for news of their ship and their departure for Australia.

With the arrival of February, the weather had improved. The wind dropped, the rain stopped, and there was some sunshine, all of which raised the spirits of the passengers enduring their wait in Cork. Mr McCabe brightened spirits further when he met Teddy and others at St Augustine on Saturday, the 1st of February.

"I have received word by electric telegraph from Holyhead that the *Erin go Bragh* is due to depart Holyhead today and should be at Queenstown by the Tuesday next."

There was a general uproar and much cheering amongst the bedraggled passengers. Teddy's heart lightened when he realised that they would be on their way within a few days.

"Yes, this is good news; I am sure you will all agree," continued Mr McCabe. "And, I expect that the *Erin go Bragh* should be able to depart from Queenstown on or about next Friday, the 7th."

"When do we go on board?" yelled one of the men.

"Yes, and how do we get to this here, Queenstown, where the ship is leaving from?" came another query.

"Let's meet here again on Monday, in the morning, and I will have more news about when the ship should be arriving in Queenstown and when you will be boarding. I expect that if the ship arrives on Tuesday, we shall start boarding on Wednesday. Queenstown isn't far, just a few miles away, and I have organised a boat to transport you all down there on the day you leave."

Teddy and his older sons went to see Jane with a light heart. The hotel where she and the girls were staying was far from grand. It was three storeys high, and the rendered brick was painted a faded red. Inside, it was gloomy, with only the light coming from the entrance door to the reception area and two windows on either side. He climbed the uncarpeted wooden stairs to the third floor and knocked on the door of a room halfway along a dark passage with a tattered, dirty carpet running up the middle. Jane's room was reasonably sized but overcrowded with Jane and the four girls plus Peter.

Jane, who was in a miserable state with a heavy cold and a wracking cough, was sitting in the only chair while the older girls were on the bed, and Anne was walking with Peter trying to stop his whingeing. Tessie was on the floor changing the dress on her doll while William sat on the bed swinging his legs and looking bored. Maria had managed to get some hot broth from the hotel and was encouraging Jane to try a little. Teddy bent and kissed his wife's head and was relieved to feel that she was not burning with a fever.

"Just keep yourself warm and let Anne and Maria care for you, my love, and you should be better in a few days. And you'll need to be, as we will be sailing on our ship and heading for Australia by next Friday."

"Oh, Teddy, really? You mean the ship is going to be coming soon?"

The girls and William were also excited and crowded around Teddy, bombarding him with questions.

"Well, with the weather easing, the ship will be leaving Holyhead today, God willing, and should be arriving in Queenstown by next Tuesday, if all goes well."

"So, when can we go on board?" piped up William, who was anxious to go anywhere to get away from the tedium of being confined to Jane's room.

"Well, we're to meet Mr McCabe again on Monday when he should be able to tell us when we will actually be boarding, but he thinks we may start boarding on Wednesday if the ship gets in on Tuesday."

"This is welcome news, Teddy. Now, did you get some more money to help us with our room and food?" said Jane.

"To be sure I did, Jane; another two guineas, that's two pounds and two shillings for another four days to next Wednesday, which is mighty generous of this here Black Ball Shipping Line."

"That's as may be," replied Jane. "But how were we expected to exist here in Cork after they told us the ship would be leaving the day after we arrived, and then there's no sign of it? Let's hope this is the end of the shenanigans with this ship and the voyage."

Teddy nodded at his wife's outburst, knowing she was like a mother hen protecting her brood against all outsiders and circumstances.

Jane continued, "Now, we must all go to mass tomorrow over at this mighty fine church they have near the river. It's called Holy Trinity. And we'll pray that we don't sink in some storm and safely arrive at our new home in this Queensland."

All agreed that this would be a fine thing to do, and Maria said she would enquire as to what time mass would be.

Teddy looked over at Maria, who had now finished coaxing Jane to have some soup. He thought she might be only twelve this month, but she was already showing herself to be a very caring person with a light heart. Rarely did anything seem to get her down.

I really am blessed with my children, he thought. *Anne was so unselfishly caring in looking after baby Peter. Kathrine was more fun-loving but also helped out, and his two older sons were hard-working young men any father would be proud of, though Andrew could be a bit hot-headed and reckless on occasion.*

****

After mass on Sunday, the whole family explored the area along the quay by the River Lee, where the church was situated. The rain had stopped, and the sun shone, which, although the air was still chilly, seemed a good omen for the trip ahead. After days of dismal, stormy weather, it could not fail to raise spirits. So, with lightened hearts, they gazed with interest, and sometimes awe, at the sights, often so different and far grander than anything they had seen in Kings County.

Further downstream along the wide quay that opened on to the river stood massive warehouses of grey stone, some two-storeys high. Upstream were solid three or four-story houses belonging to well-to-do merchants, some rendered and painted yellow or blue, others displaying the grey solid granite, representing the solid status of the occupants; and all along the quay were ships of many types: large sailing ships, their masts and rigging reaching for the sky, small sail work boats, plus a few steam vessels with their tall funnels. But, it being Sunday, all was quiet with little activity, except for a steam ferry moving down the river belching smoke from its funnel.

As the family slowly walked along the quay to the stone bridge spanning the river, they were wary of the occasional carriage or riders. Jane and her daughters admired the dresses of some more affluent citizens also out for a Sunday perambulation. On the south side of the river, on broad cobbled Main Street, they passed by several shops all shut, and Jane asked Teddy if, on the morrow, he could purchase a new pot and a ladle for cooking on the ship.

****

On the following day, Monday the 3rd of February, Teddy, again with John and Andrew, walked over to St Augustine's. On the way, they passed a bakery from where delicious savoury smells emerged. So, Teddy decided that they should treat themselves to a meat pie each. Why not enjoy a bit of luxury while they could, and the money provided for their room and board was sufficient for a few extras. Buying the pies made them late in arriving at St Augustine's, and Mr McCabe was already addressing the passengers. "When she arrives, she will need two or three days to load up cargo and then the passengers. So, if all goes well, you'll be boarding on Thursday, then sailing on Friday."

Teddy turned to the man beside him and asked, "So, when's the ship coming in?"

"That's to be tomorrow sometime."

There was a general air of excitement and anticipation and several questions about how and when they would be boarding and where the ship would be. Mr McCabe patiently answered these as best he could and told the assembled passengers that they should meet again early on Wednesday morning when he would have spoken to the ship's captain and would know more precisely when the ship would be leaving and when passengers could board. He also advised that they would get more money for room and board, taking them up to Thursday.

The rest of Monday and Tuesday passed quietly for the Ryan family. Teddy, accompanied by his three boys, made some purchases as dictated by Jane - a new pot and ladle, some blankets, a few items of clothing to see them through the voyage, and some food items that would last, including tea and sugar.

As the sun rose on Wednesday, Teddy, John, and Andrew made their way once more to St Augustine's church, not stopping for pies this time. A noisy throng had already gathered around and in front of the church steps when they arrived, but it wasn't long before both Mr McCabe and Father Dunne came onto the steps, and the latter raised his hands for silence.

"My friends, the time has almost come to start our journey to Australia, and I am terribly sorry for all the hardships that the weather and the late arrival of the *Erin go Bragh* may have caused you, particularly those with young children. But the kind assistance of the Black Ball Line in providing money for your accommodation and food is, I am sure, greatly appreciated. It looks like we shall be boarding the *Erin go Bragh* tomorrow, about which Mr McCabe will now tell you."

Mr McCabe shuffled several papers he had in hand. Then, after perusing them for a minute, addressed the gathering. "I have spoken with Captain Borlase, and he has asked that passengers start boarding tomorrow as he would like all loading and boarding to be complete by the end of the day so he can be prepared to sail on Friday morning. Queenstown is some sixteen miles from Cork. So, Father Dunne has organised that a Citizen's River Steamer Company's boat will take you from Cork to Queenstown."

At this point, Father Dunne continued. "Everyone must be at Kennedy's Quay at half past seven in the morning. That's just before sunrise. And bring all your baggage and goods with you. Make sure you are there if you plan on sailing the following day. When we get to Queenstown, you will be given your tickets for the trip on the *Erin go Bragh*."

Back at Jane's hotel, Teddy gave her the exciting news. "Myself and the boys will be here tomorrow morning at six thirty when you all must be ready to leave. I know it should take less than half an hour to get to the quay, but we want to be sure we don't miss the boat."

"That's a wretched hour to be going abroad, Teddy. Why so early?" asked Jane.

"It's going to take a while to get to Queenstown; then we have to all get aboard the *Erin go Bragh*, which will also take some time."

"Are we really going on this big ship to Australia tomorrow, Father?" asked Tessie, in a voice that expressed some doubt after all the delays they had suffered.

"Yes, Tessie. Tomorrow, we sail on a big ship to Australia, and God protect us and keep us all safe."

Boarding

The following morning when Teddy and his sons arrived at Jane's hotel, she was not ready. Baby Peter was crying and, at times, screaming, and Jane was distraught with her temper just below the surface following an almost sleepless night.

"What's the problem with Peter?" asked Andrew.

Jane rounded on him. "What do you think's the problem? He's got colic, you numbskull, and he's kept us awake half the night, even though I gave him some of that cordial. And now we have to take him on this boat journey. It's too much, I tell you!" And with that, Jane collapsed onto the bed with her hands to her face.

"Well, we have to go, Jane, if we are to catch this boat," explained Teddy patiently.

"I can't move any faster, and if you want us to get away, don't just stand there but give a hand in getting things ready while I see to Peter. Goodness knows what we're going to do with him carrying on like this and no end in sight. I shall give him some more of that cordial, though I don't like using it as it's got laudanum in it, which ain't good even for adults. And we need to get some more of it to take on the ship."

"I don't know how and when I can do that, love, but I'll try."

"Well, you'd better because otherwise, this here baby is going to be keeping the rest of the ship awake at night."

Teddy knew he had to somehow get some of the opium cordial, maybe in Queenstown, before they went on board. He, John, and Andrew joined the older girls and packed up all the baggage, then gathered everything together. Jane had managed to quieten Peter and was wrapping him and herself with her shawl.

They set out from Jane's hotel on Main Street, with everyone carrying some item of their baggage and goods.

It was still dark, and the lack of stars indicated there was cloud cover. Trudging along the wide thoroughfare, they were joined by some locals on their way to work and increasing numbers of passengers for the *Erin go Bragh*. A number of these Teddy recognised from their train journey down from Tullamore. Jane's cold was on the mend, though she wore her heavy shawl over her head and shoulders to protect against the morning chill.

At the quay, the passengers were being directed by Father Dunne. There was a lot of animated talk about the trip and nostalgic expressions on many faces, as this would be their last day in Ireland, their birthplace and homeland until now. Ahead was the unknown, both the voyage and their destination. Perhaps some were having doubts about their decision to leave.

As dawn broke, Teddy could make out the ships at the quayside, including the ferry that would take them to Queenstown. It was a steam launch about seventy feet long with a covered area astern of a high wheelhouse and room for passengers on a railed deck on top of the covered passenger accommodation.

Teddy and the family pushed forward as passengers started to board the vessel, but Father Dunne, standing on the top deck, shouted that there would be two trips as there was not enough room on the boat for all the passengers. Could families with small children be allowed to get on the first trip.

This was greeted by shouts of abuse and disbelief, although to any casual observer, it should have been apparent that the boat could not take on board the throng of passengers on the quay.

Teddy, Andrew, and John used their weight to push through, yelling that they had small children. Teddy helped Jane across the gangway onto the ferry. But there was not much room for them in the sheltered accommodation, and Teddy managed to squeeze Jane,

Peter and Tessie in under shelter, then took to the open top deck with the rest of his children. It had started to rain again, a light shower, but enough to dampen their clothes and spirits.

Two hours after leaving the Cork Quay, their ferry arrived at Queenstown. As they approached the busy port, Teddy gazed over at the town, which rose from the waterfront to a low hill, with two or three-storey stone houses lining narrow, cobbled streets. Some of these were shops selling all manner of goods that might be needed for ships and voyages. Others were houses for both the rich and poor, the latter having drab-looking tenement buildings or small cottages, while the former were located more towards the waterfront and were of more solid stone construction.

Several sailing ships were tied to the quay with their masts and rigging partially obscuring the cloudy sky and two steam vessels. Then Teddy spied a large ship with three tall masts. Its hull was painted black with a white band in the middle. This must be the *Erin go Bragh*, and it looked enormous.

Surely such a ship could not sink in a stormy sea, he thought.

Their ferry docked at the quay, and the passengers disembarked but stayed in a group as Father Dunne then proceeded to hand out the tickets for their voyage and directed them towards the *Erin go Bragh*. Teddy collected his family's tickets, then led them through crowds of noisy dock workers and around carts carrying a cargo of every description. As they neared the ship, he saw they were loading cargo. This was piled on the wharf adjacent to the ship, and as they passed, Teddy saw there were kegs of nails and shot, barrels and hogsheads of beer and ale, and even cases of ham.

At the gangway up to the ship, they were halted by a crew member who was explaining in a loud voice that they couldn't board yet as their accommodation was not ready for them.

"What are we supposed to do now, having heaved ourselves out of bed before daybreak to get here?" complained one of the more vocal passengers.

"I don't care what you do, but you can't come on board till the captain says so."

"And when might that be?" demanded another passenger, loaded with his belongings.

"Maybe around noon or early this afternoon, the way I sees it!" came the reply.

Jane turned to Teddy. "So much for being here early to board the ship and walk the streets while it was still dark. All we seem to get so far with this trip is delays but never leaving! It is almost like a bad dream."

Teddy chose to ignore Jane's outburst and suggested they move away from the dock to find some shelter to wait; while they sheltered, he, John and Andrew would try and find some more cordial for Peter's stomach problem.

There was no shelter near the quay, so John left Jane, and most of the children huddled in the lee of one of the warehouses. He was back about an hour later with two small bottles of laudanum cordial, for which Jane was most grateful, for Peter was again crying while Anne endeavoured to calm him.

It was a wet and sorry group of passengers, including the Ryans, who approached the gangway in the early afternoon. They were allowed to board this time, and the family climbed up the steep gangway and onto the scrubbed, wooden deck of the *Erin go Bragh*. As they stepped onto the deck, the family were confronted by a stern-looking man with a dark-blue seaman's jacket and peaked cap.

"Welcome on board the *Erin go Bragh*. Could you please register with this gentleman here," he said as he indicated another serious-looking man seated at a small table on which was an open book.

This man eyed Teddy and his family, then said, "First, let's see your tickets. Then I need the names of all your family, their ages, their occupation and where you are from."

Teddy handed the tickets to the man, who placed them on the table. Let's let's start with you, mister," indicating Teddy. "What's your name?"

"My name is Edward Ryan. I'm fifty one. You had better put down I'm a labourer, though up till last year I was a farmer with my own plot of land. We're from Kilclonfert in Kings County."

The man checked Teddy's ticket before Teddy then proceded to give the same information for the rest of the family.

Having completed giving their names and information for the ship's passenger log and receiving their tickets back, the family moved further onto the deck. They stood looking around at their surroundings with a mixture of wonder and interest. It was a totally new experience and environment for them all.

Teddy saw that the wooden deck was a good-sized open area with a raised deck to the stern, under which was a door at each side. There were three tall masts with sails furled on wooden spars, and everywhere were ropes connecting parts of the masts or sails. As he looked up at the masts, he spied some figures high on one of the spars. Staring in amazement, he watched these men work their way to ladder-like ropes attached to the ship's sides. Then they swiftly slid down these ropes to the deck.

One of the seamen glanced over at Teddy and observed his slack-jaw wonder at what he had just seen. He walked over to Teddy and, smiling at him, said, "Yer liked that performance of shimming down the riggin, did yer?"

John, who was beside Teddy and had also been watching the seamen, exclaimed, "That was amazing, how they balance themselves so high up then come down them ropes so easily!"

"Well, it takes some practice and ain't for the faint-hearted, and sometimes they do lose their footing up there if the seas are rough," explained the seaman. "So, you're gonna be sailing on this here, *Erin go Bragh* all the way to Moreton Bay, are you?"

"We're going to Brisbane. I've not heard of Moreton Bay," said Teddy.

"Yer, well, that's as maybe. But it seems like Moreton Bay is where the ships mostly anchor if you're getting off at Brisbane."

"You seem to know something about these ships and sailin', and this ship looks to have an awful lot of sails," said John. "Does that mean it can go fast?"

"Well, now. I'm what's called the boatswain, and I've been sailin' since I was a lad, all over the place. It's my job to know all there is to know about how this ship works as I have to be tellin' the crew what to do after the officers decide what to do. This here ship has the right number of sails to move it through the water as fast as possible, though how much sail we actually puts on depends on the wind and the weather."

"This here is the main mast," said the boatswain, pointing to the massive timber that soared over one hundred feet from the ship's centre. "Then there's the foremast towards the bow; that's the front of the ship," he said as he pointed to a mast almost as tall as the main mast. "Back towards the stern, that's the back of the ship; there's the mizzen mast. Then, each mast has them cross pieces, called spars, from which the sails hang. All them ropes hangin' down supporting the masts are called shrouds. And those shrouds that are made up like ladders are called ratlines. There are also those other lines coming down that are used to alter the sails, and they all have different names."

"To be sure, it's confusing for us, who haven't been on a ship before," stated Teddy.

"Well, you'll get to see how it all works when we set sail tomorrow. Right now, I'd best be getting on with me work before the captain there blasts me head off."

Teddy turned to see on the deck towards the stern a stout man of medium height with long sideburns and a ruddy complexion that could have been the result of numerous tots of rum but also be due to almost constant exposure to the elements at sea. He was dressed in a long navy-blue coat with a dark blue peak cap and had a commanding presence, though his demeanour at this point was somewhat thoughtful.

Captain Borlase had witnessed the scene before him many times over the last dozen years, first as an officer, then as captain of migrant ships, the last five years being with the Black Ball Line. As passengers came on board, he observed the usual motley collection of emigrants, most down on their luck and carrying what few chattels they had to start a new life in a foreign land. Well, good luck to them. He turned to a well-dressed and well-endowed middle-aged woman beside him. "These poor creatures seem worse off than many we have seen in the last few years, my dear."

Mrs Borlase, who would rather travel with and share her husband's hardships on his many voyages than be a grass widow for long periods, eyed the milling passengers.

"I fear you are right, George. This does seem like a particularly down-at-the-heel crowd. Heaven help them, particularly those with babes and young children, with such a long voyage ahead."

The tangy smell of the sea arising from the deck and the ship, in general, was completely alien to the Ryan family and the other passengers. As they stood, taking in the sight and smell of their home for the next few months, an officious-looking sailor approached them and asked for their tickets. Having looked at the eight tickets, he directed them to a hatchway to one side halfway along the deck.

"As a family, you'll be in the mid-section of steerage. The fore-section is for single males, and the stern section is for single females. We don't want those two mixing, do we or we might have some trouble?" he remarked with a sly wink, to which Jane showed her disapproval.

"But before you go below, the captain, there," he said, nodding to the stern, "would like a word with all the passengers. So, just hang on for a while here."

Eventually, after some time and the deck had become crowded with milling passengers, the captain moved to the quarterdeck rail and looked down on his passengers.

"I would like to welcome all of you aboard the *Erin go Bragh*. My name is Captain Borlase, and I am in charge of this ship on our voyage to Brisbane in Australia. It is going to be a long voyage and may get rough at times, both the weather and your comfort, but that can't be helped. When it does get rough you may be told you can't come on deck. This is for your own safety, but also it stops passengers getting in the way of the crew going about their tasks. Now, for things to run smoothly, we have some rules that need to be followed to maintain cleanliness and order. I believe that cleanliness on a ship helps to prevent sickness. The stewards will explain these rules to you. And, one final thing. I'll not have any fighting on my ship, and anyone who starts a fight will suffer the consequences."

As the captain turned away, the sailor who earlier checked their tickets turned to Teddy. "Now, when you get yourselves settled in the tween deck, a steward will tell you about what food you can expect from us on board, plus how you can cook any food and some other matters that you'll need to know as well as them rules the captain was talking about. In the meantime, just to let you know, there are five privies along each side of the ship for everyone's use, plus there are two privies up forward just for the use of females and children. You can't miss any of those as your nose will guide you."

Teddy led his family towards the hatch that opened onto some stairs going down into what seemed a rather dark hole. The stairs were steep and weren't easy for Jane, but she had handed Peter to Anne, who, in turn, gingerly made her way down to the tween deck.

As he stepped off the stairs and peered into the gloom, Teddy's first impression was of a large dim space overcrowded with twin narrow, wooden bunk beds. These jutted out along each side with a space of about two feet between them, and then there were two rows alongside each other down the middle of the deck with two aisles on either side six feet wide. Each set of two bunks was divided by a wooden partition to make a sort of cubicle.

There was about nine feet of headroom, which made the deck appear more spacious, though there was only some three feet above the upper bunk, while the lower bunks were about a foot off the deck. Between each set of bunk beds was a small wooden table that could be raised and stowed against the bulkhead. Light came from open square portholes along each side, though it was still gloomy given the overcast nature of the day. He could see that several families had already arrived and claimed bunks.

The Ryan family found several bunks close together midway along the deck. Teddy told Jane to take the lower of two bunks along the side. He informed William and Tessie they would have to share a bunk, which William grumbled about, but was made to accept. Peter was grizzling again, and Jane sat on the bed to breast feed him as best she could, but after several minutes of suckling, he was crying again as Jane had no further milk. She was distraught and weeping herself.

"I've got no milk, Teddy," she said, sobbing. "And I don't seem to have the energy to care for him properly."

Teddy looked at Jane and saw a woman who was worn out, malnourished and filled with guilt at not being able to feed and care for her child. "Jane, my love, we have to get you stronger somehow. Perhaps, some good food and then the sea air might help. But don't blame yourself. We didn't ask for an eighth child, so it's up to God to provide."

"Teddy Ryan, don't you go talking like that and blaming God. That'll get you nowhere but a place in hell. No, we'll manage somehow, God willing."

"Well, you rest up a bit, and I'm going up into the town to see about getting us, particularly you, something wholesome to eat. Goodness knows when we'll get some food on this here ship."

With that, Teddy and John went ashore and found some shops where he bought bread, radishes, a few onions, some cheese and some milk in a bottle. Back on board, he convinced Jane to have some food while the others in the family devoured a good portion of the food he'd bought.

As they were finishing their meal, Father Dunne came down with a crew member in his twenties. He walked around talking to the passengers. Then he asked if they would all pay attention as he stood on the steps to the deck.

"My fellow travellers, we've made it on board the *Erin go Bragh* at last, thanks be to God, and we're supposed to be sailing tomorrow. Now, this here gentleman is John Condron. He is one of four passenger stewards on the ship. He will keep you informed of what is going on and what you need to do, particularly if the weather gets a bit rough. He is also responsible for prohibiting any consumption of alcohol on board."

At this last statement, there were a series of protests from many of the men. "How are we expected to stay sane over four to five months cooped up down here if we can't have the odd tot or two?"

John Condron held up his hands and when there was quiet said, "Look, I ain't an ogre, and I like a drink myself. So, what the eye doesn't see, ain't happening. You get what I mean. And then there'll be times when some liquor is needed for medicinal purposes. But I ain't tolerating any drunkenness or brawling, do yuh hear? Part of my job is maintaining order and strict morality, so don't forget it."

"Now, I can also tell you that there's three passenger cooks on board. Their job is to bake bread, keep the fires alight in the cookhouse, cook food for some passengers, and organise for passengers to cook their own food. However, after today, you will all be responsible for cooking most of your own food."

At that, there were several shouted comments about, "Where do we get the food to cook as we only bought a few supplies on board?" And, "How is it going to work, cooking our food when there's so many of us?"

"Okay, okay, quieten down!" yelled the priest. "The ship has food supplies for all the passengers to last for the whole voyage. It may not be the sort of food you might like, but then they have to carry supplies that won't go bad, or, at least, not rot too much."

John Condron continued, "You are going to have to organise yourselves into what they call messes. These should be about ten adults, which, in this deck, would mean two or three families combining. Each mess will draw rations together, cook, and eat. You are to select a mess captain to collect your rations and keep order in your mess."

"There'll be two meals each day, dinner at one p.m. and tea at six p.m. But if the weather is rough and stormy, no fires will be lit, so you'll have to make do with cold rations."

"Now, you may not like it, but there are rules for while you are on the ship. That's to make sure that everything is done in an orderly manner and things are kept clean and hygienic. And here's what them rules are: each morning, you must be out of bed by seven o'clock unless you are sick. Steerage passengers – that's you, also have to clean their own berths and keep everything down here neat and tidy. That includes emptying any buckets you may have used to relieve yourselves or throw up into."

There was a sullen silence.

"Finally, lights will be turned out at eight p.m. when you should all be in bed."

Father Dunne now spoke up, "For the children, we shall try and organise a schoolteacher so that your children can attend some lessons and keep learning. And there is also a surgeon on board to help deal with any sickness, but he can't do anything about seasickness. You'll just have to get used to that."

"What's seasickness, Father? Is it when you're pining for mermaids?" asked one of the men as his wife gave him a dirty look and slapped her hand across his chest.

"Oh, it's got nothing to do with mermaids, James Wren, but a lot to do with the sea when it's all furious," was John Condron's reply. "There's buckets you can see down here. Make sure you use them when the time comes; otherwise, the deck gets awful slippery."

Father Dunne again addressed the passengers, "My cabin is at the rear of the ship, under the raised quarterdeck, if anyone needs to talk to me at any time. Now, we'll leave you to settle in and make yourselves as comfortable as possible."

While Kate and Anne helped to arrange the family's belongings, Teddy went exploring to find out how and where meals would be prepared and when some dinner might be available.

The deck was crowded with a mixture of passengers and crew; the latter mainly involved loading cargo into two holds opening onto the deck towards the bow and aft of the main mast. There was a strong wind blowing in from the southwest across the harbour, raising white caps from which salty spume was being blown across the ship, and Teddy found he had the tangy taste of salt on his lips.

He made his way to the stern, where he could see smoke rising from a chimney on the side of the quarterdeck. Inside a cramped and somewhat smoky space were two large iron stoves into which a burly, almost bareheaded man with a filthy apron was adding charcoal from a sack against one wall. Several large pots and pans hung from hooks on the ceiling, and two pots were already on the stove. The aroma of a lamb and vegetable stew came from them, sufficient to make Teddy's mouth water as he realised he had not eaten much all day.

The man, whom Teddy presumed was the cook, glanced up as Teddy came in. "Supper ain't ready yet. That'll be around sundown or five o'clock."

"I'll be back here then to get a bit of that stew for my family. It's starting to smell quite tasty. But what about us cooking for ourselves? How's that work?"

"Well, I keeps the fires going, provided that there ain't rough weather. When that happens, there's no fires as we don't want to burn the ship to the waterline. So, when you cook something for yourselves, and most of the family passengers do, then you brings it up here or to the other galley on the other side of the ship and cooks away to your heart's content. Though there's enough room for a few messes to cook at once, you don't want to be spending too much time on your cooking; cos others will also want to be cooking."

Having understood how meals were prepared, Teddy strolled to the side of the ship and looked down on the dock. Workers were milling around and loading all sorts of cargo, including, he saw, some of the baggage and goods that the passengers had brought with them. As he stood watching, he was joined by Tessie and William.

"Baby Peter is crying so much and making such a ruckus, I wanted to get away," explained Tessie. "Anyway, it is sort of exciting being on this ship, and I would rather be exploring or seeing what is going on than sitting down in that dark place where we have to sleep."

Teddy felt guilty that he wasn't helping Jane with Peter, but then Maria and Anne were there, and what could he do anyway. The poor bub had colic or was hungry, and Jane didn't have the milk to feed him properly. *But what will we do about caring for and feeding Peter, and we're just starting out on this voyage?*

William wanted to know what the dock workers were doing and when they would be sailing. So, after spending some time explaining, Teddy left the two of them in the care of each other with an admonition not to leave the ship and to stay out of harm's way. He made his way down into the gloom of the tween deck, where he could hear Peter still quietly sobbing, being too tired now to do more than that. Jane was sitting on one of the bunks holding Peter, looking weak and exhausted.

He suggested that Anne take Peter onto the deck for some fresh air, hoping that might help, while he put his arm around Jane and tried to think of how he could help her. At a loss for anything helpful to say, Teddy held his tongue and continued holding her.

The tween deck was now swarming with families who had moved in and settled into their cubicles and bunks. Peter was not the only child crying; three or four others were howling their unhappiness at the unfamiliar situation or demanding to be fed.

As dusk approached, with grey skies still hanging low over the town, the gloom in the tween deck deepened. Somewhere on deck, a bell rang just twice.

Maybe that's dinner, thought Teddy and eased Jane up, urging her to come and get something to eat.

The stew was hot and quite tasty, and Teddy, with Jane and his children, stood around on the deck eating from the wooden bowls they had brought with them, using wooden spoons. Teddy spied a more smartly dressed man that he took to be an officer and approached him.

"Are we going to be sailing tomorrow, as we've been told?"

The man eyed Teddy and recognised a down-at-the-heel but respectable man. "We were hoping to have sailed with the morning tide about dawn, but that won't happen as there's still some cargo to come, and we need a clearance from the harbour master as there was a leak coming over from Liverpool that we think we've fixed. Perhaps we'll make the afternoon tide, but it depends on the winds, as we need to clear the harbour mouth while it's still light."

More delays. Teddy found his patience wearing thin. Would they never leave? It was as if some force or fate was playing with them, having offered a brighter future, then keeping it just out of reach. And this news would not help Jane's mood, as she was already fed up with all the delays and shenanigans hindering their departure.

He walked back along the broad expanse of the deck to the stairs or companionway that led down to their accommodation. He thought, *best see how everyone is doing and get them all settled for the night.*

The only light in the tween deck came from several enclosed oil lamps. But these were enough for Teddy to see his family had allocated the four bunks in each of the two cubicles amongst themselves and were preparing their bedding. They only had six thin straw mattresses, which were shared with Jane, Teddy, and the older girls. Blankets were also being handed around to cover themselves and provide some cushioning on the wooden boards of the bunks that stank of carbolic soap and vinegar after being washed down earlier.

Peter was now asleep in Anne's arms and was given to Jane when she was ready for bed. As the family settled down for the night, there was low murmuring amongst the passengers, with the occasional fart and loud curse. Teddy lay with William and listened to the unfamiliar, almost rhythmic sound of waves lapping against the ship's side.

This is it. We are on our way, or, at least, tomorrow we will be. God preserve us all and keep us safe and, oh please, God, may this not be a wild and useless adventure but lead to a much better future for us all.

****

He awoke sometime later to Peter's screams and Jane's frantic attempts to quieten him. Moving to her bed, he took Peter from her. Better to scream to the night outside than disturb the folks down here. Having wrapped Peter in a blanket, he made his way up the companionway to the deck above. The deck appeared deserted, and the night air was chilly, with some stars seen through the openings in clouds. After pacing the deck for some time, eventually, Peter quietened, and he brought him back down to Jane.

The scene was repeated towards dawn as Jane failed to give Peter enough milk, and a bleary-eyed Teddy saw the light appear in a grey dawn that promised rain sometime soon. As he was trying to console Jane on his return to the tween decks, Mary Gavan, the wife of Teddy's friend John, came into their cubicle.

"I don't wish to intrude, but I see and hear you have a problem with your wee babe, and I might be able to help."

Jane looked at Mary, who was in her thirties and well-endowed. "Aye, I do have a problem, Mary. I thought the babe may have had colic, and we have been giving him some cordial. But that seems to have hardly any effect. It's really that there's not enough milk in my paps for the poor lad, and I'm at my wit's end as to what I can do. But why do you say you can help?"

"Well, I sees how you don't look too strong and having the babe and all. So, I thought there's no doubt the child isn't getting enough milk, poor little mite. No wonder he's crying and fussing so much. I have a wee babe myself, though he's older than yours. I thought I can share some of my milk with your wee one."

Jane looked like she would protest, feeling it was her responsibility to feed her child. But Teddy spoke up first. "Jane, to be sure, this would be a godsend! You know you don't have the strength or the milk to satisfy Peter, and if Mary here can help, that would be good for both Peter and you, and you can stop your fretting. After all, tis a long voyage to Australia, and Peter crying all the way would drive us and the rest of those down here half crazy."

"You're right, Teddy," said Jane wearily. "I just can't cope, and it's wearing me out. Perhaps if I can get some more rest and some food, the milk will come. Thank you, Mary. You are an angel in disguise sent by the Blessed Mother Herself. Would you like to take Peter now or sometime later?"

"I can give him a feed for a bit now, then see when I can do it later in the day." And with that, she took Peter in her arms and moved back to her cubicle.

Teddy set about organising a mess with Tony Molloy and John Gavan's families. The men and wives agreed that Teddy should be the mess captain, so he set about getting information on what rations he could get for them by visiting the cookhouse.

On this occasion, he found a different cook, a younger man in his twenties. Teddy explained that he was the mess captain for his mess and wanted to get food rations for the first few days.

"What's your name?" asked the cook, wiping his hands on a non-too-clean brown apron. "My name's Patrick

Langan, and we'll call your mess after your name. But it's not me that'll be giving out the rations; that'll be ole skinflint Daniel Baxter, the storekeeper. And he's gonna want to know how many adults, that's those over the age of fourteen, plus those between four and fourteen, 'cos they get half rations each."

Teddy set off to find the storekeeper, who was lounging at the rail watching some more cargo being loaded, including several cows and pigs. These were being led to pens on the forward deck.

Daniel Baxter was an unremarkable-looking man, except he did not appear to suffer from any lack of victuals. In fact, the ruddy complexion of his unshaven face and the veins in his red nose indicated that he also had access to a good supply of liquor.

Teddy approached the storekeeper and told him what he wanted. "There's twelve of us adults over fourteen and fourteen that are between four and fourteen."

Baxter eyed Teddy and felt that this was a man from whom he could make some money.

"You know there's only supposed to be no more than ten adults in a mess, and you've got nineteen when you count the younger ones for half an adult each. So, I can only give you the rations for ten adults, or you can reduce your mess to enable everyone to eat proper like."

"We are all friends, and we thought it best if we stuck together. And what would you do with the rations for the other six adults?"

"Well, you can make a mess of your friends, but the rules state there's only supposed to be ten in a mess. And what I do with the rations for the other six is my business. Of course, if you would like to pay something extra, I can make sure you get enough rations for your whole mess."

Teddy was stunned. He or the others could not pay extra for rations for the mess above that allowed for ten adults, though he recognised this was likely a scheme the storeman had devised to make money.

"But it is our business 'cos we want to be fed properly," came a third voice, and they turned to see that John Gavan had joined them. "I'm not having my family starving 'cos you are using some rules to make yourself better off, Mr Baxter. I can't see that it's any skin off your nose if we have nineteen in our mess, except that you can try and make some money by takin' food out of the mouths that deserve to have it. And we'll take exception if you try and short us on the rations. So would other families in our tween decks, many of whom will also have more than ten in a mess, as there are some mighty big families on this here boat, and we're fed up with getting pushed around by uppity, greedy people! We had enough of that back in King's County."

Baxter saw he wasn't going to win this one and agreed, with ill grace, to give the full rations to the mess, despite its size. He led the two men down to a large locker towards the bow of the ship.

As they made their way along the deck, John Gavan quietly said to Teddy, "I thought I had better come and give you a hand, but it seems like you needed a hand in more than carrying the rations."

Teddy expressed his thanks and relief that John had turned up. "I wasn't going to let the bugger get away with a swindle, but you saved the day, John."

Down in the locker, amidst barrels, sacks, and boxes of foodstuffs, the storekeeper doled out their rations and gave them a sack and a wooden box, into which he started placing various items.

"You're entitled to some flour or hardtack biscuits and oatmeal, peas and potatoes, plus tea, sugar and salt as well as a small portion of raisins, suet and butter while they last. And there's fresh meat from the cows and pigs we brought on board to which you are entitled till that's all gone, then it's gonna be potted or salted meat. Also, each day, you can draw a ration of water to drink and cook. The children can also get a quarter of a pint of preserved milk a day."

Having selected sufficient rations, the two men carried them back to the tween decks, where the women proceeded to plan meals based on the available rations and using what they had brought on board themselves. The first would be dinner that day, so a start had to be made almost immediately.

Later in the morning, Teddy emerged onto the deck with John Gavan, William and Tessie. The last few barrels and boxes of cargo were being winched or carried on board and down into the holds. Then, shortly after the last cargo was aboard, an order was shouted from one of the officers, and preparations commenced for their departure. William was fascinated by the men scrambling up the ratlines and then working their way out along the yards where they were loosening the sails, though not unfurling them.

Then, nothing more happened, with the sky darkening and the wind rising. A passing crew member told them they were waiting for the ebb tide and for a steam tug to come and move them into mid-stream. Teddy saw the women in his mess head towards the cookhouse with ingredients for dinner in a box. Then, a few minutes later, Jane approached him, scowling. *What is it now?* Teddy thought.

"We can't have no dinner cooked today on account of we're about to set sail, and we're told we will all get in the way!"

"That means we shall have to be eating some cold food. How about some of that blood sausage and boxty we brought with us, and there's still some bread I got from the cook this morning. We won't starve, and at least we shall be on our way soon. Then we can have something hot for tea this evening once we've set sail."

Jane let out an exasperated sigh and was about to go off to prepare some cold dinner with the other two mothers and the older girls when Teddy put his hand on her arm. "But come back here soon, my love, so we can watch leaving Ireland together."

Teddy went below to the tween deck shortly after with William and Tessie for some dinner but was soon back on deck, as were William and his two older sons. A steam tug had come alongside, and ropes were being thrown to her. The gangway had been raised on the landward side, and men were standing by the bow and stern lines, ready to cast off. Aloft, the crew swarmed in the rigging, ready to unfurl some of the sails.

This is finally it, thought Teddy. He had mixed feelings; huge relief that, after all the planning and procrastinations, they were finally on their way. That was combined with a tight knot of fear in his gut about what might lie ahead for himself and his family on the voyage, and on their arrival on the shores of Australia. But there was also a sense of excitement and anticipation about a better future for them all. Overall, though, there was a deep feeling of sadness. He was leaving his Ireland, his home, with its familiarity gained over five decades.

Leaving Ireland

The deck was crowded with passengers, rugged up in woollen coats and shawls against the chill wind blowing from the west. Most were looking towards the dock, many with glum faces. Some women were weeping. For them all, despite the promise of a brighter future across the oceans, they were tearing themselves from their homeland and, in most cases, from family and friends.

Jane came up to stand by Teddy, as did the girls, except for Anne, who was below minding Peter. As the bow and stern lines were cast off and hauled aboard, Teddy felt deeply saddened as if this meant cutting all ties with his birthplace.

"This is it, Jane. There's no going back now. It's a mighty big venture we've taken on, and I pray to God and all the saints that we've made the right decision."

"Now, don't you go doubting yourself, Teddy Ryan. We've made our bed, and we're going to have to lie in it, though I am sore afraid myself. It's not just the long voyage, but what may await us at the end, at the other side of the world."

Teddy put his arm around Jane's shoulders and held her tight. "We'll do it together, my love, and take the consequences together."

As he said this, Teddy felt the ship move, with the tug pulling it away from the dock. The cold fear in the pit of his stomach intensified. Progressing slowly southward towards the harbour mouth, he could feel the ship reacting to the waves with some slight rocking. This was a new sensation for him and others on the deck.

William asked, "Is it going to get much more bumpy than this, Father?"

"I am sure it will get much bumpier, William, when we get into the open seas. But don't you worry. You'll soon get used to it."

The steam tug left them midway to the harbour entrance, and as it moved away, the orders went up to the sailors in the rigging to unfurl the sails. As the heavy, dirty-white canvas fell from the yards, the wind immediately filled them with a loud thump. The *Erin go Bragh* now began to make its own way, heeling slightly to the port side as it increased speed.

This was a novel experience for the passengers as none had been on a boat at sea before. Many had not even seen the sea. Several of them moved to the rails on both sides to watch the bow cut through the grey, choppy harbour waters. As Teddy and Jane watched, they slowly made their way to the harbour entrance. And, as they approached this and the open sea beyond, Teddy could feel the deck move more underneath him as larger swells advanced through the entrance. By the time they had cleared the harbour, the ship was well and truly in the grip of a mounting sea. But it was a beam sea, coming at the ship's side from the west, causing it to roll with each wave that passed under it.

Neither Teddy nor Jane spoke, each overwhelmed by their thoughts, as they clung to the portside rail and watched the green hills of their homeland slowly ebb away in a misty rain. Then, looking very pale, Jane said, "I feel awful sick, Teddy." And with that, she vomited onto the deck, bringing up her dinner.

Teddy held her until she was done, then suggested they go below. In the married section of the tween decks, Teddy led Jane to her bunk, where she lay down. The ship's motion had changed as it altered course to the southwest, with the sea coming on the bow quarter. It was a frightening experience as the bow lifted then plunged into the next wave, sending a mighty shudder through the ship. Teddy himself was only slightly queasy and hoped it would pass. They were on their way, but it felt like the ship might break apart each time it hit a wave. Knowing there would be a lot of this rolling, pitching and shuddering of the ship, and probably worse when they were in a storm, meant it would be an extra long and arduous voyage.

On the quarterdeck, Captain Borlase walked over to the mate, Walter Meyler, who, as the officer of the watch, was eyeing the sails and wondering if he should make some changes.

"We'll need to take a westerly course, Mr Meyler. Though, this wind from the northwest and the swell from the west will make it slow going. Keep her close hauled, but not too much canvas."

"Aye, Captain," was the mate's terse reply as he moved away to shout orders to the crew.

As the afternoon progressed, the ship's motion remained much the same, and Teddy went back on deck to see what it was like and get some fresh air as the tween decks were getting stuffy. Many passengers felt it would be better to lie down than be upright with all the motion, but that didn't stop nausea and the sweet, acrid smell of vomit permeated the tween deck, even when buckets were being used.

With the wind and sea on the starboard bow, Teddy found the sensation of the big sailing ship making its way through the grey, white-capped waves exhilarating. It was heeled slightly to port, making it difficult for Teddy to maintain his balance. As the massive sails powered the ship through the water, it rose to the peak of a white-capped grey wave before plunging down the other side and into the next wave, sending spray flying over the bow and forward deck.

His elder sons joined him, and together they stood by the starboard rail to take in this new adventure, bracing themselves against the roll and heel of the ship.

Andrew was particularly taken with the experience and commented, "This isn't too bad. In fact, it's sort of enjoyable. Perhaps being a sailor wouldn't be so bad."

"I have a feeling this is an easy ride compared with what it could be like when the weather is misbehaving," replied John, who had to steady himself as the ship hit a larger wave.

Teddy looked to the west, where the clouds looked darker. "We should start preparing some tea before the weather gets nasty. Come along, lads. Let's get something cooking," and with that, he moved back down to the tween decks.

After talking with Jane and the others in his mess, he collected the ingredients for a simple stew and headed to the cookhouse. Mary Gavan and Lizzie Molloy joined him, as did John.

They found others were already there but set about peeling praties and dicing meat on the deck outside while bracing against the ship's motion. Then, when their turn came, they quickly put their pot on the hot stove and waited while it cooked, stirring occasionally. The pitch and roll of the ship was increasing and they had to make sure that the pot did not overturn on the stove. A two-inch metal flange around the stove's edge was there to prevent pots from sliding off.

In time, the meal was cooked, and Teddy gingerly carried the pot below deck, together with some bread he had obtained from the cook. The tween deck now smelled of several hot meals floating in the air, but this was also mingled with the smell of vomit as several passengers felt decidedly queasy. Jane and Anne were among them and would only take some dry bread. Despite the increased motion of the ship in the mounting sea, Teddy and the rest of the family finished the meal between them.

Back on deck, after seeing that Jane and Anne were as comfortable as they could be, Teddy noticed how the wind had increased. The ship was now being driven faster, the bow smashing into waves, sometimes with a shuddering jar that went through the entire ship. The crew were aloft in the rigging furling the large mainsail and fore course. He gazed with awe as they balanced on the ropes below the yards and then made their way rapidly back down the ratlines to the deck, despite the increased motion of the ship. He wondered if anyone ever fell off, as it seemed they had little to support themselves except the line under the yard on which they were standing and their bare hands.

He didn't stay long on the exposed deck as rain now accompanied the increased wind, and his coat was soon soaking wet. He stumbled down the companionway to the tween decks, struggling to keep his balance on the now-wet stairs. A scene of near chaos and misery met him in the dim light as passengers endeavoured to secure their belongings while keeping upright. Others, having succumbed to *mal de mer,* retched into buckets or any receptacle they could find or straight onto the deck, which was usually the option for many children. Others lay huddled on their bunks. But the eyes of many showed utter terror for this new and uncontrollable experience they were going through.

As he watched the turmoil, a loud voice behind him yelled to close all the port holes. The steward Condron stood with his legs apart, braced against the ship's rolling motion. "There's a storm coming up, and you don't want to let water in to make life even more miserable!" he shouted.

The men heeded his warning. But darkness descended on the deck with the port holes closed, except for the faint light from a few enclosed oil lamps or candles. Slowly more lanterns were lit, although not enough to provide more than an indistinct viewing of one's surroundings. Teddy found his way to the family's bunks. Jane was lying and looking quite ill, as were Catherine, Anne and John, the latter leaning over a bucket and spewing up his dinner. Teddy felt a bit queasy, and the smell of vomit added to his queasiness, but he had things on his mind other than sea sickness. He sat by Jane and smoothed her brow.

"How are you feeling, Jane?"

She opened her eyes and stared at him. "And how do you think I am feeling, you dolt? I feel so sick I think I must be dying, and this ship is moving all over the place and probably not in the right direction. It ain't natural, I tell you. And I'm scared, Teddy. Are we going to sink, as I can't see how the ship can stay floating in this storm?"

Well, thought Teddy, *she hasn't lost her spark*. "They tell me you can get used to it after a while, and then you just carry on like a sailor," he said, trying to placate her. "I am sure we're not going to sink. I was up on deck, and the ship may be bouncing around a lot, but it doesn't look like it's sinking."

"And who would those be that tell you these fine words about getting used to this ship's motion?" asked Anne. "Do you know if they've ever been to sea in rough weather?" At which point she promptly leaned over and dry retched into a bucket.

Teddy chose to ignore the comment and proceeded to make sure that all their belongings were secure before lying down on the bunk above Jane, where William was already sitting, watching and listening to all that was going on.

****

That first night at sea was a rough baptism for the migrants on the *Erin go Bragh*. The storm increased in intensity as the ship made its way almost due west from Cork into the Atlantic. For the passengers in the tween deck, it was a terrifying nightmare. In almost total darkness, they literally clung to their beds, many suffering the misery of seasickness as the ship's motion became increasingly violent. When it plunged into yet another wave, a vicious shudder would shake the vessel through its length, convincing those passengers capable of rational thought that the ship must surely break apart.

They could hear the howl of the wind in the rigging, where only storm sails now gave the ship steerage. She was close-hauled with the wind on the port beam and the sea coming onto the port bow. The result was a violent corkscrew motion making the helmsman's job difficult to keep a steady bearing.

The rain and sea spray made life on the deck for the night watches unpleasant, but they also added to the discomfort of life below decks as water dripped through the closed hatches and air vents. Soon, a number of the bunks were sodden, and passengers were crowding into drier parts.

Dawn and some light from open hatches revealed the married tween deck sodden with water and slippery, in places, with vomit and urine. Many could not get to a water closet or find a bucket, so 'needs must'. At least the sea seemed not to be as rough, although there was still a noticeable roll, and they could hear the crash and feel the shudder as the bow dove into another wave, pushed on by more of a following wind on the starboard quarter.

Teddy climbed down from his bunk and sat next to Jane. She smiled at him, though she still seemed weak.

"Jesus, Mary, and Joseph, I thought that night would never end, and I was sure we would all perish. I don't know how the ship can take such a beating, but it seems calmer now, and I don't have that feeling like I want to throw up all the time."

"Would you like something to eat, Jane? It's been some time since you've put something in your stomach, and whatever was there has long since come up."

"Aye, I could maybe have a bit of boxty. That would go well with some hot tea, although maybe it's still too rough to be lighting a stove. But how's Peter? I haven't heard from him at all during the night?"

"Peter's fine. Mary Gavan, God bless her, took him in hand for a bit during the night, and I guess she gave him a feed. Then, he didn't seem too worried about the movement of the ship. Maybe he's too small to understand and thought it was just someone rocking him to sleep. Now, I'll go and see about making some tea."

With that, Teddy checked on the rest of his family, told Maria to get her mother some of the boxty they brought, and then made his way up on deck.

The rain had ceased, and the wind was less fierce, although the sea was still grey and angry with towering waves topped with wind-whipped white caps. He noted that more sails had been added, and, as a result, the ship was ploughing through the waves sending spray flying over the bow. Several other passengers were on deck, taking the air after a night cooped up in the tween decks, and Teddy greeted a few as he made his way to the cookhouse.

There, he found that the stoves had been lit, and the smell of baking bread was in the air. Patrick Langan was there as a cook again and allowed Teddy to boil some water in a kettle. Then as Teddy was due to depart with the boiled water, Patrick handed him a loaf of freshly baked bread and a pat of butter wrapped in paper.

Teddy looked at him in surprise, but Patrick just shrugged. "Well, I liked the way you stood up to that storeman, Baxter, the sly bastard, and I hears you have a large family with a newborn."

Teddy thanked him profusely and hurried back to the tween decks, where most of the three families immediately pounced on the bread and butter. Teddy managed to coax Jane into having a small portion with her hot tea, which had a good amount of sugar.

Peter was whingeing, so Jane took him to her breast and was able to give him some milk, after which Teddy suggested Anne and the other older children, who felt up to it, take him up onto the deck. He asked Maria to stay behind, and the two of them tidied up their bunks and belongings, putting what they could out of the way next to the ship's side or under the bunks, which had about ten inches of clearance below the bottom bunk. Some items were placed on the bunks to be removed, if necessary, to sleep.

With many variations, this was the start of what would be a daily routine. Teddy met with the other adults in his mess and discussed how they would organise meals for themselves and what provisions they would need if they were available. Then, he, John Gavan and Tony Molloy found Baxter, the storekeeper, and fetched his mess's daily ration of water, which amounted to three quarts for each adult for personal use and a gallon for the mess for cooking. Around noon, they collected what rations the mess was entitled to, including some already cooked items.

The ship was making heavy weather of it, with the wind now coming from the northwest onto their starboard bow. Their course was roughly west-south-west, with the ship having to tack, causing it to heel to the lee or port side. This was another novelty for the passengers, many of whom were on deck, with the less stable needing to hold onto something to keep their balance. But some, like Andrew and Maria, were finding their sea legs and discovered the swift, plunging movement of the ship, a somewhat thrilling novelty.

Around one p.m., announced by two clangs of the ship's bell, dinner was organised with Lizzie Molloy and Mary Gavan going with Teddy to get the cooking done in the cookhouse. The families in Teddy's mess again ate in the tween decks, sitting on their bunks and balancing pots and bowls in the none-too-steady conditions.

During the afternoon, a few of the passengers in the married tween decks organised some card games, which caused a few raised voices as disputes or exclamations of disbelief rang out. Other families just sat on their bunks or stood around talking. Anne had met one of the single women on the voyage while walking on deck, and she ventured down to the single women's quarters to see how they were, and there, the two young women sat and chatted for some time.

Tea was organised at five p.m, which was again announced by two bells. After that, the sound of a fiddle could be heard, and shortly after that, this was joined by another, with a couple of the men in the married quarters playing a lively jig. Many of the passengers gathered around with much foot tapping. The night was less rough than the previous one, and there was less seasickness. A feeling of comradery among the many families seemed to be developing, with children mixing and playing together.

****

The following morning saw a change in conditions with strengthening winds from the south. The ship was still tacking on a westerly course, and they were now well into the Atlantic, with a heavy swell from the southwest. The *Erin go Bragh* was rolling with it while ploughing into the wind-swept swells, much to the discomfort of the passengers. These adverse conditions meant the ship struggled to make more than three to four knots. Teddy and Andrew came on deck to find waves coming over the deck at the bow, and an officer warned them to go back below deck for their safety. They didn't hesitate as it was difficult to maintain their footing on the wet and violently moving deck.

The rough sailing continued throughout the morning and afternoon, and there were no meals cooked, not even tea, which meant the passengers existed on hard tack or the hard ship's biscuit with butter. But many felt ill again due to the rough seas, so eating was often not something they missed.

Life was claustrophobic and crowded in the married tween decks, with only dim light when the portholes were shut. The weather meant all the passengers were present, either lying down, sitting on the floor where it was dry or standing. Some were playing cards. Others were talking, reminiscing about the land they had just left, or speculating what it would be like at the destination. An increasing number of adults just sat staring vacantly at nothing.

Although the hatches to the deck were supposed to be kept closed in rough weather, they were often left partially open to allow in some fresh air. But that meant sea water and rain made their way through, and when some individual came or went, necessitating fully opening the hatch, often water would slosh down onto the tween deck. The smell of numerous unwashed bodies, sweat and a general mustiness from damp wool clothes and blankets hung in the air. Although some air did come down through vents in the upper deck and through the partially opened hatch, the atmosphere was becoming increasingly fetid.

Towards evening, the steward, Condron, appeared on the stairs to the tween deck and announced that small groups would be allowed on deck for short spells to get some fresh air. The seas were still rough with a strong wind blowing, and Condron told them not to go near the ship's rails but to stay inboard. He also told them to empty buckets or containers while they had the chance but warned them to be careful and not throw the contents into the wind.

Teddy told John and Andrew to take their nearly full buckets and accompany him up for some air. As they headed up the stairs together with Tony Molloy, John Gavan and half a dozen others, they were careful not to slop too much out of the buckets. Teddy noted that the rain had eased to a drizzle, though this still stung as the wind whipped it into his face.

The deck was wet, and the ship pitched into the waves sending windswept spray over the deck. But the fresh air was welcome as they clung to whatever post or hatch they could find. Teddy made his way to the foot of the aft mast and, hanging onto a belayed line with his feet apart, he surveyed the scene. The white-capped waves, as high as the side of the ship, rolled in from the west, and the wind filled the main and fore topsails and top gallants as well as a genoa at the bow. He could feel the force of the wind driving the ship forward, but also making it heel to the lee or north. As he looked down the length of the ship, he watched the deck rise and fall, with each fall ending in a shudder as the bow ploughed into a wave.

As he stood there, alone now, watching as his sons carefully negotiated emptying their buckets, the boatswlain came up to him. He was a small man, though Teddy could see that he was also well-built, like a boxer, wearing a shirt, woollen jacket and the mid-calf linen slops familiar to many sailors for some time. He also exuded confidence, despite appearing to be an ordinary seaman.

"You're a brave one, standing up here on deck in this here weather!" he exclaimed in a friendly manner.

"I needed some fresh air, but, to be sure, there's something grand and also frightening about the waves and how the ship seems to get through it all without sinking."

"Ah, so you're not one of the sops that's continuing to puke up their innards down below. And I grant you it does get a rather rich odour down in the tween decks after a few days of being confined there. My name's John Judd, and we were talking before when you boarded the ship. As the boatswain on this here ship I'm in charge of all the regular seaman, including all the riff-raff they hire to come on a trip like this. Some are useless as shite, but most end up doing a half-decent job. So, you're planning on starting a new life down in Queensland, are you?"

Teddy liked this man and his friendly manner. "Well, we were having a hard time of it after we were evicted from our crofter plots, and there doesn't seem like much of a future for the likes of us in Ireland now. I hope starting a new life in Australia will be good, not just for my wife and me, but more particularly for my sons. Perhaps they can really make something of themselves down there. But tell me, Mr Boatswain, ain't you ever afraid the ship will get swamped and sink when you get the wild weather like we had the other night, with waves higher than the ship's deck and pouring water all over the ship?"

"To be sure, sometimes, I get sore afraid in a real violent storm. But I've been a sailing now for nigh on twenty-five years, and you get to trust your ship, and it helps if you have a good captain, as Captain Borlase is, who you can also trust. It's rough now and will be for a few days till we head south into the warmer waters. Then, you won't be complaining about rough seas no more, as it will be getting awful hot, particularly for the likes of youse who haven't been south of Cork in your lives."

"So, we have to go south, but then, don't we need to go east or west to get to Australia?"

"Aye. I ain't sure of the exact route the captain is gonna take, but it's likely we'll sail roughly south till we near the coast of Africa, about the Canary Isles. Then we'll probably pick up the trade winds and head southwest towards the coast of South America. I know that sounds like we'd be heading in the wrong direction, but the winds and current along the coast of Africa make it difficult for sailing ships like ours to sail down south along the African coast. Once we get near the coast of South America, we'll head south until we pick up good winds coming from the west, and then we'll be heading east towards Australia. The farther south we go, the stronger the winds will be, but then the seas are also rougher, and it can be mighty cold, particularly during the winter down south."

With that, John Judd, boatswain, suddenly turned away and yelled at a seaman. "You dumb arsehole, you don't throw the feckin' slops into the wind! Now look what you've gone and put all over the deck," as most of the stinking contents of a slop bucket ended up on the deck and over the seaman. "Ah, some of them have nuttin' between their ears, but he's just learned a lesson." With that, John Judd moved off down the deck.

Alone again, Teddy viewed the sea with its powerful, grey-green waves that stretched as far as he could see. He could not help but reflect on how alone and vulnerable they were on this vast ocean, probably hundreds of miles from the nearest land, and they had so far to go. At least at the moment, the captain and John Judd were in control of the ship, but it seemed to Teddy that this control was a tenuous one that, with an increase in sea and wind, could be lost, and the sea would then take control. It was a frightening thought, although he also felt that a seaman, like the captain, must also experience a certain exhilaration in using or somehow controlling nature to power their ship through the ocean.

As the groups made their way onto the deck, the hatches were opened to allow more fresh air below. By the time Teddy returned to Jane and the family, the air was somewhat fresher.

Jane looked at Teddy and exclaimed. "You're wet through, and you stink of salt water!"

Teddy just smiled. "Oh, Jane, it is such a sight up there, with the wind and the waves. I wish you could see it."

"No, thank you very much. I am more than content to be down here and dry, though it isn't the best of places."

After their sparse tea, some passengers again started playing a couple of fiddles. Another brought out a tin whistle to add to the music, which now had many tapping their feet and some dancing where they could find a space.

Dancing was somewhat precarious as the ship's motion, which was quite violent at times, made even standing difficult. But the camaraderie that the music engendered helped to dispel, to some extent, the passengers' plight in the dim and smelly atmosphere of the tween deck. Even Jane tried some foot tapping while Andrew joined in the dancing.

****

The weather had not improved next morning. If anything, it was worse. Rain squalls sweeping across the sea and the ship's deck meant the hatches were kept shut. It would be another day without hot food, thought Teddy after he had surveyed the scene. He, Jane and Anne had spent a harrowing night as Peter had been fussy and crying quite a lot, even screaming at times, as if there was something seriously the matter with him.

But by daybreak, he had fallen into an exhausted sleep, and when Mary Gavan came by to see about giving Peter a feed, Jane suggested it would be better to wait until he had woken.

At least, now, there is some peace, thought Teddy. *If one could call it peace with the way the ship is pitching and rolling and the wind howling.*

The Troubles Start

The rough and stormy weather continued for several days as the ship headed southwest into the Atlantic and into the path of winter storms. With the winds coming mainly from between south and west, the ship was tacking quite often, making life for the passengers miserable. The continual rough corkscrew motion of the ship and spume flying over the main deck, then dripping down to the tween deck below, made life more oppressive by the day.

Captain Borlase was on the quarterdeck with his wife and daughter during a break in the rain. They stood surveying the sea and the ship as it made heavy weather of ploughing through waves higher than the ship's deck. Moving to the quarterdeck rail, the captain yelled to the third mate, James Green, who had the watch.

"She seems sluggish in responding to the helm, Mr Green, and slow in righting herself after heeling over."

Green was a slim man of average height with a pock-marked face that forever seemed to be scowling as if he was at odds with all in the world. He was dressed in a long, grey-green oil-skin coat, open at the front to show a rather dirty waistcoat and a sou'wester hat on his head.

"I've been noticing that myself for some little while now, Captain. Ain't sure what's causing it. We don't have too much sail, though the seas have a nasty cross chop to the swell."

The captain's experience from many years at sea and at least a decade as master of several sailing vessels similar to the *Erin go Bragh* made him think it might be a ballast problem.

"Mr Green, I think we need to check the bilges. We seem to be too heavy, and that's why she's slow to respond to the helm. Send someone down to have a look below if you please."

Green yelled to the boatswain, who shortly after was on his way below to investigate. He was back ten minutes later, moving as fast as he could across the deck towards the captain and third mate.

"Captain, we got a leak. There's nigh on two feet o' water in the bilges. I just had a quick look, but it's hard to see where it's coming in, though we definitely have a leak."

The captain's face turned pale at the mention of a leak. It was the last thing he needed to hear, particularly in the rough conditions they were experiencing.

"How the hell have we got such a leak after fixing that one we had coming over from Liverpool? It sounds like more than just seepage between the timbers. And the ship has a relatively new copper bottom."

"I wonder if it's the same leak we had going from Liverpool to Queenstown started again?" thought Green aloud.

"Perhaps you're right, Mr Green. Maybe something or someone back in Liverpool got it started. So, if that's the case, it can't be a large leak. We've been at sea now some eight days, and if the water is only at two feet, it's not coming in very fast. Still, we need to see if we can find out where the leak is and if we can deal with it. We also need to pump out the bilges to help us find the leak and improve our sailing capabilities. I want the pumps manned continuously until we clear the bilges or as near as clear."

Green ordered a roster of men to man the hand pumps as the captain strode off after checking to see that his wife and daughter were secure and happy to remain on deck. He also reassured them that they had nothing to worry about, as his wife had heard the conversation about the leak and expressed her concern to her husband.

He found the first mate, Walter Meyler, in his cabin. Meyler was an experienced sailor of medium height and slim though sturdy, tanned appearance, with the practised gait of a sailor who has weathered some rough weather at sea. He had served on several other migrant ships, including two previously with the captain.

Captain Borlase explained the situation to the first mate, who exhibited the same worried look as the captain.

"We have to see if we can locate the leak, Walter. Maybe we can fix the problem," said the captain.

"Have you considered turning back for Queenstown?"

"Of course, I have, but it doesn't seem that serious at the moment, and I feel we can keep it under control with some extra pumping. Besides, we have a schedule to meet. And what could they do in Queenstown to fix it in a hurry that we couldn't do while sailing that wouldn't take a month of Sundays? And if we had to spend time in Queenstown, what do we do with all these passengers? No, Walter, we carry on and make the best of it, hoping it doesn't develop into a more serious problem, which I am convinced it won't."

****

Six days at sea and some five hundred nautical miles west-south-west from Cork, the ship turned to head almost due south. It was also the day that tragedy struck.

Teddy heard the keening coming from further along the tween deck. He walked down to see what it was all about. Several passengers were standing around observing the scene of a distraught mother cradling her infant to her breast while the father stood with a forlorn expression trying to comfort his wife. They were a young family, in their twenties, with two young boys, who seemed to be twins, holding on to their father's trousers while asking what was wrong with their wee brother, James.

At that point, the ship's surgeon, James Long, pushed through those standing around the cubicle with the dead child. He gently took the child and laid it on the bunk. After a cursory examination, he straightened up and said to the parents, "I'm afraid the cholera has taken him. I am so sorry. I shall organise with the captain for the burial." And with that, he moved away down the length of the tween deck to the companionway with the air of a man who has seen such deaths too many times to affect him, although there was a sadness about his face. As he was about to climb up to the main deck, he waited as Father Dunne, having heard the sad news, was coming down.

"It's cholera, Father, and I'm afraid there's going to be more such deaths, particularly among the little ones," explained the surgeon.

"Thank you, Mr Long," said the priest as he nodded in understanding and then proceeded down the tween deck, putting the purple stole around his neck, prior to giving James McQueen, aged seventeen months, a final blessing.

The burial was late that afternoon, with Father Dunne reading the service. Captain Borlase was by his side, dressed in his formal dark blue captain's uniform with his long coat uncovered by an overcoat despite the cold wind.

Many passengers had also gathered to observe and comfort the weeping parents and their two surviving sons. They gazed at the captain's sombre, though not unkind, face recognising in him the man who was their guide and master on this voyage. Many sensed that this would not be the last such death on board. But death had always been so much a part of life in Ireland that there was an acceptance of its presence, although this did not diminish the anguish suffered for the loss of close relatives, particularly children.

As the ship headed south, Teddy noted that their progress was not as fast as with the stormy conditions encountered earlier. The less turbulent conditions, though, allowed hot meals to be eaten, much to the relief of the passengers who had been existing on cold fare for several days. This also made Jane feel more comfortable and spend time on deck with Teddy. She was overawed by the wide horizons of the seascape with nothing but blue-grey waves all around for as far as the horizon. For them both, this was a dramatic contrast to the more confined but variable vista of the rolling hills around Tullamore.

More of a routine was now being established with the various messes procuring their rations daily, meals being prepared, and sometimes eaten in groups on deck if the weather and seas were kind enough. Katherine and William began school lessons under Mary Killen, a twenty-four-year-old single governess.

At first, it was too chilly to hold classes on deck, even on fine days, so they were held during the morning for a few hours in the tween deck married quarters. The position varied almost daily, depending on what space was available. Mary initially decided to teach those children, both boys and girls, between eight and thirteen years of age, of which there were forty among the various families. Many had received little or no education, with some already working to earn money for their families. A few of these, though, were not interested in learning, and their parents weren't interested in their being educated, particularly the girls.

Mary decided to divide her classes into two. One group would consist of children with no or very limited education. The second group consisted of those who had already been attending school. She obtained a board made of several pieces of timber fastened together, plus some chalk. With this, she proceeded to get her classes underway. With no means of writing, her pupils were limited to learning by rote or by using the board to practice their writing.

Mary was not the stern, no-nonsense governess type. She was a slight woman with a good figure who carried herself well. Her pleasant, slightly round face invited confidence, and she had a twinkle in her brown eyes. She was also a born teacher, and it was a profession that she loved. So, although her tools were very limited, she was determined to succeed in providing some form of education to the children under her care.

Being a good storyteller, like many Irish, she found this gift was a great help in her teaching. Her tales told of Irish history, other countries' history, geography, and some of the basic sciences. She would describe how a tree or other plants needed roots both to hold it in the ground and to provide water and food so it could grow, and without water, it would die. She used her stories to help with basic maths.

"Now, a farmer was bringing four horses to town to sell. But when he came to the marketplace, he could only sell three horses. He wasn't too sad about this because at least he had one horse left to ride home."

Within a short time, Mary's classes became very popular, not only with the children, who often could not wait to attend, but also with some adults, who would hang around on the edge of the class to listen and, perhaps, to learn, although, some of the young single men seemed to have more on their minds than learning.

Each morning, Teddy and others in his mess would clean their cubicles, mop the deck and arrange belongings as neatly as possible. Jane, of course, had to join in as she always felt the men did not do a thorough job. This routine was affected by stormy weather when passengers could not go on deck, but still, Teddy endeavoured to keep his area somewhat tidy, for which he earned much begrudging praise from Condron, the steward.

Others in the tween deck were not so conscientious, with some areas being not just untidy but with the deck covered with the spilled contents of the bucket that had been used as a toilet, usually after rough weather; and this was despite the mess captains receiving numerous tongue lashings from Condron. Teddy and Tony Malloy had also added their protests, partly because of the smell and because they felt it wasn't healthy, not with young children often playing on the deck.

When the ship ran into rough and rainy weather several times over the next two weeks, the mess and stink from one end of the tween deck were exacerbated by the inability to clean properly and the closed port holes and hatches.

Teddy's concerns were justified a few days later when some infants became ill with fevers, vomiting and diarrhoea. Their crying and screaming could be heard throughout the tween deck while their parents were frantic. The surgeon, James Long, diagnosed that they had infant cholera.

Like many doctors of the time, he had no great knowledge of the disease or its effective treatment. Only eight years previously, in 1854, John Snow had discovered a link between cholera and poor sanitation, following several severe outbreaks of the disease in London. But his ideas were slow to catch on, and many still believed the disease was caused by a 'miasma' or poisonous vapour in the air.

The treatment of cholera was often based on ridding the body of the poisonous entity, and this was done with great vigour by applying emetics to cause further vomiting, plus purges and enemas to evacuate the bowel. Of course, this greatly hastened the loss of water from the patient, leading to dehydration. In some cases, a tincture of opium was given, which would have had some calming effect on the stomach as well as on the overall condition of the patient.

Mr Long tried all of these treatments on the infants, though to no avail on three of the infants, who were nine months, eleven months, and two years old. A day later, dehydration had left the skin on their tiny limbs dry and shrivelled, like paper, when pinched. The following day, the 25th of February, they mercifully succumbed to the disease and their tiny bodies were committed to the deep on a calmer day, with blue skies and white scudding clouds.

However, James Long was a practical man who had read John Snow's theory on the connection between cholera and poor sanitation. So, he ordered that the tween deck be thoroughly cleaned, particularly where the infants had died. Most passengers not involved with the cleaning crowded onto the deck, where they found the sun provided enough warmth to make it comfortable, despite a wind blowing across the deck from the west.

****

Over the proceeding ten days, the first mate had been monitoring the stinking bilges daily, and he found there was still more water accumulating than could be accounted for from seepage, despite the increased pumping regime that had been established. He reported this to the captain in the latter's comfortable cabin with glass windows looking out astern.

"I'm sure we have some further leaks, whether from the wearing of caulking between the hull planks or some other cause, I don't know. But I'm gonna have another good look to see what I can find when the weather is calmer, and we can move the ballast."

The captain's face showed concern. "Damn and blast, Walter. This here ship's been doing the Atlantic crossing for the Black Ball Line for some years, and I'll wager they've never given the hull a good checking. Now, they expect me to sail halfway around the fucking world in a leaky sieve of a boat and do it on time. Let's see if you can find those leaks, and then we'll try and stop them. I'm wary of putting on too much speed or being heeled over too much to the lee, as this might worsen the leaks. So, watch our speed and keep her from heading too close to the wind."

The following day, the 26th February and the eighteenth day at sea, another of the infants, a one-year-old, died of cholera. When no more deaths occurred for a few days, passengers started to feel that the miasma may have passed. But on the 1st of March, a year-old girl died again from cholera.

By early March, with the ship approaching 30 degrees north latitude and much calmer seas, the first mate, with three experienced seamen's help, found the leaks' main cause. The water level in the bilges was now relatively low, and the pumps were only being worked once every twelve hours. It was still hard to find a leak as a series of heavy iron ingots lay along the lowest part of the bilge, two or three layers thick. This was the ship's ballast, and the iron ingots were used as a means of transporting iron to the Australian colony.

Then towards the stern, one of the seamen spied an area of cleaner water in the otherwise rather dirty bilge water. On closer observation and using his hands he could feel about 4 round holes in the hull.

"Mr Meyler, I think I've found our leak, sir."

Meyler came as swiftly as he could with the confined head space and the jumble of iron ballast. "Well, well, well. What have we here?" He bent down and felt the holes, which could now be partially seen with more light from another lantern. "These look like they've been drilled. This isn't just seepage through plank separation or poor corkage. No. These here holes have been deliberately drilled. From what I can feel, they seem to be about half an inch wide."

They continued searching and found leaks between boards where the caulking had worked its way out, particularly in rough weather.

The captain was aghast when informed about the nature of the leaks by the mate. "What the hell! Someone was intent on sabotaging this vessel. But why?"

"It must have been one of the workers on the docks," was the mate's suggestion. "They're the ones most likely to be able to come down and do such a thing while the ship was in port. I doubt it would be one of the passengers on the ship now. They wouldn't be that fanatical to risk their own lives in case the ship sank."

"I think you're right, Walter. It's likely to have been someone with a grudge against the Irish in Liverpool," said the captain. "The anti-Irish feeling in Liverpool has been running high since hundreds of thousands came over from the famine and afterwards. The English workers don't like 'em one little bit as they think they're takin' jobs from the locals, and they work for less pay. It could be one such worker, who, knowin' this ship will be carrying a load of Irish to Australia, decides he's gonna take his revenge. Maybe it was personal, someone in his family missing out on a job to an Irishman. They also blame the Irish for a lot of the disease that's been taking people's lives. Then the Irish can be a rough lot, so maybe this man or someone close to him got beaten up or even killed by the Irish."

"Well, one thing we can be thankful for is that whoever drilled these holes either didn't realise the ship had a copper sheath on the bottom, or his drill couldn't get through the copper, 'cos when I pushed a stick into the holes, it hit the copper bottom, which was whole," volunteered the mate.

"That's as maybe. But we're still taking on water. It must be coming through between the copper sheath and the wooden hull as the copper only comes up to just below the waterline, and it is only sheets nailed on. So, with rough weather, there could be a separation between the individual copper sheets allowing water in."

"I agree, Captain, and with more rough weather to come, particularly down south, we could be in for a problem if we don't plug those holes tight enough to stop the leak."

****

The first mate organised for the holes to be plugged with wooden dowels covered in pitch while oakum[3] was used to caulk the leaking gaps they could find between the hull timbers. It was hard work in poor light and with the foul-smelling bilge water sloshing around. This seemed to stop the leak from the drill holes, although there was still the slow accumulation of water through poor caulking between the planks, which was harder to stop completely. Water was also seeping down to the bilges from seawater coming inboard during rough weather and then finding its way below deck, usually accumulating a mixture of human excrement and other delectable substances as it proceeded through the living quarters. The pumps needed to be operated at least once a day in rough weather and once every two days when conditions were calmer, but the stench in the bilges grew over time to be a miasma on its own.

Meanwhile, the deaths continued, one each day, for the next week, although not all were from cholera. On the 2nd of March, a four-year-old girl died from measles, and on the 6th of March, Tony and Liz Molloy's eighteen-month-old boy died of consumption, or at least that was what the surgeon said.

Both Tony and Lizzie were overcome with grief, and Jane and Teddy did what they could to comfort them. "I knew he was sick," sobbed Lizzie to Jane. "He'd been coughing, feverish, and sort of weak for some time. And we thought maybe being at sea would help him. But how could this stinking cesspit of a ship help him, being locked down here and freezing to death and filthy half the time; even when it's not stormy, it's been so rough it's hard to

---

[3] Oakum is **a preparation of tarred rope fibre used to seal gaps**. Its main traditional applications were in shipbuilding, for caulking or packing the joints of timbers in wooden vessels, both in the hull and on the deck.

stay on your bunk. The poor mite. He hardly complained, though, and now the angels have him, so at least there's that to be thankful for."

The surgeon had ordered a thorough cleaning of the tween deck with carbolic soap and vinegar in water. But this seemed to have had little effect. James Long may have had some inkling of the connection between good sanitation and cholera, but none of the passengers had any idea. A day of rough and rainy weather had them mostly confined below decks again with little ventilation, and the stench from faeces slops, which often spilled onto the deck from the buckets, was overbearing, particularly as the temperatures were warming up as the ship headed south. At the same time, the cries of feverish infants were constant and grated on the nerves of many, although they also may have had young children.

It wasn't just the young children who were ill. Several older children and adults also succumbed. Their vomiting and diarrhoea added to the stench and mess on the deck. But these older passengers seemed to recover after several days of torturous fevers and fluxes. The surgeon used the only known treatment at the time on those patients that would accept it, which was emetics and purging. He didn't seem to realise that the bodies of those sick with cholera were already losing fluids, particularly water, and such treatments only exacerbated their plight. The disease at this point was confined to the married tween deck, and many of those healthy enough spent their time on the open deck, some even sleeping there, so as to be away from the fearful miasmas that they believed were causing cholera.

****

In the first week in March, Walter Meyler reported back to the captain on another survey of the bilges.

"I'm afraid it ain't good news, Captain. I've found a number of points where we have more leaks coming through between the planks. The rough crossing from

Liverpool probably added to the problem. The caulking's poor at some places, and if it wasn't for the copper sheathing, I reckon we'd be in much worst trouble. There's also a couple of places where it looks like the Toledo worm has got in behind the copper, maybe where it's worked loose, and them worms have put a few holes in."

"Why didn't you find these leaks earlier, Walter?"

"Well, I guess once we found the bored holes and caulked a few leaks between timbers, then we stopped looking. Besides, this time we moved a lot of the iron ballast, which is a bastard of a job, and stinking too, where the bilge sludge that doesn't get pumped out has built up. That's where we found the wormholes and some other leaks, more down towards the keel line."

"Do your best to patch up the leaks, and we'd better increase our pumping to ease the water coming in. Let's hope we don't get a lot of rough weather between here and Moreton Bay 'cos that's gonna cause more problems."

"Aye, Captain. I'll get some lads on to it, and we'll do what we can, and I'll keep a closer eye on it from now on."

With that, the first mate left a dispirited captain with much to consider. The voyage had not started well, with the gales and storms delaying their journey from Liverpool to Queenstown. Then it seemed as if there was a lot of sickness with this cholera that had caused the death of several young ones. Moreover, he had found his ship was less than fully seaworthy with a leaking hull, and some of those leaks seemed likely to have been caused by sabotage. *Would something else turn up to mar this voyage?* he wondered.

****

Jane and Teddy were deadly afraid of Peter and even Tessie catching cholera, as, although several older children and adults were unwell, some quite seriously, it was the really young ones who were succumbing and dying.[4] They tried to stay isolated from the other passengers to the extent possible, and Jane, Teddy or Anne would take Peter on deck when they could. The fresh, salty breeze and the ship's rolling motion seemed to calm him down.

Jane regained some of her strength and was able to provide Peter with more milk. However, on the 6th of March, she noticed that Peter was more fretful, and as she tried to coax him to suck on her breast, he turned his head away. As she held his head, she noticed it was warm, and his face flushed and feverish.

Her heart sank, and when Teddy came down to the tween deck, she tearfully told him she felt that Peter was ailing and had a fever. Teddy immediately took the babe, explaining he was taking him to the surgeon. He climbed the companionway as fast as he could, cuddling Peter and trying not to weep.

He found the surgeon in the aft quarters of the ship, where he was sharing a tot with the first mate. Teddy burst in on them and thrust Peter at the surgeon, demanding, between breaths and sobs, to know whether Peter had cholera.

The surgeon looked annoyed at having been disturbed, especially by one of the steerage passengers, but he was not an unkind man, and he noted Teddy's obvious concern. Taking the baby in his arms, he felt the flushed face with the back of his hand.

"I'm afraid your babe is suffering from a fever, and he's also got a bad case of the shits, so it's probably cholera," he said quietly as he gingerly handed Peter back to Teddy.

"Is there anything we can do? Is there any treatment you can give to help him?"

---

[4] This may have been because the infants became dehydrated much more easily than the older children and adults following persistent diarrhoea and vomiting, and there was no means of rehydrating them effectively.

James Long looked at Teddy with weary sadness. "If he were an adult, I could try purging him or giving an emetic, but I don't feel that would work on such a wee babe. Just pray; that's all I can suggest. Some do beat the disease, so just pray and tend to him as best you can. Oh, and try and get some water or milk into him as he's drying out."

Sick at heart, Teddy slowly returned to their cubicle on the tween deck. "The surgeon says it's likely cholera, but there's naught he can do for Peter except to try and get some water or milk into him," explained Teddy to Jane.

"Well, that's as may be," exclaimed Jane as she took Peter from Teddy and laid him on the bunk before putting dry cotton clout on him. "He's not taking any milk, and it's hard to get water into him; but we are going to beseech Our Lady, St Bridget, and God Almighty to save Peter. So, all of us will be on our knees with our beads till he gets better. And we'll start with a novena to the Blessed Virgin, who should understand what it's like having your child threatened with dying."

Teddy went and found John, Andrew, William and Tessie. He explained Peter's plight to them as gently as possible to not overly upset the young ones.

"To be sure, your mother is mounting an assault on God, the Blessed Virgin and all the saints to get help curing Peter, and you're all to join in. Best, come on down below."

The family gathered around the bunk where Peter lay, tossing and whimpering in obvious discomfort, with Jane alternating between trying to get him to suckle or take some water and bathing his head with water from a pot Teddy had brought. Once on their knees, with their rosary beads in their hands, Jane started on the Our Fathers and Hail Marys that formed the novena. They all joined in, moving from one bead to the next as each Hail Mary was completed, seeing this as the only hope for baby Peter.

The prayers continued through the night, with all but the youngest taking their turn at the side of the bunk. At teatime, Teddy went with Mary Gavan and Tony Molloy to get some food, which they brought back to the tween deck. Teddy forced Jane to eat, explaining that she needed her strength to care for Peter, but thinking that all the prayers and caring would not help Peter now as he looked at the tiny body of his son that seemed to have shrunk even more so in the last few hours.

Neither Teddy nor Jane slept much that night, although Lizzie Molloy came and insisted Jane get some rest while she minded Peter.

The next day and night were extremely hard for the whole family as they knelt or stood around the bunk on which Peter fought for his life. He was no longer crying. It was as if he had no energy to do so. Jane, Anne and Lizzie Molloy continued to bathe his face and head with cold water to try and keep the fever that raged in him down, though it seemed to have little effect. There was no longer a need to change his clout as no fluids were left to be evacuated, though that didn't stop the griping pains that caused him to whimper and twist on the bunk. His skin was like thin parchment.

Teddy had spoken with Father Dunne early in the day about Peter's condition, and the priest had spent some time by the bunk with Jane and Teddy, both consoling and praying with them. Now, he came down to the tween deck again. When he saw Peter's condition, he told Jane and Teddy that he would administer the last rites or extreme unction to Peter.

As the family gathered on their knees again, joined by several other passengers, including the Gavans and Molloys, he anointed the tiny body as it squirmed with pain. He quietly said the Latin prayers that accompanied the anointing.

When he had finished the short sacrament, he turned to Teddy and Jane, and there were tears in his eyes as he said, "He is in God's hands now. Have no fear; he will be with the angels." He had buried an even dozen children since they had left Cork, and despite his faith, he found it hard to reconcile the loss of so many innocent children.

Peter seemed to be calmer after Father Dunne left. He just lay there with Jane and Teddy watching over him for the night. It was early morning on the 8th of March when he breathed his last. Jane hardly noticed that he was not breathing. Then, with an anguished cry, she hugged Peter's lifeless body as she quietly sobbed. Although she had known for the last two days that Peter's life was ebbing away, she still felt a sense of utter loss now that it had happened, and there was also a growing sense of guilt that she had not been able to provide for him sufficiently to keep his strength up enough to defeat this horrid disease.

The surgeon came and pronounced Peter dead. He then told Teddy and Jane that he would arrange for the burial at sea. This brought fresh sobbing from Jane, who exclaimed that it didn't seem right for her baby to be just cast overboard and then eaten by fish. James Long explained that the body would be sewn into a canvas shroud with a weight, so it would be safe from being eaten by any fish and sink to the bottom of the ocean. Father Dunne, who had arrived, also tried to comfort Jane by telling her that Peter's body would rise on the last day, but his soul was now undoubtedly with God and free of any suffering.

Peter's burial was held that afternoon with several passengers present, particularly from the married tween decks. Teddy was beginning to be liked by many on that deck for his leadership and for standing up to the storekeeper. The captain was present, having earlier offered his condolences to Teddy and Jane, though Father Dunne read the burial service. Teddy held Jane as they watched the small canvas-wrapped body slide from the board into the ocean, creating barely a ripple. The captain and the surgeon certified Peter's death, which was entered in the ship's log as having occurred from infant cholera at the age of two months at latitude 23.43 degrees north, longitude 22.16 degrees west.

Where the Butter Melts

Neither Teddy, Jane, nor the other passengers realised it, but the latitude at which Peter died is referred to as the Tropic of Cancer, or the Northern Tropic, and is the most northerly circle of latitude at which the sun can be directly overhead. They were now just past the point the old mariners, who crossed the Atlantic some two hundred years earlier, referred to as "where the butter melts." It was here they picked up the northeast trade winds that would carry them across to the Caribbean, and that is what the *Erin go Bragh* was doing. The Canary Islands had recently been passed to their east, while ahead lay open ocean all the way to the Antarctic in the south and South America to the southwest.

It was a warm sunny day with a fair wind from the northeast filling all the ship's sails. The sea was now a deep blue with a moderate swell, and the breeze did no more than cause tiny wavelets to sparkle in the sun. Despite being filled with grief, Teddy could appreciate that this was a welcome contrast to the rough, stormy, gloomy days that had tormented them for the first three weeks of the voyage. Like most passengers, the Ryan family was on deck soaking up the sun's warmth. Like many men, Andrew and John had shed their coats and had their sleeves rolled up. The women and girls could not shed the heavy wool dresses, so they found the sun overly hot and sought the shade offered by the sails.

More days followed like this, with the steady trade wind pushing the *Erin go Brah* towards the equator. Then, one morning, as Teddy and John Gavan were crossing the deck to collect their rations, an excited shout went up from some passengers towards the bow.

"Look! Would you look at that! That's amazing!"

Teddy and John hastened to the ship's rails and saw a pod of dolphins swimming and jumping from the water, keeping pace with the ship's bow. They were mesmerised.

"Have you ever seen or heard of anything like this before, Teddy?" exclaimed John.

"No, I've never. What sort of fish are these, or are they some sort of other sea animal?"

A passenger nearby yelled, "One of the crew called them dolphins!"

"Well, they are certainly playful creatures. It seems like they want to keep us company," said Teddy. "Wait here, I'm going to fetch Jane and the others, and I'll tell your Lizzie too."

And with that, Teddy hurried across the deck and down to the tween deck, returning shortly with Jane and the rest of his family, plus Lizzie, and her children. The dolphins were still playing along the bow, and it was becoming so crowded with passengers that it was difficult to get a space to see. Somehow, Teddy managed to elbow his way through to the rail while dragging Jane with him.

"Will you look at that, Jane! Isn't that a marvel to behold?"

Jane was suitably impressed. "Tis a far cry from Kilclonfert, looking at such marvels. And the warmth of this sun on this deep blue ocean is also not something you'd see in all of Ireland."

But the more clement weather didn't stop the deaths, though there was only one more from cholera.

Three days after Peter's death, Ellen Dempsey, aged eighteen months, succumbed. Then, three days later, fourteen-year-old John Quiskelly died of a fever.

The ship was now well into the tropics, and the temperatures had risen accordingly. None of the passengers had experienced such continuous heat, with only the occasional rain squall in the afternoons to cool the conditions. The northeast trade winds continued to blow, and Captain Borlase kept the *Erin go Bragh* on a south-south-west course that took full advantage of the wind, with the ship reaching over five knots at times.

Except for the hottest period, around noon to two p.m., most passengers spent considerable time on deck. Below on the tween deck, the open port holes and air vents provided some fresh air, but conditions tended to get quite hot and uncomfortable. The woollen garments that had served them well in the cold Irish conditions were now a burden and uncomfortable, particularly for the women who wore long skirts with long sleeves. Although such garments may have protected them from being burned by the sun's rays, they were far too hot for the conditions. With little bathing, the aroma of human body odours joined the other smells in the tween deck.

Water was in constant demand to slake thirst, and the ration of three quarts per day[5] per statute adult was sometimes insufficient to meet the demands, as some of it was used for bathing their faces and sharing with the children. Children between one and twelve years old were considered half an adult and, therefore, only got half the water ration of an adult, even though their thirsts might be roughly the same.

Not being used to such hot and sunny conditions, many passengers were badly sunburnt after the first few days, and the accumulated salt on their exposed skin added to the discomfort. Some used some precious water to pour on their arms and sponge their faces and necks to cool themselves and wash off the salt.

On the 19th of March, Catherine Deering, aged fourteen, succumbed to a fever. She had been sick for a few days with a sore throat and temperature, then a red rash started to cover her torso. The surgeon expressed his opinion that it was almost surely scarlatina or scarlet fever

---

[5] Three quarts is equivalent to three and a half litres.

and that there was little he could do except to try and keep her cool by sponging with water. By now, the *Erin go Bragh* was almost at the equator, and the daytime temperatures were so hot the caulking in between the deck planks began to melt. The ship's black hull absorbed the heat, while the breeze from the northeast did little to cool the temperature in the tween deck, despite all the portholes and hatches being open.

The sombre sea burial of Catherine that day was followed the next day by raucous festivities as passengers and crew celebrated 'crossing the line'. The significance of the occasion had to be explained to the passengers. But after the ship's officers and crew, as well as Father Dunne, had informed several of the passengers of what the occasion meant, the word spread with many exclaiming, "To be sure, it's a wondrous thing it is to be crossing the middle of the earth."

Captain Borlase officiated as Neptune for the equator crossing ceremony. He looked impressive with a blue flowing robe, a long false beard, a pasteboard crown and an improvised trident, seated on the top of a bale set on top of two large boxes. One of the single women had been chosen and dressed in a flowing white robe and pasteboard crown as Neptune's wife, Amphitrite. Four men who were deputised as his assistants stood beside the captain, looking suitably stern.

Two large canvas tanks had been set up and filled with seawater. When all the available crew and passengers had gathered on deck, King Neptune announced, "All men who have not crossed the equator before are known as Pollywogs. To earn the right to be a trusted Shellback, you are required to undergo an initiation. When your name is called you are to step forward, and my assistants will proceed with your initiation."

As King Neptune read out the names, each man came forward, some somewhat reluctantly but usually urged on by their companions. They were then led by two of King Neptune's assistants to one of the canvas tubs. There a bucket of seawater was tipped over them to the great amusement and much cheering from the assembled passengers and crew.

Led back to King Neptune, they were then presented with a shell by Queen Amphitrite, who called out to them. "Welcome to the other side, Shellback."

After the first few initiates had received their line-crossing baptism, most took off their coats if they were wearing them, and some took off their shirts to keep them dry, though they were still wearing an undershirt, despite the heat.

That's what Teddy, Andrew and John did, much to the disapproval of Jane. Then, Teddy welcomed the drenching of salt water, though it was rather tepid than cold, as he had expected. He knew the salt would dry on his clothes, though he reckoned that this would make little difference as much of his clothing was already laced with salt from dried sea spray and a lack of fresh water with which to rinse them. Many others faced a similar situation, and some men had developed nasty, red rashes on the inner thighs from the salt, while lice bites added to the discomfort.

The crossing-of-the-line ceremony took several hours, with some young boys joining the fun. As Teddy and the family were wandering away from the festivities, where a number of the men and boys were now engaged in throwing water over each other, he heard several shouts from the opposite side of the ship. He saw people pointing and, following the direction they were indicating; there, some 200 yards from the ship three spouts of water were erupting into the air.

Intrigued, he asked Andrew and John, "What is going on there?"

Both sons shrugged their shoulders. But once they had come up to the ship's rail, Teddy heard one seaman present say, "They're whales all right. And there's a whole pod of them, see. Maybe they will come closer, and we can have a better look."

At that moment, a massive creature with a black top and white underside rose out of the water, then slid back under. As it did so it raised an enormous tail high in the air.

The passengers stared in awe, with many more gathering along the ship's rail. Someone remarked that they seemed like gigantic dolphins, and the first mate standing nearby informed them that, indeed, they were related somehow to dolphins, though most did not seem to have teeth, while he had heard that in some cold waters near Canada, there were smaller whales with teeth that would devour whole seals at one gulp.

****

Having crossed the equator, the *Erin go Bragh* continued on a course south-south-west towards the coast of South America, with variable winds that gave it a speed of about four knots. Their speed to date was slower than Captain Borlase would have liked, and he considered calling in at Rio de Janeiro to get fresh supplies and water. But he then felt they could make up time in the southern latitudes and, if necessary, they would resupply in Cape Town before the long haul across the Southern Ocean.

On the 25th of March, six and a half weeks out from Cork, the *Erin go Bragh* was some fifty miles off the coast of Brazil. It was also the day two young boys, Peter McQueen and William Hellion, died from scarlatina. With several other children and adults in the married tween deck sick with what appeared to be scarlatina, the surgeon ordered a thorough cleansing of that deck with carbolic acid in water. As there were only light winds and it was hot and sunny for much of the time, the passengers congregated on the main deck while the mess captains, under the guidance of the surgeon and Mr Condron, proceeded to cleanse and disinfect the tween deck, leaving the distinct sweet-sour smell of phenol, the disinfecting agent in the acid.

The cleansing came too late for two-year-old Anne Flanigan and four-year-old Essy Dempsey, who joined their maker the next day. That day was another hot one; the wind had died to a light breeze. When Teddy came on deck in the morning, he noticed they were heading into the sun to the east. He wondered why this was the case but thought no more about it as he collected his mess's daily rations. The fresh meat had long gone, and they were now being supplied with potted meat instead. This was a gooey mixture of some unknown meat cooked in butter, after which it had been pounded, placed in an earthenware pot, heated again, and then covered in clarified butter to seal it. The problem was that the tropical temperatures tended to soften or even melt the butter, which could break the seal, thus spoiling the contents. Salted pork was also on the menu, though this was a last resort food and not something to consume in the tropics, with thirst already a problem among the passengers.

On the 27th of March, there were two more deaths: two-year-old Patrick Walsh from scarlatina and fifty-eight-year-old Jane Kelly from a fever. As Teddy came on deck that morning, he was surprised to see that the sun was now on the starboard or right side of the ship, whereas for all the days except the previous one, the morning sun had been on the port or left side, if they could see it. Surely this was the wrong direction to be travelling. What was going on?

James Green, the third mate, was standing up on the quarterdeck, eyeing the luffing sails in the light breeze as the vessel struggled to make any headway. His surly nature put many people off approaching him.

But Teddy wasn't intimidated and approached the quarterdeck before calling up, "Mr Green, why are we heading towards what seems to be north? Ain't that the wrong direction?"

"It's not your business to be worrying about what direction we're taking. That's for the likes of the captain and me. But if you must know, with these contrary and light winds here and not having the luxury of havin' one of these new-fangled steam-driven propellers to drive us anywhere we wish, we have to go looking for a decent breeze. And we need to get a move on as we're lagging behind where we should be, though that's my reckoning, dat's all."

This worried Teddy; the whole sense of the unknown, out on this ocean, at the whim of the weather and skill of the captain and officers. Dry land had a lot to recommend it. When he was with John Gavan and Tony Molloy, he couldn't help but voice his concerns. But the former had a cynical streak in him.

"What are we doin' over near South America? We should have headed down past Africa. Ain't that how all the ships go when they're sailin' to Australia?"

"I don't know too much about it, Jono," replied Teddy. "But it does seem awful strange that we're going round in circles here and doin' it awful slow when we've got so far to go. We've also gotta cross over to the other side of the Atlantic now. And have we got enough food and water on board for all these here people if we're going to be longer on this voyage than planned?"

However, Teddy was heartened to see the next day that they were heading back in a more southerly direction and with something of a breeze that at least filled out the sails, giving the vessel some headway.

There was another death from scarlatina that day. However, the surgeon was doing what he could to isolate passengers that showed symptoms of the disease, all so far in the married tween deck. But this wasn't easy, with so many passengers crammed below decks. With the captain's approval, he urged those closest to the sick passengers to spend as much time on deck as possible, even sleeping there if the weather permitted. There was little rain, though also not much wind, as the ship headed now on a south-south-easterly course.

It then altered course to the southeast and averaged about four knots in moderate winds for the next few days. This continued slow speed, about twice as fast as a fit person could walk, worried Captain Borlase as they lagged behind their estimated trip duration. What hampered progress was that they were heading into the southeast trade winds, which blow steadily during the year, though more strongly in the cooler months. This meant constant tacking on the part of the ship to make progress.

This was a relatively pleasant phase of the trip for the passengers, including Teddy and Jane's family, with temperatures still warm though cooling somewhat at night. There continued to be little rain, which was another concern for the captain as they were already nearly two months into the voyage. They still had a long way to go, so would the water last the distance?

The deaths continued almost daily, with two more on the 30th of March and four again on the 2nd of April. The saddest aspect of the deaths was that most were children from nineteen months to seven years of age. The almost constant burial services, conducted mainly by Father Dunne, had become so commonplace that few now attended, apart from immediate family and some friends. On the married tween deck, these deaths had also produced a melancholy lowering of the spirit. Even if one's child had not succumbed, there was a constant number of sick passengers - young children, older children and adults - acting as a reminder of the spectre of death hanging over the deck, from which there seemed to be no release.

Teddy was now more aware of the direction the ship was travelling by looking at the sun's position relative to the ship in the early morning. On the 3rd of April, he noticed that they seemed to be heading more in a southerly direction. As he stood pondering this on the slightly heaving deck with Andrew and John that morning, he saw the second mate, William Harvey, strolling towards him. Harvey was a man of medium height with a pleasant, somewhat rounded face and a congenial disposition. He was in shirt sleeves and could have been mistaken for an ordinary seaman if it wasn't for the peaked cap he wore at an angle over his thick blonde locks. As he approached, Teddy stepped towards him.

"Good morning, Mr Harvey."

To which Harvey replied, "Tis a good and fair morning, is it not, though a mite more wind would be good."

"Mr Harvey, why are we now headin' more towards the south? Shouldn't we be heading more to the east, cos that's the way to Australia unless I'm mistaken."

"Well, you're right about the direction we're travelling now. That's very observant of yer. And you're right about the direction to Australia. What's yer name?"

"It's Teddy Ryan, and these here are my sons, Andrew and John."

"Well, now, Teddy Ryan. We are headin' south, actually a bit west of south or south-south-west, cos there's a current that flows south along the South America coast hereabouts, and we want to make use of that. Also, we're heading south to catch the westerlies coming in as we get down to around 30 degrees south latitude. You know about latitude and longitude, do yer?"

Teddy shook his head with a frown of some bewilderment on his face. His sons shared the same look.

"Well, latitude measures how far we are from the equator, either north or south. You know, the equator is that line that sort of runs around the middle of the earth like a belt around the belly of a portly gentleman. It's where youse got inducted and drenched to celebrate crossing it."

Teddy and the boys grinned and nodded.

"Well, the further you get south below the gentleman's belt towards his balls, the higher the degree of latitude, with his balls being at 90 degrees. It's the same up north. When you get to his neck, which is sort of like the north pole, it's again 90 degrees from the equator, which itself is zero degrees. Do you follow that?"

By now, Teddy and his sons were grinning and nodding, though still with some mystification in their eyes. "What's a degree?" asked Andrew.

"A degree is just a way of measuring that distance of latitude. One degree of latitude is about the same as sixty miles. So, if you are 30 degrees south latitude, you're roughly one thousand eight hundred miles from the equator."

"That's an awful long way, though, if you ask me," ventured John. "Why it's nigh on a hundred miles, we travelled from Tullamore to Cork, and this here ship ain't going near as fast as that train we were on. So, how much further or how long is it gonna take for us to get to Queensland?"

"That I don't know, lad, though we've already been at sea some fifty days, and we've a mighty long way to go. Once we pick up the westerlies, we must cross the South Atlantic and pass the bottom of Africa. Then it's a long stretch of open ocean after that till we arrive at the southeast of Australia or the island of Tasmania. But those westerly winds can be pretty fierce and drive us along at a fair speed if we're lucky."

Harvey did not wish to alarm the passengers, as any dire news would spread like wildfire through the tween decks, but he was also concerned that they were behind schedule and that the food and water would not last the distance and time it might take to get to Queensland.

As Teddy talked to the second mate, he noticed two men by the side rail of the quarterdeck. One had a reel of line that he was paying out over the side, and the other had a watch. As he looked, the seaman with the watch called, "Mark."

The seaman with the reel of line then yelled something to the seaman with the watch, which sounded like, "Three and a quarter."

Harvey saw Teddy watching the men and explained. "They're measuring how fast the ship is going."

"How on earth do they do that?" asked Andrew.

"Well, you see that line? That's got knots and flagging marking every fifty-one feet. Do you remember I was talking about nautical miles and degrees? Well, there's 6,076 feet in a nautical mile. Now you could let out a line marked every 6,076 feet over an hour to find how fast you're going, but that ain't practical. So, they put these marks at fifty-one feet, which is $1/120^{th}$ of a nautical mile. Then they throw out this piece of board with a lead weight on one side. It is called a chip log. They see how far it is dragged out by the ship in thirty seconds, which is $1/120^{th}$ of one hour. That way, we get the number of nautical miles per hour or what we sailors call knots."

"I sort a get it," said a slightly dazed Teddy.

Though John, who had more of a brain for figures, nodded and said, "That's a smart way of doing it, though kind of cumbersome."

"It isn't that accurate," said the second mate, "but it's the best we've got, and they've used the same system now for the last three hundred years."

With that, the second mate wandered off along the deck, leaving Teddy and his sons to ponder the wonders of navigation.

John, who followed Mr Harvey's explanations most closely, marvelled, "It is just amazing that these seamen can find their way across the oceans and around the world with no landmark or sign to guide them but the stars, the sun and a couple of small instruments. Some of us couldn't find our way to Rafferty's Pub on a dark night if it wasn't for the hullabaloo coming from there as the poteen goes down."

"Aye, you're right, John," answered Teddy. "Talk about putting one's trust in the captain and crew to get us to Queensland, but that we have to do."

Dire Straits

April slipped by as the *Erin go Bragh* continued to the south.

It had reached 33 degrees south latitude on the 19th of April, where they should have picked up the westerly winds that are a consistent feature of latitudes from here south. Although the winds were generally from the west, they varied in direction and speed and rarely exceeded a strong breeze. So, the ship continued to move slowly east, making no more than three to four knots.

Easter was on the 20th of the month, with Father Dunne saying an Easter Sunday mass on the foredeck. The number of deaths had lessened, though they were still occurring, one every few days, mostly from scarlatina. Life on the married tween deck continued with the routine established earlier in the voyage. For most, it was a monotonous drudge with the monotony broken by sickness and death. The continuing occurrence of scarlatina also meant that as many healthy passengers as possible were sleeping on deck, provided the weather cooperated. And for a large part, it did with not a great deal of rain. When it came, the rain was in squalls and thunderstorms that usually lasted less than an hour.

Passengers also spent as much time on deck as possible as it was a relief from the dense overcrowding, the lack of air flow in the tween deck, and the overpowering stench of sweaty bodies that had rarely seen a wash since leaving Ireland. The odour from the water closets also added to the unsavoury atmosphere.

Teddy ran his mess with the help of John Gavan and Tony Molloy. Recently, there was an almost daily confrontation with the storekeeper, Daniel Baxter, who persisted in trying to make a bit extra on the side by providing food and water supplies. He continued to raise the point that a mess was not supposed to have more than ten statute adults and that Teddy's mess had seventeen. But Teddy stood his ground, often backed by John or Tony.

Captain Borlase found the mate, Walter Meyler, on the quarter deck the afternoon of Easter Sunday.

"What's our speed today, Mr Meyler?"

"We're averaging just under three knots on the chip log, Captain."

"Damn, that's not good enough. It's got me worried, Walter. We should have got some good westerlies this far south, but where are they? And I don't want to go much further south in case the seas and weather cause more problems with our leaks. It's a cruel situation. Mayhap, I shudda stopped in at Rio when we lacked a good wind there, but I thought we'd make up speed once we got further south."

"Well, there's always Cape Town."

"You're right, Walter. If we don't get a consistently good wind from here on, we will have to stop there, though the company won't like it. They're stingy as hell with spending money on provisions, and they never leave any room for delays. But you can never tell with the weather on these long voyages, sometimes it's plain sailing, and sometimes it can be a nightmare for the captain, crew and passengers. And, of course, the time of the year makes a difference."

"Captain, how about I get the crew to set up some rainwater catchment holders? We can use the canvas pools we set up to dunk those crossing the line and put a spare couple of small sails to catch the rain when it comes. That could help replenish some of the water we've used."

"Excellent idea Walter. Then let's pray for some rain to cross our path."

But there was no change in the weather, with the winds still light and the ship making little more than three knots over the next week. The only rain came from brief squalls that swept in and were gone within half an hour, providing just a few inches of fresh water in the canvas tubs.

Being a sensible man, the captain decided it was necessary to start rationing the foodstuffs and water.

He explained to the first mate, "Before we left Liverpool, I certified that we had food and water for one hundred and forty days or twenty weeks for three hundred and eighty-seven statute adult passengers plus crew - enough if we completed the voyage in the usual time of four to five months. Part of the problem is that we have some four hundred and fifty passengers on board, including about eighty children under twelve years of age, with an adult being defined under the Passengers' Act as twelve years and older. That means for some eighty children, there's no provision for rations, and many of them can eat as much as an adult. But that's what this Passengers' Act states, that I only have to provide food and water for the adults, not the children. And the company wouldn't let me add on extra for the children, even though I knew there would be a number of them, though not as much as eighty. So, we have been eating into our provisions faster than anticipated, and we still have a ways to go."

When the steward, Condron, announced that there would be some rationing of food and water to the occupants of the married tween deck, there was, not unexpectedly, an uproar. Jane was one of the first to voice her concern.

"I ain't worried for myself, but it's the young ones that need their food, and if they don't get it, there's more chance they'll get sick. This here, scarlatina, is a frightful disease, and we don't want our Tessie or Billy getting it."

Jane's concerns seemed justified when on the 25th of April, eighteen-month-old Patrick Gavan, the son of their good family friends, died. He had been sick with scarlatina for some days, with his parents, John and Mary, beside themselves with worry. There'd been two other deaths around the same time, one from scarlatina. Patrick appeared to have beaten the disease, but several days of fever had significantly weakened his emaciated body, and he just seemed to have decided that life was no longer worth living, and so had passed away.

John and Mary Gavan had seven children, and the three youngest, Teresa, Catherine and Lucy, took Patrick's death the hardest, questioning why their young brother had to die when he was getting better. Jane, who was so grateful for Mary's help breastfeeding Peter, did what she could to comfort her. The Ryans and several other families gathered on deck that afternoon for Father Dunne once again to perform a burial service before committing Patrick's small body to the grey-blue ocean.

****

Towards the end of April, there was a violent storm. It was late afternoon, and those on deck could see the dark clouds massing to the southwest. William Harvey, the second mate, who had the watch, ordered most sails to be furled, the portholes closed, and hatches battened down in preparation as the wind increased and the sea began developing white caps. The passengers were ordered below to keep them out of harm's way and out of the way of the crew handling the sails.

When the storm struck, Teddy and his family clung to their bunks as the fury of the squall tossed the ship about. During the first month, most of the passengers had become accustomed to the violent movement of the ship in rough weather. But for the last six weeks, the weather had been much calmer. Some wondered if they were entering another period of prolonged rough weather.

An hour later, Teddy emerged onto the sodden deck to a brilliant red sunset covering half the sky in hues of red. Though rough, the sea was no longer whipped by strong winds. In fact, the scene was almost peaceful. However, a casualty of the squall was several broken water barrels. Having had relatively calm weather for a few weeks, the crew had become more nonchalant about securing the barrels not in use. The result of not being properly stored was evident in the stoved-in barrels and flooded deck.

The captain was not impressed when a rather guilty-looking second mate reported the water loss.

"Damn it, man! They should have been properly secured, Mr Harvey. We were already likely to be short of water given how slow our progress is. Now, we will definitely be short."

"You're right, Captain. It was one thing I forgot about when I saw the squall approaching, and we have not been diligent enough in ensuring the barrels were more secure even in the calmer weather."

"Well, there's nothing for it, but we will have to call into Cape Town and get some more water. We can't carry on to Australia with what we have. And while we are at it, we'll see about adding to our food supplies. Ask the first mate to see me and we'll work out a course for Cape Town."

The ship, which had been working its way to the east and south, was now at 36 degrees south latitude. The captain ordered a course slightly south of east. This heading would put them somewhat south of Cape Town, but he wanted to make the most of what he thought would be more favourable winds at a lower latitude. As it transpired, the ship only averaged four knots over the next eleven hundred nautical miles.

****

When Teddy and Tony Molloy came to get their day's rations next day, Baxter, the storekeeper, gave them more food than he had over the last few days since rationing had started.

"What's the deal, Baxter?" asked Teddy. "Have you suddenly found more food you had hidden away for a rainy day?"

"No, Mr Ryan. It's because we're gonna be calling in at Cape Town to get more fresh water after them barrels got staved in during the storm yesterday. And the captain is also planning to get us some more provisions."

"Are you serious, Baxter?" asked Tony.

"To be sure, Mr Molloy. That's roughly where we're heading now. And it's a good thing, too, 'cos this ship is going slower than my nanny's perambulator, and you all are eating us out of the supplies. We'd never make it to Australia if we carried on like we are."

"Well, that's grand news, isn't it, Teddy?" exclaimed Tony. "We might even be able to get off this ship for a while and walk on solid ground. "Twoud be marvellous if we could."

"Aye, it would be, Tony. We could all do with havin' our feet on solid ground for a bit."

There was general rejoicing when Teddy and Tony broke the news to others in the married tween deck. The fiddles were out that night, and much music and dancing took place to celebrate a possible temporary reprieve from their confinement at sea.

With the weather being much cooler, there was less demand for the shrinking water supply. The second mate had the watch when Captain Borlase approached him on the quarter deck on the 7th of May. He had just attended the burial of young Rody Wren, who had died of a fever earlier in the day.

"We seem to have more of a wind today, Mr Harvey."

"Indeed, we do, Captain. And I've had the fore, and main top gallants unfurled. The ship log speed was up to six and a half knots at the start of my watch."

"Well, let's hope the wind stays with us to Cape Town. The passengers are getting restless with the reduced rations, even though I have eased the rationing a bit. I don't want any trouble on board."

"I think we may already have some trouble by the looks of what's brewing down there on the deck," the second mate replied as he nodded towards amidships.

The captain turned to find a scuffle had broken out between some of the passengers. Four men were holding boxes of rations, while several other men were trying to take the boxes, shouting that they had more food than they had a right to. Two or three supporters of those carrying the supplies had intervened, and punches were being thrown.

The captain swiftly descended onto the main deck and advanced on the fight. In a loud voice, he demanded to know what was going on.

One of the assailants, a small, ferret-faced man from the single men's quarters, replied in a whining voice. "It ain't fair, Captain. Look at all the grub these here family people are getting, while us single folk are having to do with barely some hard tack and that potted stuff you call meat. There ain't even enough tea or sugar for us to have more than a cup a day."

Teddy was one of the men carrying the rations, and looking the captain squarely in the eye, he said, "These are all our rightful rations, though they ain't as much as we were getting before. We've got three families in our mess. Now, I know it makes more than the ten adults we're supposed to have. But we wanted to be together as friends to help each other. And the way I see it, we're all entitled to the same rations per adult, so I don't see that it makes a difference if us three families, as friends, combine to a mess and then get our fair share of food and water."

A number in the enlarged crowd that had now gathered were nodding their heads in agreement, while several others were shaking their heads in disagreement with scowls on their faces and mumbling to those nearby.

The captain was a fair man, and although rules or regulations had been put in place for a reason, which reason often escaped him, he was intent on keeping the peace. They had a long way and maybe three months yet to go, so it would be best to quieten any dissension.

"I hear what you're saying, Teddy Ryan, and there's some logic to it. We're all still going to be on tighter rations for a couple of weeks until we can call into Cape Town on the Cape of Good Hope and get some more supplies and water."

"The winds haven't been what they should be or normally are, so we've been going a lot slower. That means our supplies for the journey won't last till we get to Queensland. It's already ninety days since we departed Queenstown, and we have another sixty or maybe as much as ninety days till we arrive at our destination. We can pick up some supplies in Cape Town, but we also need to conserve what we have, as I am not sure how much food supplies we can get in Cape Town. That's why I ordered the rationing. Now, it's best if you all go about your business, which does not include abusing others over food."

The crowd dispersed slowly, but one man, slightly better dressed than most male passengers, turned back and addressed the captain with a worried look.

"Captain, can you tell us about this here leak we have? We've been hearing about it for some weeks now. Are we in danger of sinking, and shouldn't you get it fixed if we're going be in this here, Cape Town?"

Captain Borlase smiled grimly at the passenger, thinking, *I knew the leak problem would get out eventually.* And he knew this small, red-headed man as one of the more intelligent among the passengers.

"It's Sam McQueen, isn't it?" The man nodded. "Well, Mr McQueen, first off, we aren't in any danger of sinking. Yes, we do have a leak, but it's not much of one, and our pumps are able to keep it under control. Most sailing ships, like the *Erin go Bragh,* that have been around for a while develop leaks cos the caulking between the planks in the hull works its way out, particularly in rough seas. But we do have a copper bottom, which helps to slow any leaks and even to prevent them. We will endeavour to put more caulking where the leaks are while in Cape Town. And they couldn't do more than that unless they take the ship out of the water, and there's no need for that. I plan on sailing this ship to Moreton Bay and then sailing it back to Liverpool."

The captain's explanation seemed to satisfy Sam McQueen and several other passengers who had remained behind to hear the answer. The captain had felt it best not to mention that they were watching their speed because of the leaks, not wanting to exacerbate the problem.

****

A week later, early on the morning of 14th May, a lookout on the round top yelled down that he could see land dead ahead. The passengers flocked onto the deck, towards the bow and the ship's sides, to get a glimpse of the first land they had seen in two months since sailing by the Canary Islands in early May.

As they approached the coast, the captain steered to the northeast. Those on the starboard side could see in the distance a high mountain range with rocky cliffs plunging down to a more gentle slope that was clothed in green vegetation, reaching all the way to the sea. Further north was a massive, cloud-covered mountain, taller than any mountain any of the Irish passengers had seen before.

"With the wind from the southwest, we should be able to make a straight run into Table Bay," volunteered the first mate, who had the watch.

"I agree, Mr Meyler," came back the captain. "It would be better to go south of Robben Island as the charts show we have better depth there. Have you got that list of provisions we need? And then there's water as well? I don't wish to spend more than two or three days here if we can help it."

"Aye, Captain. I've made the list and will get ashore as soon as we can anchor tomorrow. Hopefully, we can get a berth at a wharf to load the supplies."

"I'll come with you and pay my respects to the harbour master and see what he can do for us. Black Ball must have an agent here we can use to get our water and food supplies."

The first mate yelled to the boatswain. "We shall be making a run straight into Table Bay once we reach the entrance, Mr Judd. We'll have the fore and main courses and mizzen with two jibs. But be ready to alter sails as we move into the bay as the winds could change."

Touching his hat, the boatswain replied, "Aye, Sir."

Then he was yelling orders for the crew to stand by braces, tacks and sheets. At the same time, the first mate ordered the helmsman to bring the *Erin go Bragh* onto a course heading for the southern entrance to Table Bay.

Cape Town

Most of the passengers were on deck to watch the arrival into Cape Town, eager to catch a glimpse of land after three months at sea. There was also anticipation about what this land in southern Africa would be like and what sort of people lived there. Teddy and Jane, with the rest of the family, had joined the throng of people now crowding towards the ship's bow and along its sides, although being kept away from where the various ropes used to adjust the sails were belayed.

As the sun rose higher into a clear blue sky over the land to the east, Teddy watched the grey outline of the massive mountain. It was covered with clouds that seemed to drape over the edges, almost like a white cloth on a table. Other lower ranges of hills extended into the distance.

After some time, the ship altered course to roughly northeast. The crew hauled on the braces to adjust the sails to make the most of the now southerly wind, which had strengthened, with small white caps appearing on the long low southerly swell. As the *Erin go Bragh* made its way towards the entrance to Table Bay, south of Robben Island, the passengers watched as the low cloud slowly dissipated to reveal the fantastic sight of a flat-topped mountain that rose precipitously from near its base. On either side were smaller mountains, the one to the north was almost as high as the table-top mountain, while that to the south was lower and sharply pointed. The lower slopes of the mountain range seemed to be only covered in bushes, while the steeper slopes were bare rock.

"That's called Table Mountain. Ain't it a magnificent sight, now?" And Teddy turned to see the second mate just behind him.

"To be sure, it is at that," replied Teddy. "I have never seen a mountain that high before. How long are we staying here at Cape Town, Mr Harvey, and will we be able to go ashore, do you think?"

"I know the captain wants to replenish supplies and leave as soon as possible, so it might just be a few days. It depends on how quickly we can get the food and water supplies we need. As for going ashore, I don't think that's likely. You can see the number of ships in the bay, so it ain't likely we'll get a berth, so we'll have to anchor in the bay."

The *Erin go Bragh* sailed south of Robben Island before the first mate gave the order to come about to a heading of southeast. As they advanced towards already anchored ships, Mr Meyler ordered reduced sails, furling the main course, although the wind had lessened somewhat in the lee of the land and mountains. They made their way between several vessels to a point some half a mile from the town's shore.

Cape Town in the 1860s had the air of a flourishing and prosperous town. Numerous white-painted or grey stone single or two-storey buildings could be seen from the ship. It was late morning on a Wednesday, 14th May, and the streets and harbour side were busy with people and various modes of transport. Teddy could make out that some people were black and pointed these out to Jane.

"These must be some of the natives from these here parts." To which Jane nodded as if mesmerised by the scene before her.

"Tis a grand town this. I wonder if Brisbane will be as grand when we get there?"

As they stood staring at the unfamiliar landscape, a small sailing boat, a shallop, approached them through the thirty or so ships in the bay. As it came close by the *Erin go Bragh*, it lowered its sail, and a man standing towards the bow yelled across the slightly choppy waters.

"Ahoy there, *Erin go Bragh*!"

The captain moved to the ship's rail and yelled back, "Ahoy there! We're the *Erin go Bragh* out of Liverpool and Queenstown, bound for Moreton Bay in Australia."

"The harbourmaster sends his compliments and requires to know if you have any cases of fever on board."

"No, we've no case now, though earlier in the voyage, we were sorely troubled by cholera, then scarlatina."

"Could I come on board, so we can learn your reason for calling into Table Bay and how we might be able to assist you?"

"You're welcome to come on board, sir." And the captain immediately ordered a rope ladder to be lowered over the side.

The shallop pulled alongside, with the help of four rowers manning the oars, and a middle-aged man with a blue pea coat and peaked cap clambered expertly up the rope ladder and over the side onto the deck. As he landed, he turned towards the captain, his expression serious but relaxed, and extended his hand.

"I'm Nelius Eksteen from the Cape Town harbourmaster's office." His accent sounded quite foreign to the passengers, including Teddy, who had gathered to see this man from Cape Town.

"Captain George Borlase. And I'm pleased to make your acquaintance. Would you care to step this way to my cabin, Mr Eksteen?"

The two men made their way aft through the throng of passengers and into the captain's cabin at the stern. "Could I offer you a drop of rum, Mr Eksteen?" asked the captain. "I'm afraid there's not much, as we're running short of supplies. In fact, that's our reason for calling into Cape Town. We've been three months at sea and still have a way to go to our destination. With some four hundred and thirty passengers to feed, plus my crew of sixty, we've been using up our food and water supply." As he said this, the captain filled two crystal glasses with rum and handed one to Nelius Eksteen.

The latter looked around at the well-appointed cabin - the fine woodwork around the walls, the plush leather seats and the well-polished table.

I'll wager most of those poor migrant passengers I saw on deck have nothing like such comfortable quarters, he thought.

Sipping on the rum, which he found wanting in flavour, if not in strength, he said, "Captain, Cape Town can certainly provide you with water supplies and some food provisions, though with so many vessels requiring provisions and your arrival unplanned you may not get all you need. And how would you pay for the food supplies?"

"I understand the Black Ball Line has an agent here. I plan to make arrangements through him to purchase the food and water supplies and a few other items."

"Yes, I believe the agents are James Baine and Company, with a Mr Daniel Fox as manager. You'll find their office along the foreshore. So, what is your expected date of departure, Captain?"

"I would like to leave as soon as possible. I presume there is no chance of getting a berth alongside a wharf to make it easier to load supplies. If not, we shall have to organise a tender to bring out the goods, which will take longer."

"You are correct. We have a certain amount of wharf space, but, as you can see, this is a busy port and priority is given to regular vessels and those that are prepared to pay. Might I suggest that you avail yourself personally of some of the excellent brandy we produce here in the Cape. You won't find better brandy anywhere, except perhaps, for a few of the ne-plus-ultra French cognacs." And with that, Nelius Eksteen took his leave and returned to his shallop.

I guess he didn't like my rum, thought the captain. *But then, I don't blame him. It ain't the best, though it's good for keeping the cold out and the crew happy.*

He set about organising with the first mate to lower and man a longboat, in which he was shortly on his way, dressed in his best, freshly brushed uniform coat and cap. Before he left, the captain ordered the second mate to thoroughly inspect the hull in the bilge to search for and repair the leaks that were still causing problems. "We'd best take this opportunity of being at anchor to see what we can do to stop the leaking, and if you need any supplies to achieve it, let me know."

Most of the passengers were on deck, where they would rather be than down in the dingy, dank and smelly depths of the tween decks. They watched as Captain Borlase and the first mate were rowed ashore by six crewmen.

"What wouldn't I give to be on that there rowboat," said John Gavan, who was standing next to Teddy by the rail, towards the bow of the ship. "It would be heaven to put my feet on dry and solid land for a change and maybe even find a pub where one can get a decent drink."

"I'm with yer there, Jono," replied Teddy. "Just a few hours ashore and away from the stench of this ship would be great, but I don't see it happening, not while we're stuck out here in the middle of this bay."

"Well, at least we should get some fresh food on board for a change," replied John.

Meanwhile, Captain Borlase was nearing the shore, and the oarsmen shipped their oars as they glided alongside some stone steps. He and the first mate jumped onto the steps and made their way onto the dock, where they surveyed the busy scene. Several ocean-going ships were moored further along the key with gangs of dark-skinned men busily carrying goods of all sorts on board, expertly balancing their headloads as they navigated the none-too-stable wooden gangways. There were wagons carrying goods to be loaded, drawn by large draft horses, either waiting their turn or making their way to a berth-side destination. There were also groups of better-dressed men deep in discussion, whether about cargos, politics or sea stories the captain could not tell. And overlaying all the bustle was the babble of voices and shouts, some curses and some commands.

The captain and first mate walked towards a group of three men holding an animated discussion, which the captain interrupted by asking if any of the gentlemen could direct them to the offices of James Baine and Company, agents for the Black Ball Shipping Line.

The gentlemen turned an annoyed look on the pair that lasted several seconds, then one of them said, "So, you want the James Baine office. Well, go down there and take the first street that runs off the dock," he said, turning and pointing. "The office is in a stone building on the left of that street. It is easy to find. Did you just arrive in that black-hulled, three-masted ship?"

"Thank you, and yes, we did. I'm Captain Borlase from the *Erin go Bragh,* and this here is my first mate, Mr Meyler. We're on our way to Australia but have been making slow progress of it from Queenstown and need to stock up on food and water."

"Well, good luck, Captain Borlase. I am Captain James Burke from the *Ben Nevis*, bound for Melbourne, Australia, with a rowdy bunch of gold diggers. I hope you get what you want, although supplies are short at present. As you can see, there are many ships going somewhere in the bay, and most want food supplies."

"My thanks, Captain Burke, and good luck to yer." And with that, the captain and first mate made their way across the cobbled foreshore to the street that had been indicated. They found the agent's offices on the first floor of an imposing grey stone building, up a wide, ornate, highly polished wooden staircase.

Knocking on a heavy wooden door with "James Baines and Company" etched in gold letters on a metal nameplate, they opened it to a wide reception area divided by a wooden railing from an office space with several clerks busy at desks. One of the older clerks near the railing spotted the captain and rose to ask how he could help them.

The captain introduced himself and Mr Meyler and explained that they needed to arrange food and water supplies for the *Erin go Bragh*.

"Ah, well, we weren't expecting you, Captain. But let me take you to meet Mr Fox."

With that, he opened a gate in the well-polished railing and ushered the two men through to one of several doors at the rear of the room. He knocked and, on hearing a voice saying, "Enter," he proceeded to open the door for the captain and first mate to enter.

Mr Fox was a man of average height, with a girth straining the buttons on his silk waistcoat of a man familiar with good food and wine. His face, enclosed in mutton-chop sideburns, had a florid appearance, also indicative of a considerable consumption of alcohol. He rose and extended his hand across a large polished wooden desk.

"Daniel Fox at your service, gentlemen. How can I be of service?"

The captain introduced himself and the first mate. Then on being directed, he took a seat in a comfortable leather armchair. In fact, the entire office portrayed an establishment of some financial consequence.

"I am very pleased to make your acquaintance, Mr Fox, and we certainly need your assistance. I understand that your firm is the agent for the Black Ball Line?"

"That is correct, and I assume you have just arrived in that fine three-masted vessel that anchored this morning?"

"Yes, sir. We are from the *Erin go Bragh* out of Liverpool and then Queenstown. Unfortunately, our voyage to Moreton Bay is taking longer than we had planned and provisioned for. Firstly, we were delayed by gales by a week before reaching Queenstown. Then unfavourable winds and discovering several leaks in the hull have meant a slower-than-normal passage so far. We've also lost several casks of water during a violent storm. As a result, we are very low on water, and our food supplies will not be sufficient to see us through the long passage ahead to at least Hobart Town."

Mr Fox was frowning and looking through papers on his desk, then asked the clerk, "Do we have any notice that the *Erin go Bragh* was to call into Cape Town for reprovisioning, Mr Stewart?"

"I shall check, Sir, but I don't think so."

At this, the captain intervened. "We weren't scheduled to call into Cape Town. We called in because we were running short of water and food. So, can you help us, Mr Fox?"

"All right, Captain, I shall see what we can do. Though mind you, as we weren't expecting you and there's a lot of demand for provisions from all these ships in the bay, we may not be able to offer you much in the way of food. Water, though, should be no problem. Have you got an idea of what foodstuffs and how much you require?"

The first mate handed his list to Mr Fox, explaining, "We desperately need flour and meat of any kind, plus if we can get some fresh fruit and vegetables, that would help cut down on the scurvy."

Mr Fox took the list and perused it. "I shall get my clerks onto this immediately, and by tomorrow morning we will know what you can have and how much. I shall also organise for a lighter or pinnace to transport the goods out to you tomorrow, all of which will be billed to the Black Ball Line, and for that I shall need your signature once everything is finalised."

"Thank you, Mr Fox. I much appreciate your assistance, and so will my crew and passengers. Now could you tell us of a good place to get a meal while we're ashore?"

After Mr Fox explained the way to a nearby tavern, the captain and first mate headed there and ordered two plates of roast beef with potatoes and vegetables, plus a tankard of ale each. As they sat devouring their meal, Mr Meyler suggested that it might be worth their while to look elsewhere for foodstuffs, if only for themselves and the crew, as it seemed Mr Fox may not come up with sufficient food.

"Let's ask here in the tavern, where one might get food to take on board, both fresh and preserved."

The captain agreed, and when they approached the burly figure of a man in a dirty apron and wild red hair behind the bar, he suggested they first try the farmer's market gardens on the outskirts of the town.

"The main one is the Oranje Zigt Farmstead, and you're in luck as today they are selling. I heard the bell sounding this morning, and they fly a flag from the tower in Homestead Park when they have produce to sell. You head out of town to the east. Just ask anyone and follow the people going and coming. There are other farms with fruit and vegetables, but this is the biggest, though you'd best get yourselves a carriage as it's a hard walk up to the farm."

The two hurried back to their boat and told three seamen to accompany them while the others minded the boat. Setting off east through the bustling business streets of the town, they hailed the first carriage they saw. This took them out through quiet residential neighbourhoods with houses of all descriptions, some quite grand, almost palatial. On the way, they saw several people obviously returning from the farm. Some white women or men had sacks of fruit or vegetables being carried by dark-skinned men, presumably servants. The carriage driver explained that the dark men were Cape Malays who had been brought over from the East Indies. There were also merchants, or ship's officers being trailed by Cape Malays, pulling hand carts loaded with rich assortments of fruit and vegetables.

"Damn it, we should have got ourselves a cart or two!" exclaimed the captain. "We'll be hard put to carry much between us, even with this carriage."

"Let's see if we can hire one out there. Perhaps we'll be lucky," suggested the first officer.

And they were lucky. Inside an ornate white arched farm gate were several carts drawn up with Cape Malay attendants standing beside them. The captain and first mate checked their cash situation. Having ascertained from a nearby white attendant, who was directing the flow of buyers, that English pounds were acceptable to purchase goods, they hired a cart with an attendant. The attendant would bring the cart back to the farm.

They then strolled around the tables and casks that displayed numerous fruit and vegetables, a few of which were unfamiliar to the men from the *Erin go Bragh*. Some produce, like potatoes, was just heaped on the ground. Deciding that fresh fruit and vegetables such as green beans, cabbage, onions, leeks and carrots were desirable to keep down the scurvy threat, they purchased a reasonable quantity of each. They then filled the rest of their carrying capacity with several sacks of potatoes, the two sailors helping to load the cart and becoming loaded down with fruit and vegetables themselves.

"This all isn't a lot, given the complement of crew and passengers, but it may help to supplement what Mr Fox is going to get for us," explained the captain. "Perhaps we can also check other fresh food sources, though our cash funds are limited."

They made their way back to the wharf and loaded what they could into the longboat, but it would take several more trips with different crews to ferry the remainder of the food to the ship. When he saw the first boatload arriving, the second mate ordered several seamen to carry the various boxes and bags of fruit and vegetables to the store while others, under the boatswain, were detailed to keep the passengers from snatching the goods. Despite this, the sight of fresh apples and oranges for passengers separated from such luxuries for three months or even much longer was too much for a few passengers. Scuffles developed as various mess captains and individuals tried to grab some of the fresh food. Some even overpowered the seamen to do so before order was restored.

Teddy judged that getting first in line at the ship's storeroom to get his mess's share would be better and set off there with Tony Molloy in tow. Others had the same idea, but not many and Teddy and Tony joined the short queue.

As the boxes and bags of fruit and vegetables were carried in the storekeeper's eyes lit up. *Now here was a way to make a bit on the side*, he thought.

When the time came to dole out the foodstuffs, he started handing out very meagre portions. There might not have been a great deal on offer, given the limited funds and transport available to the captain and first mate, but Teddy and some of the others at the head of the queue weren't having it, knowing that Baxter would be trying to swindle them.

"Give us our fair share, you thieving bastard," yelled one of the men.

Teddy joined in. "A quarter of a cabbage and two apples ain't a fair portion, Mr Baxter. And unless you want a riot and the officers getting involved, you had better give us our fair share for each mess."

Baxter scowled at them with a look for Teddy that was pure hatred, but he then went ahead and handed out a fairer share, although it was still not much. A couple more apples, two oranges, an onion, and two potatoes were handed over for Teddy's mess.

"You'll get some more tomorra, and the captain says we're getting much more supplies tomorra."

Even this small extra ration added to the few other staples they were still entitled to from the ship's original food supply was very welcome. The children benefited from a small piece of apple, and Teddy ensured Jane got a quarter of an orange while the onion and potatoes went into a stew with some salted beef.

****

Early the next morning, the captain and second mate went ashore to see how successful Mr Fox had been in finding foodstuffs to supplement their supplies for the remainder of the voyage to Moreton Bay. The James Baine and Company office was a hive of activity as they entered, but, on enquiring with the same clerk as yesterday, they were informed that Mr Fox was not in.

"I expect he shall be back shortly, perhaps in another hour or so," volunteered the clerk.

So, Captain Borlase and Mr Harvey decided to explore the town for a bit and perhaps find other useful foodstuffs for the voyage. They were back an hour later and met Mr Fox as the latter climbed the stairs to the first floor.

"How successful have you been, Mr Fox?" asked the captain.

"Let's go into my office and I shall explain the situation," replied the stout gentleman as he breathed heavily, the effort of climbing the stairs being one he would prefer to have done without.

The captain and second mate looked at each other, exchanging glances that suggested Mr Fox may have bad news. *On the other hand, he may prefer not to talk and climb stairs simultaneously, as obviously, the latter was causing him some distress*, thought the captain.

Once inside the plush office, Mr Fox seated himself, with a heavy sigh, into his leather chair and, mopping his perspiring face with a large linen handkerchief, looked at the captain and second mate. The captain introduced Mr Harvey, then they both sat down in the comfortable leather armchairs.

"It's not good news, I'm afraid, Captain Borlase, though it is not all bad. With so many ships in port, getting many of your supplies has been hard. Having said that, my staff have been able to secure a limited quantity of flour, milk, dried peas, sauerkraut, tea and sugar. We have got you a goodly supply of ship's biscuits and salted pork that should see you through to Australia, plus you can have all the water you need. Unfortunately, we have only been able to get you a limited supply of potatoes, fresh vegetables, apples, oranges and grapes."

The captain drummed the fingers of his right hand on the arm of his chair. "Well, I appreciate what you've been able to get for us, and we shall have to make do with that and pray we have a faster passage than we've had so far." He felt it better not to mention that they had had some success at the fresh food markets the previous day. "Is there any chance of getting some livestock to take on board for meat, like hogs?"

"I shall see what we can do, but I can also get you a good supply of biltong, Captain. That's dried meat."

"I don't know biltong, but if it helps to cut the hunger and give some sustenance, we'll take it."

"Right, Captain. We have organised a barge to ferry your supplies to the *Erin go Bragh*. It should be alongside your ship later this morning. So, could you be ready to unload the supplies. It will need more than one trip, what with providing water as well. Once all the loading is done, please return to my office to sign for all the produce, plus labour and boat hire."

The captain and Mr Harvey came out onto the busy street and joined the mixture of sailors, white citizens, brown Cape Malays, the men with their fez-like red hats, the women in full colourful dresses with ornate headdresses, and several black Africans.

"We need to get back to the ship to organise the unloading of the provisions," commented the captain. "But, first, let's have a quick look to see what other supplies we can pick up with our limited cash."

They hailed a carriage and asked to be taken to a butcher, where they obtained a limited quantity of meats and sausages. A food emporium yielded a few more useful items, which they again arranged to be taken to the docks. Then, they proceeded with the carriage to the dock and organised their purchases to be taken on board the longboat.

The longboat was loaded with as much as could safely fit. Then the second mate stayed behind with the remaining provisions, while the captain and six oarsmen headed for the *Erin go Bragh*. As he clambered on board, the captain could sense the tension in the air. Several passengers were shouting and pushing against several of the crew who, with the first mate, were endeavouring to restrain them.

There were angry shouts from two or three passengers in particular.

"Why can't we go ashore?"

"What's the harm in giving us a break from this stinking, rotten bucket of a ship?"

"How come the crew get to go ashore, and we don't?"

These shouts and curses were accompanied by pushing and shoving and much fist-shaking. It was an ugly scene that greeted the captain as he stepped onto the deck. But he stood there and raised his arms.

"Shut up, the lot of you, or I'll throw you in the brig with only ship's biscuits and water. Then you'll see what stinking and starving is really about!"

As the noise subsided, he looked to the ring leaders. A couple he knew from the trouble they had created before over food. He sighed as he realised that the situation was likely to get worse before they reached Australian shores and that would be many weeks more of this lot cooped up on board. He couldn't blame them, but what could he do except try to reason with those who might listen? He knew that for some, their skulls were too full of frustration and mutinous thoughts or somewhat lacking in brain capacity to be amenable to reason.

"I realise that this has been a long and difficult journey for all of you. And I understand how you would dearly love to put your feet on dry land that isn't forever moving about. That might have been possible if we had gotten a berth by a dock. But we've come here unannounced to find some more food and water supplies and there's no room at any dockside. We cannot ferry all who want to go ashore using our small boats. We are getting some food provisions and a good supply of water, including, as you have already seen, some fresh fruit and vegetables. So, I just ask for your patience. But I will not stand for any more trouble. Do you hear?"

There were some mumblings from the ringleaders and others and much despondency.

"What's the bloody use? We're stuck on this damn ship. This feckin' captain don't give a rat's arse for us steerage passengers. We could just be a load of feckin' cattle as far as he's concerned." But the group slowly dispersed.

Teddy was also frustrated at not being able to go ashore with Jane, and his elder sons were also pushing for that to happen, with Andrew being quite vocal in the crowd that met the captain on his return. But he couldn't see how they'd accomplish this, and the captain's words only reinforced that.

He moved towards the bow of the ship where Jane was standing with several other women discussing the outburst from the crowd. When Teddy reached them, Jane accosted him.

"So, what did the captain say? Can we get to go ashore?"

"It ain't gonna happen. They can't get to a dock to tie up, and there's no way all those that want to go could be rowed back and forth in the rowing boats. This is as close as we get to land until we get to Queensland, so take a good look as we won't see any land before we get to Australia I'm told, and that is going be some weeks. But at least we'll have some fresh food for a bit with what I've seen them bringing on board."

"That's as may be, Teddy. But I'm not sure I can last many more weeks on this here ship. That tween deck where we live is worse than a pig pen and smells just as bad. And then we have to put up with them other passengers in the bunks nearby. There's a couple of them across the way that argues with each other till the cows come home and never a thing is resolved. Then there's poor Catherine Dempsey, that's just along from us, she's in a rare state and hardly stops weeping, while the husband looks like he's in a trance. Though it's no wonder with them having lost four of their children, and the last one just after Easter. And Ellen and Daniel Brien have lost three of their four children and are also in a bad way. Other families have lost two or three of their young ones. I fear, Teddy, that this ship's a floating death trap, especially for the young ones. And when I say trap, I mean just that, as we can't get out of it or off it. Oh, Mother Mary, when is it all gonna end?"

Teddy could feel his wife's intense frustration and fear and knew that many others, himself included, felt the same. But what was there to do? It was like they were trapped in some purgatory that just didn't seem to be ending any time soon.

"Jane, I don't know when it will end. It's maybe two more months before we get to Queensland. But we've gotta be strong and take hold of the good things we have, or that happen, small though they may be. We have each other and the children, who are all healthy." Then putting his arm around her narrow shoulders, he smiled down at her. "Now, let's get some dinner into us, hoping that the thieving bastard, Baxter, is gonna give us some decent rations."

Meanwhile, the second mate was reporting to the captain on the state of the hull in the bilges. "It ain't too good, Captain. We moved as much of the iron ingots and pumped her as dry as we could. There seems to be seepage coming through in several places between the planks, and some of that pine is sort of rotten on the edges, havin' been wet for so long. So, we patched up as best we could with oakum and tar. That should hold for a bit, but as soon as we get some rough weather and movement of them planks, the caulking's gonna ease out."

"Thanks, Mr Harvey. That's all we can do now, short of getting her ashore and careening her. Thank God for that copper bottom; otherwise, the situation would have been much worse, particularly with them holes that were bored through the hull. Did you find any more of them?"

"No, Captain. It seems they hadn't much time to do the drilling, and they would have found it hard to move the iron ingot ballast."

"Well, thank goodness for that. And you're right; we will have to watch how we sail to minimise the amount of rough weather and movement of them there planks. This means we shall have to be careful about heading too far south to avoid any really stormy weather."

As the captain was talking, a shout came from one of the crew that a boat was approaching. A steam-driven vessel, belching smoke from a tall funnel towards its stern, was making its way towards the *Ern go Bragh*. Shortly after that, it came alongside with the first shipment of the supplies provided by Mr Fox, crowding its open deck. Many passengers gathered to watch the unloading and the first mate decided to give them something to do. He organised a number of the men to assist with the unloading of the barge and carrying the goods and water into storage.

As the barge was lower than the *Erin go Bragh*, this required the use of a block and tackle attached to the main yardarm, which was mainly used for the heavier items, including barrels of water and a few of brandy. Lighter items were handed up or pulled up by ropes over the side.

The passengers were fascinated by the Cape Malays, who made up a good portion of the barge's crew. Many of the dark-skinned, turbaned men revelled in the curiosity and, flashing broad smiles, waved to the passengers while talking animatedly amongst themselves as they manhandled the cargo and helped to hoist it aboard the ship.

It was mid-afternoon when the last of the water and foodstuffs were on board. As the barge prepared to leave, its captain yelled to the first mate that they would return with the second and final load the next morning. He then ordered crew members on the *Erin go Bragh* to let go of the stern and bow lines. The one-hundred-foot-long vessel headed back to the distant docks, threading its way expertly between the anchored ships in the bay.

****

The next morning, true to its skipper's word, the barge was seen approaching from the shore not long after Teddy and his sons had climbed onto the deck, anxious for fresh air. With the ship not moving and little breeze, the crowded tween deck had become more than usually putrid - a mixture of stale, strong body odour and damp.

The barge came alongside, and once securely moored, unloading commenced as on the previous day. In addition to the other foodstuffs, several squealing hogs had to be hoisted using the block and tackle and then penned just aft of the forecastle. Some of the passengers helped with this, and there was much hilarity when a couple of the porkers managed to get loose and run squealing around the deck, pursued by several passengers and crew before being captured.

By noon, the unloading was complete, and the captain boarded the pinnace for the journey to the docks and his reckoning with Mr Fox. He ordered the longboat to be rowed to the dockside with the third mate, James Green, and there to await his return. He also ordered the first mate to prepare for sea and their departure, which he planned for first light the next morning, the 17th of May.

For the second day in a row, the passengers and crew were able to supplement their otherwise meagre rations with a limited quantity of fresh vegetables, fruit and meat. Fresh milk was also available for the children, including Tessie and William. Andrew and John found biltong very much to their liking, though Jane and Teddy's daughters were not keen on it. The dried fish was also a novelty. In fact, any fish was a rare treat for these land-locked Irish with only limited access to freshwater fish back home, and then usually at their peril as it meant poaching from one of the English-held estates.

On board the ship, there was still grumbling among some passengers; many stood along the rails and gazed at the town or the towering vista of Table Mountain.

"That would be a good climb up that mountain." exclaimed Pat McEvoy, a farm labourer in his mid-twenties, who could envision a better life in Queensland, no matter what.

"It sure would, Pat. But I'd just like to get ashore and do some roaming around before we leave," replied Larry

(Lawrence) Stones. He was an impressionable nineteen and had been a labourer on a nearby estate since he was thirteen until his dad decided he should leave and try to do better elsewhere.

As he told Larry, "There's nothing for you here. So, best try your luck in Australia." Larry had jumped at the chance of a new beginning, and though it was hard leaving his family, his mother and dad had given him their blessings.

The other two members of this little group were the brothers Thomas and Patrick Conroy. Both were older, in their mid to late twenties and Thomas, in particular, tended to boss the others around.

"I reckon we ought to wait till dark so we can steal one of them dinghies and row to shore. What do you think?" suggested Thomas, the elder.

"Count me in!" said Larry.

"Much as I'd like to, I don't think stealing a boat to go ashore is the right thing to do," Pat McEvoy quietly stated. "What are you gonna do when you get ashore in the dark? You don't know where you are going and we got piss all money to spend. Then, we gotta be back before sunup, as I heard the captain tell the first mate we are sailing then, and I don't want to get left behind."

"Oh, you're a lily-livered excuse for a man. Where's your sense of adventure? And I for one need to get off this stinking hulk and breathe some fresh air," retorted Thomas.

"Well, that makes three of us," said Patrick Conroy. "I'll ask Pat Murphy and Tom Murray if they want to join us. We'll see you by the main mast after lights out, Larry."

Teddy and Jane also had thoughts of going ashore as they stood together by the rail in the late afternoon. "The word is we're leaving first thing tomorra," said Teddy. "It's a pity we couldn't have gone ashore and explored and stretched our legs. And, to be sure, I'm not looking forward to going to sea again for goodness knows how many weeks. Some of the crew told me it can get pretty rough going across from here to Australia."

That evening, the Ryan family again had an improved tea, with some fresh pork, potatoes and onions, together with two apples, which were divided up between the younger children.

After lights out, at around eight p.m., when quiet had descended on the ship apart from a few muffled conversations, four figures stole silently across the deck to where the smallest of the rowing boats was lashed to the hatch over the ship's hold. Thomas Conroy had a sharp knife with him, which he used to slash the ropes holding the dinghy.

"OK, boys, let's get this thing over the side, but be quiet about it."

They managed to lift and carry the dinghy to the rail and were about to tip it over the side when Pat Murphy whispered, "How are we gonna row this thing? There ain't no oars in it."

The Conroy brothers looked bewildered. Not being used to boats, they hadn't thought of the need for propulsion.

"Well, where are the feckin' oars?" replied Thomas. "I can't be expected to think of everything!"

"Perhaps they're back under where the boat was lying," volunteered Larry Stones.

But as he and Patrick Conroy moved back across the deck, they were spied by the officer of the watch, the second mate.

"Hey, what the feckin' hell are you two up to?" Then, he caught sight of the other two men holding on to the dinghy at the rail. "What is going on here? And where do you think you are going with that dinghy?"

His raised voice brought two seamen, also on the watch, and the dinghy thieves knew they had been caught.

The two by the rail with the dinghy didn't know whether to run or stay, but where could they run to? So, Thomas Conroy decided to brazen it out.

"We was just gonna take a quick trip onto the shore to stretch our legs and maybe pick up one or two nice local women," he said with a lopsided smile, which didn't fool the second mate.

"We didn't mean any harm, Mr Harvey. Honest, we didn't. We only wanted to get ashore for a bit," wailed Larry.

"And how were you going to get there, you, numbskull, without any oars? And the way you are handling that boat without holding fast to the painter, you'd lose the dinghy before you even got over the side, that is, if the dinghy landed the right way up, 'cos you ain't got any way of lowering it over the side, apart from just dropping it."

The other two crew were smiling broadly, and Thomas, in particular, was feeling highly embarrassed while his companions shuffled their feet and hung their heads.

"Well, I'm gonna have to report this to the captain, so I need your names. I doubt he'll do much about it except have a laugh, which is what others are gonna do when they hear about your little episode. That'll likely be punishment enough and pretty hard to bear at that. Now, get that boat back where it belongs and get to your beds, and, mark my word, me and the other officers will be watching you for any more trouble."

The four men slowly carried the dinghy back to the hatch, where the second mate ordered one of the crew to secure it. Then, smiling to himself, he resumed his watch. He couldn't blame the young men for trying to get ashore, and this was probably the forerunner of more trouble ahead over the next few weeks as they made their way east to Australia.

A Stretch Too Far

As the sun rose over Table Mountain, which was again clothed with its white table cover of clouds spilling over the edges, Teddy, Jane and the rest of their family were on deck to watch their departure from Cape Town. The crew turned the capstan to raise the anchor while, at the same time, seamen aloft let go of the main, fore and mizen topsails, top gallants, and royals, as well as the jib and fore course sails over the bow. There was a cool south-easterly breeze, and the captain ordered the boatswain to steer southwest.

"Brace the sails to starboard, Mr Meyler, and we'll stay on this reach until we get well clear of the bay. Then, I think, we'll head due south."

As the *Erin go Bragh* left the sheltered waters of Table Bay, where there was little more than a light chop, it encountered again, like an old friend, or perhaps an old adversary, the long deep south-westerly swells. To Teddy, the feel of those ocean swells, and the movement of the ship as it rose and fell with each succeeding crest brought a dread of what might lie ahead. This was despite the fact that, like most passengers, he was a somewhat seasoned sailor by now, although few liked the experience.

Turning to Jane and his sons, he said, "This could be a rough passage to Australia, but just keep thinking of the chances we'll have there, chances we would never have had in Ireland. So, I reckon we'll just have to grin and bear it, knowin' that each day gets us closer to our new home and our own farm. Why, each of you boys could, maybe, have your own farm or business!"

"My, you're a one for preaching, Teddy Ryan. You shudda joined the priesthood to give us all a good earful each Sunday. Though you're right, we've gotta look at our future and why we're on this here damn ship," retorted Jane.

"And what about me, Father? Can I have my own farm or business in Queensland?" piped up Tessie.

"Sure, you can, Tessie," interposed John, thinking to bolster her spirits. "Why, you could be richer than the lot of us."

This seemed to give Tessie something to think about. She was no longer the little girl with her doll as a constant companion. The voyage, including the deaths of her baby brother and so many other children as well as some adults, had vastly broadened her experience, giving her a more serious nature and maturity beyond her years.

"Now don't you go thinking about owning your own land, yet, my girl," was her mother's stern, though loving reply. "You just make sure you look after your brothers first."

As Teddy and Tony Molloy walked across the now more unstable deck to get their mess's daily ration, they heard the second mate giving orders to head south.

"Turn to one hundred and ninety degrees," he informed the helmsman. "And let's get the main and fore courses unfurled and braced."

With the sails filling in the breeze, the *Erin go Bragh* heeled over on her starboard side and slightly increased speed, the bow cutting into the deep blue ocean swells under an almost cloudless, light blue sky. The land slowly dropped out of sight on the port side, and by the afternoon, they were again alone on a vast ocean. For many passengers, there was a certain nostalgia about leaving the shelter of Table Bay and the safety of being close to land.

For some, the sense of melancholia that day was heightened by the death of eleven-year-old Michael Dempsey from a fever. This was the fifth of Edward and Catherine Dempsey's six children to die on the voyage, the first being their baby, Ellen, who died from cholera earlier on the journey. Catherine Dempsey was beside herself with grief, and no kind and comforting words from Father

Dunne or her husband penetrated the pall of her sorrow. At the burial service that afternoon, as her son's body was slid over the ship's side, Catherine made a lunge for the ship's rail and was pulling herself over the rail before her husband and another man pulled her back, weeping, onto the deck.

"Just let me go, Eddy. I need to be with them," she moaned.

"They're in God's arms now, Catherine, and have the angels to care for them," murmured Father Dunne.

"What God, Father?" she screamed as she rounded on the priest. "What loving God would take nearly all my children away in just two months on this godforsaken voyage? There's no loving God, and don't you try and tell me there is, with them nice words."

Father Dunne remained silent, knowing that nothing he could say would assuage the deep grief that Catherine was suffering.

He just looked at Edward Dempsey and quietly said, "Take good care of Catherine, Edward. Keep her close. And hopefully, time will heal her sorrow to some extent."

It was a very sober moment for the other passengers present, including Jane and Teddy. Jane was frightened that these deaths would claim another of their children, feeling both fortunate and guilty that they had only lost Peter. Teddy sensed Jane's fear but was silent, not knowing what to say. He, too, was anxious that this voyage would end without the loss of another of their children, particularly their always curious and good-tempered Tessie, who provided a rare spark of light in their lives.

****

Over the next two weeks, the *Erin go Bragh* headed south-east and then east-south-east into the southern Indian Ocean. As the ship moved further south, the swell from the west increased while the weather deteriorated. On the 30th

of May, they had reached 40 degrees south latitude and were entering the roaring forties, aptly named for the often gale force winds that swept in from the west.

On the positive side, the following sea and good wind was helping to increase the ship's speed. Captain Borlase was on the quarter deck with the first mate, both dressed in oil skins with sou'westers over woollen sweaters, as the temperatures had dropped markedly since Cape Town and were now quite frigid.

"What's our speed, Mr Meyler?" enquired the captain.

"We've been averaging between five and seven knots by the chip log, Captain, and with this westerly continuing, we should be able to maintain that unless we have to reef sails in stormy weather."

"And how are the pumps dealing with our leaks?"

"We've been able to keep the water in the bilges below a foot most of the time, but that has meant pumping through the daylight hours and to some extent at night. It's cross seas that give us the most problems, causing the timbers to shift. So, let's hope we don't have too much of those, even though these swells can be monstrous at times. But they're coming from the same direction as the wind most of the time so far. The helmsman just has to be paying attention to prevent the ship from broaching with such a following sea."

"Let's keep her on this course to about 45 degrees south and see if we are lucky. Not only will we get more speed, but the distance to Australia will be shortened. But keep an eye on them bilges, and if there's more leakage, we'll have to come up north." With that, the captain went to join his wife and daughter in the relative warmth of their cabin.

For the passengers in the tween decks, the increasingly rough, windy and sometimes stormy weather had meant more close confinement below deck. It was a far cry from the sunny days they had experienced for six weeks earlier before moving into the South Atlantic, when so many passengers spent much of the daylight, and even for some, the night hours on deck. There was not as much sickness now as earlier in the voyage, but the endless days sitting or lying in the gloom of the tween deck, with the port holes closed most of the time and only a weak light coming through the hatch was a cause of much melancholia. Groups of passengers were allowed on deck for fresh air if conditions were not too rough, although balancing on the heaving deck was not pleasant under often heavily overcast skies. And many of the women and young children were reluctant to brave the deck under these conditions.

The married tween deck was crowded with thirty-eight families, a few of whom had no children or only one, while others had as many as seven to ten children. The scene was one of despondency and boredom, with most sitting or lying on their bunks, perhaps talking with family members or just staring into space. The fiddles and tin whistles were silent as nobody seemed in the mood for music or dancing, even if one could balance sufficiently. With the colder weather, the men had on their heavy Ulster overcoats and either soft caps or battered stove-pipe hats while the women wrapped their woollen shawls about themselves.

One bright and positive note was the classes still being held by Mary Killen. They kept the younger children occupied and helped them gain some knowledge. It was a slow process, with few tools to help with the teaching. But Mary was patient, and using her chalkboard, she helped many of the children either start learning how to write or improve on skills and knowledge already learned. Arithmetic was also taught with a chorus of voices reciting the times' table, and the same was the case with history or geography when Mary would get them to recite dates and events or places and countries after she had explained about these mysteries.

"William of Orange beat James the Second at the Battle of the Boyne in 1690," went the chorus of voices.

The lessons also provided some adults with a distraction, entertainment, or learning experience. Mary was not a stern, overbearing teacher but was patient with poor students and taught by inviting participation. She continued to make her classes fun with stories and encouragement for her pupils. Many young men, like John and Andrew, found her highly appealing, and they made a point of trying to attend most classes. This was noted by others in the family and invited some ribbing from their older sister, Anne, and their father.

"So, tell us what you learned about Bonnie Prince Charlie, then?" asked Anne, with a mischievous smile. "Or were too distracted by watching the teacher to follow the the lesson?"

As the ship headed further south, the weather worsened. The winter months were not a good time to be sailing below 40 degrees south latitude. The massive swells rolling across from the west could be fifteen to twenty feet high, and frequent storms also lashed these latitudes, becoming increasingly vicious the further south one went. An almost constant strong wind blowing from the west increased markedly as part of each passing storm. The result was that the *Erin go Bragh* was able to maintain an improved speed of up to eight knots in these latitudes, but at the expense of comfort to the passengers and hard work for the crew, who were required to change sail configurations with the changing weather. At the same time, there was the constant need to man the ship's pumps to keep the level of water leaking into the bilges to a minimum.

There were now few deaths occurring, despite the deteriorating wet and cold conditions in the tween decks. But on the 30th of May, Patrick Byrne passed away. He was only two days old and was the third of Catherine and

James' eight children to have died on the voyage. The two youngest had been lost earlier through scarlatina and infantile cholera. Then, to compound the family's woes, Catherine succumbed to pleurisy on the 7th of June. She left her distraught husband, James, and their eldest daughter, Maria, to care for their four remaining children. The seas were too rough for more people other than James Byrne, Father Dunne and the captain with several of the crew to attend the burials.

Before Catherine Byrne's burial service, Captain Borlase had been on watch and eyeing another approaching storm from the west when the first mate approached him.

"Captain, I fear the leaks are getting worse. We will either have to have almost constant pumping or get away from this rough weather. You can actually see the leaks increase in places with the hull movement caused by these rough seas."

"All right, Mr Meyler. We've had a good run now for these last ten days, but best be careful. Let's bring her up a few points to port and lay a course for the Great Australian Bight. That will get us a good deal north of 40 degrees south."

Teddy's mess as well as others found that the fresh provisions obtained in Cape Town had been consumed faster than they thought they would have been. The ration handouts for each mess now consisted of the hard ship's biscuit, salt pork and the odd potato. Some biltong was still available in limited quantities for those who liked it. Bread was no longer baked through lack of flour, at least for the steerage passengers.

Shortly after the ship had altered course to a more northerly track, Teddy and John Gavan headed to the store to collect their rations. They were earlier than usual as they were taking advantage of a break in the stormy weather, which could make crossing the deck a somewhat hazardous venture. Walking across the wet deck they saw two male passengers emerge from the door leading to the storeroom with a box containing dried, salted fish and several other items supposedly no longer available.

Teddy was intrigued and suspicious, given his former dealings with the storekeeper. "Now, what do we have here?" he asked the two men.

They looked at him guiltily and started to turn away. "None of your feckin' business, you nosey busybody," replied the larger of the two men, who was Teddy's height but of broader build.

"But, to be sure, it is our business, isn't it, John? Here we families with children are getting nothing but mouldy biscuits and half-rotten salt pork, and you two are about to enjoy some nice fish with a couple of potatoes, and I can see you've got some tea there as well."

"Aye, it sure is our business," joined in John Gavan. "My clann haven't had a good meal for days now, and here, it looks like you are going to be feeding your face."

"Well, we pay for it, see," replied the shorter of the two men in a truculent voice. "We give ole Danny Baxter a shilling or two, and he gives us some of the better food he's stored away."

Teddy and John's faces showed their anger at the storekeeper's greed and trickery. "The thievin bastard!" growled Teddy, who was so angry he considered doing some serious physical damage to the storekeeper. "And how long has this been going on?"

The big man replied, "Just a couple of weeks this time. But maybe others have been getting special favours afore that."

"What do you mean, 'this time'? Has he been doin' this before on the voyage?" Teddy wanted to know.

"Well, I'm not really sure. But we was getting some extra rations back before we got to Cape Town. Mind you, it was costing us money," the smaller man replied.

"This is bloody disgusting," interjected John Gavan. "Wait till I get my hands on the bastard. And to think our clann have been doing without so this man can line his pockets!" And with that, he marched through the door to the storeroom with Teddy following, equally incensed.

They found the storekeeper in the storeroom, portioning out ship's biscuits to be collected by the various messes. John Gavan came into the room and said in a deceptively calm voice. "Morning, Mr Baxter, we've come for our mess's rations."

There was a cunning look in the storekeeper's small eyes that looked up at John and Teddy as he said in a surly tone. "Well, you're early, and it ain't ready yet. Yer can see I'm only just doling out the biscuits."

Teddy looked Baxter in the eye and said, "It ain't just biscuits we're after. We understand you've got some nice dried, salted fish and praties we could have."

Baxter looked startled, but his tone was brazen. "Who told you that?"

"Never you mind, Mr Baxter. We would just like some of them victuals for our mess, particularly for our children," said an increasingly irate John.

Baxter felt he was at a disadvantage, so he tried his commercial storekeeper tone. "All right, then. I've got a few extras that I put aside. There ain't enough for too many people, so I thought it best to give it to those that can pay for it. So, where's your money then?"

"We're not paying anything for what should be rightfully ours, you thieving excuse for a storekeeper," came back Teddy.

"Well, then, you ain't getting anything but your regular rations."

John Gavan had had enough, and stepping around Teddy, he grabbed Baxter by his coat lapels and threw him back against the bulkhead, which he hit with a dull thud. At that point, two more mess captains appeared at the door to the storeroom. Teddy recognised Pat Bolger and Tom Colgan from the tween deck. They stared at the scene, with Pat uttering an exclamation.

"Be Jesus, was Baxter here giving you some lip, was he?"

John Gavan turned at the voice and uttered, "The thieving bastard has been stashing some of the better food away and then selling it to those with some money to buy. Now, we just want what should be ours by right."

"Has he now!" said an astonished Tom Colgan. "I suspected he might have been up to some tricks the way he was treating our mess and some of the others, but makin' money from our misery and that of our clann. That is a hanging offence!" In two strides he was opposite Baxter and then landing a punch to the storekeeper's head.

Teddy yelled for calm. "All right, lads. It ain't our business to punish this thieving bastard."

But both Tom Colgan and John Gavan were deaf to his pleas. Only the voice of the second mate stopped their pummelling of Baxter. "What the hell is going on here?" William Harvey shouted.

A babble of voices tried to explain to him what they had discovered. "Quiet! I'll listen to one at a time, please. Now, Teddy Ryan, you tell me why our storekeeper is being knocked about within an inch of his life."

So, Teddy explained how they had discovered that the storekeeper had been secreting some stores and selling them to passengers who were prepared to pay. While he talked, Baxter stood unsteadily on his feet with a scowl on his bruised face, although he knew it was the end of the line for him and his money-making scheme.

"All right, Mr Baxter, you are coming with me to see the captain. The rest of you get out of here. I'll send one of the stewards to act as storekeeper, and he'll dole out your rations. I'm also going to find out how much food has been put aside and how best to distribute it."

Teddy and the other mess captains, and there were several additional ones there now, moved back out onto the deck. They stood around talking amongst themselves with an increasing volume and many exclamations and curses, all of them angry at having been deprived of some precious food items.

****

The *Erin go Bragh* was making heavy weather of it through the southern Indian Ocean as they now slowly made their way towards the southwestern coast of Australia, some two thousand miles to the east. Monstrous swells, up to thirty feet high and well above the level of the deck, rolled in from the west. And with the almost constant strong winds or gales creating white caps on the peaks and sides of the swells, the sea seemed to many frightened passengers to be perpetually angry. The *Erin go Bragh*, which seemed so big when they boarded in Queenstown, now appeared small and fragile and in danger of being enveloped by these seas. Luckily, the swells were still coming from almost directly astern.

As they moved slowly into lower latitudes, the winds decreased in strength to between twenty and thirty knots from the west or southwest. To help prevent too much movement in the hull timbers the captain had ordered sails to be reduced. This meant that their average speed dropped to around four knots. This was slower than the swells, which required careful handling of the ship to prevent broaching and being capsized by a following swell. It also meant rougher conditions for all those on board and a longer time at sea for the already distressed passengers.

Despite the reduced speed, the effect of the winter storms that swept in from the west continued to shift the ship's hull planks, slowly causing the leaks there to increase. During such bad weather, constant pumping was needed to keep the water level in the bilges from becoming dangerously high. This was also affecting the crew, with much grumbling and mutinous talk. Captain Borlase was a worried man. He was in command of a leaking ship in rough weather. He had a near-mutinous crew. He was forced to proceed slowly, which meant that food supplies, particularly for the steerage class passengers, were diminishing fast, and there was increasing agitation among some of these passengers.

As he paced the quarterdeck mulling over what to do, Mr Meyler, the first mate, approached him. "Captain, some of the crew are refusing to work the pumps as they say they didn't sign up just to pump a leaking ship."

"We have to keep the pumps going, Mr Meyler, especially during the rougher weather as these leaks seem to be multiplying. What options do we have to lessen the load on them? And I agree it is a great deal of extra work they're having to do."

"Can we ask some of the more able-bodied men among the passenger to give a hand? After all, it's just manual work that doesn't require much skill."

"That's a brilliant suggestion, Meyler. Approach some of the more amenable passengers who seem capable of doing the job and put it to them. We can draw up a roster. It will also give them something to do, rather than sitting and festering down in the tween decks, thinking about not having enough to eat."

Mr Meyler proceeded to round up about thirty men from amongst the passengers, including John and Andrew Ryan. They jumped at the chance to do something useful. Some oilskins were borrowed or were spare and made available to these passengers during their pumping shifts, and the first mate showed the willing men how the pumps worked. A joint roster was set up using the passengers and crew, with one-hour shifts and two men to each pump, there being six pumps. This seemed to ease the disquiet amongst the crew, some of whom shared shifts on a pump with passengers.

****

For three weeks, the *Erin go Bragh* made its slow way towards the land that would be the future home of the weary passengers. Gradually the winds eased further, and the temperatures crept up above freezing. The passengers began spending more time on deck. Although, every so often, storms would plunge the ship into a maelstrom of tossing waves whipped into a white-capped fury by the winds, with rain and hail thundering on the deck. Sometimes, the storms would last two or three days, with only the pumping volunteers and mess captains permitted on the heaving decks to collect their meagre rations of mainly ship's biscuit and salt pork.

The cold, wet and cramped conditions were too much for some and bronchial ailments multiplied.

It was thus that an enfeebled William Birmingham succumbed to an "inflammation of the lungs" on the 28th of June.

It was a chilly, though sunny winter's day, but not nearly as cold as it had been a week or two earlier. The seas had moderated further over the last week, and the wind had dropped considerably, sometimes being no more than a breeze of about ten knots, though storms would still move in from the west, greatly increasing the wind speed and the wave action. The combination of shortening sails in rough weather and lighter winds meant their speed was now averaging less than four knots.

After taking sightings with a sextant, the second mate determined that the *Erin go Bragh* was at latitude south 37 degrees 15 minutes and east 122 degrees 18 minutes. Marking his coordinates on the chart, he found they were approximately two hundred nautical miles south of the southwestern Australian coastline. When the captain came on deck, the second mate informed him of their position.

"We will need to head for Hobart Town to get some decent food and replenish our water supplies. That means we will have to head south again, Mr Harvey. We need to get down to 44 degrees south latitude and then I'd like to take her on a direct course for the south of Tasmania. However, this wind from the east is making that difficult. So, let's try her on a course of 150 degrees until we can get a more easterly bearing. It'll be slow going, but there's aught else we can do."

"Aye, Captain. I'll bring her up as close to the wind as possible as the sooner we get some fresh food and water, the better we'll all be, but particularly them steerage passengers who must be close to starving now, with the meagre rations they're getting."

The poor state of the rations was continuing to affect the health of the passengers. Teddy watched as many of those on the tween deck became more listless. Some developed stomach complaints from eating rotten meat, and on the 3rd of July, Eliza Quaid died from dysentery. It was almost the last straw. The passengers had complained to Father Dunne, but he could do little. Now they took their grievances straight to the captain.

A small delegation, including Teddy, John Gavan and Tony Molloy, went aft to the captain's cabin. They knocked on the cabin door and were told to enter. On entering, they could not help but gawk at the spaciousness of the cabin and its fine fittings, which contrasted with their abysmal conditions in the tween deck. Mrs Borlase and Miss Borlase were seated by the wide window that extended across most of the stern, and they looked up enquiringly at the motley group of poorly dressed men who had invaded their privacy. The captain had been studying charts laid across the broad expanse of a solid polished oak table. He looked up as the men entered and eyed them warily, knowing that they weren't here on any good mission.

"Gentlemen, what can I do for you?"

Teddy spoke for the group. "Captain, we want to register a complaint about the lack of proper food these last few weeks. In fact, it's not just a lack of proper food, which was scarce before, but of any food. People are hungry, and we also only have a limited ration of water, so they're often thirsty too. This can't go on much longer. Some people are getting sick 'cos the meat we're getting is half rotten, and there's a man that's died from that today."

The captain was at a loss as to how to deal with a situation over which he had little control at the moment. All he could offer them was some hope.

"I know you are all having a tough time of it, and I'm sorry the food supply is not what it should be. I could offer you excuses by saying that we have had to slow our speed to limit the amount of water leaking into the bilges, so we are way behind our schedule. But that doesn't help you. All I can say is that we are heading to Hobart Town now to replenish our food and water supplies, and we should be there in about a week. I'm just asking that you be patient till we get to Hobart Town."

Teddy looked at the other men in the group. They weren't satisfied, but what else could the captain or they do?

"I hears what you're saying, Captain. But isn't there anything you can do to ease the situation for the next week, even just for the children? What about the better rations that those in first class or the crew get? Can't some of that come to us?"

"The crew are also on short rations though not as short as yours. But then they have to work, so I am not taking any more from their rations. I can see about getting some extra food from that allocated to first-class passengers. It won't be much, but it may help. As you say, mainly for the children."

The men had to be satisfied with that and shuffled silently out of the cabin with resigned but downcast looks.

As the door closed, Mrs Borlase spoke up, "George, these people are having a nightmare of a voyage. What with so much sickness and death earlier on and now they're starving. It's been the children that have suffered the most, and it's them I'm fearful for now. I know you are doing your best, George, but this voyage has been the worst I have been on with you."

"You are right, my dear. I do feel for these steerage passengers. They've had a hard time of it. I'm surprised we haven't had more complaints and violence. Perhaps it's the saner heads amongst them, like that Teddy Ryan, that are helping to keep the lid on it. The situation would be a lot better with a more seaworthy vessel. This tub probably shouldn't have left the port without a proper inspection and repairs to the hull. It might have a copper bottom nailed on, but it's getting on and the hull being made of pine doesn't help."

****

Having reached 43 degrees south latitude on the 3rd of July, the next week saw the ship alter course to almost due east, heading for the south coast of Tasmania. Steady westerly winds enabled the *Erin go Bragh* to increase her speed to just under six knots.

Then, on the sunny but chilly morning of 9th July, the lookout on the round top yelled, "Land off the port bow!"

With a feeling of near euphoria, the passengers already on deck rushed to the port rail to try and see for themselves. Teddy was there but hurried down to the tween deck. Climbing down the companionway, he yelled before he got to the bottom.

"Jane, Jane, they've spied land. It's Australia! Or at least Tasmania."

"Now, you're sure this be what they are seeing and not some cloud or fantasy?"

"I haven't looked myself, Jane. But let's you and I go and look. If this be Australia, then our journey is almost over; thanks be to God!"

Teddy helped Jane up the companionway followed by the rest of his family and quite a few others from the tween deck. They found a spot not far from the port rail and, shading their eyes, could just make out a low, dark mass on the horizon. There was an excited buzz among the other passengers as they all craned to make out the slowly emerging land.

What was it going to be like? Were there still savages roaming around? What wild animals would there be?

At noon they were no nearer the coast, but closer to hand, an island appeared not far from the ship, with two or three more visible in the distance to the north. But there was no sign of habitation to be seen on the islands. They were each a mass of blue-green forest-covered hills, coming right down to the sea, with no building in sight. As time passed and the passengers realised they would not get closer to land, at least for a while, they drifted away to other parts of the deck, and the mess captains went to get what supplies they could for their dinners.

By late afternoon they were closer to the coast, and passengers could make out the same green forest mass covering hills, though here and there was the odd plume of smoke. There was speculation among passengers as to whether these were from native campfires or other settlements.

Teddy asked the third mate, James Green. "What do you make of them there smoke plumes coming up from the forest, Mr Green?"

"I ain't got a clue. Could be just them thieving savages roastin' a sheep they've stolen from some innocent settler."

Perhaps, thought Teddy, *but then, Mr Green seemed to have a bias against a lot of humanity, so maybe it was something more innocent.*

****

The next morning dawned clear and sunny. The passengers again crowded onto the deck to hopefully see more of their promised land, but, to their disappointment, the coast had diminished to a smudge on the port quarter as the ship maintained an easterly course.

"What's going on?" demanded Andrew of the boatswain when he saw him approaching. "Ain't we gonna head into Hobart Town here in Tasmania?"

"Oh, calm yourself, young man. To be sure, we're gonna head to Hobart Town. But first, we gotta make sure we don't go too close to the coast here. The captain ain't been this way before, and though he's got charts, he ain't taking no chances of running up on some rocks we don't see soon enough or getting driven onto them by a sudden squall. I reckon we'll be in Hobart Town by tomorrow sometime."

Andrew and the other passengers who had been listening had to be content with that. Meanwhile, the euphoria of sighting the coast of Tasmania was dampened by yet another death – that of ten-year-old Bernard Dunne. The talk was he had died of a fever, at least that's what the surgeon had said. But most knew it was some sickness he'd got from eating rotten food and not having enough strength to fight off the illness.

Jane said to Teddy as they stood on the deck for the burial service. "Oh, Teddy, it's a crying shame. He almost made it to a new life and then lost his."

Then she hardened her tone. "If it weren't for the lack of proper food and not being able to stay warm. Well, he would have made it. This shouldn't happen if those who are in charge did their job proper like. It's nigh on criminal it is. You could call it murder, you could, murder of innocent children, as the poor lad isn't the only one to have died from lack of what they should have had on this voyage."

"I feel you may be right, my love. Father Dunne never said that the voyage would be so hard and that so many people might die. And he's already been on a voyage between Ireland and Australia. So, perhaps this voyage is worse than what they usually are."

That afternoon, the captain was conversing with the first mate. "Mr Meyler, given our current position, I feel we can now head towards the mouth of the Derwent River, which will get us to Hobart Town. I calculate we are some forty-five miles from the mouth of the Derwent, and a course of 340 degrees will get us there. With the winds now from the southwest, it should be a straight run with the sails braced well to starboard, though the winds will likely change once we get in the lee of the land. We don't want to get too close to land during darkness, so let's limit the sails and take it slowly."

"Aye, Captain. But might I suggest we proceed slightly more to the east on a heading of 345 degrees. This will take us clear of Bruny Island and keep us safer in the dark."

"Make it so, Mr Meyler, though make sure the watches keep a sharp lookout!"

Hobart Town

During the night, the *Erin go Bragh* slowly made its way to the north, passing Bruny Island to the port side, and by morning it was abeam of North Bruny Island and heading towards the Derwent River estuary. When Teddy came on deck to a dull grey morning with clouds hanging low, he eyed the scene they were now passing. But the vista on either side of the ship was nothing like Ireland.

To his left, the landscape alternated between low hills and flat land and all was covered in dense forest, though not the sort of forest he had seen before. On the right, the ship was approaching a rather flat tree-covered peninsular. After some time, they entered a wide bay, and as they slowly advanced up the bay, Teddy could see the odd house in land cleared amongst the trees on the left.

"This here be the mouth of the River Derwent," said a voice behind Teddy, and he turned to see John Judd, the boatswain. "They named it after a river not far from my home in the Midlands. Don't show much imagination these here people who name things in new places, or maybe they just wanted to make themselves feel at home. And over yonder," he said as he pointed to the starboard, "there's that nasty place they used to put the worst convicts, Port Arthur."

Teddy looked with interest across the flat land with rolling hills in the distance and thought, *This whole place has had a strange beginning with convicts being the first main inhabitants, if you didn't count the savages who were here from God knows how long. And now we're coming here to build a new life and, I guess, help improve it all.*

The ship moved slowly up through the wide mouth of the Derwent, and Teddy watched as increasing signs of habitation occurred on the left bank. Then, he noticed a small sailing vessel approaching from upriver. When it was within hailing distance, a man in its prow yelled across to the *Erin go Bragh*.

"What ship are you, and where have you come from?"

The captain ordered the first mate to hove to and then advanced down the deck to the bow. "We are the *Erin go Bragh* out of Liverpool via Queenstown."

"Thank God for that!" came the reply. "We thought you might have been lost at sea as you are so late in getting here. We have the medical officer here and request permission for him to come on board to check on the health of your passengers and crew."

"Permission granted."

And with that, the small sailing craft expertly made its way alongside the *Erin go Bragh* while the latter remained hove to, having turned into the wind. A rope ladder was lowered over the side. A small, stout gentleman with a suntanned face, dressed all in black except for a white shirt, clambered up the ladder with more agility than his figure would have earlier indicated he was capable of doing.

Stepping over the railing and onto the deck, he advanced towards the captain. "You are the Captain, I presume?"

"Indeed I am. Captain Borlase."

"My name is Dr John Martin, medical officer for Hobart Town. You are long overdue, Captain. You must have had some problems along the way?"

"The winds weren't kind to us, Dr Martin. And then we've been nursing some serious leaks, which have slowed us further. This has all meant we are running short of provisions and water. That's why we've called into Hobart Town."

"Well, before you'll be allowed to land, we need to make sure you haven't any nasty diseases that could spread through the colony here. So, with your permission, Captain, I would like to first have words with your surgeon. If he assures me that you have no infectious diseases among your passengers, I would, then, like to inspect your ship, the passengers and the crew."

"Of course, Dr Martin. I'll send for the surgeon, Mr Long, and he should be here presently. If you agree, I shall ask my first mate here, Mr Meyler, to escort you on an inspection of the ship while I arrange for the passengers and crew to assemble on deck."

Thanking the captain, Dr Martin waited for John Long to arrive, which was not many minutes. After a brief discussion with the surgeon and having been assured there were no infectious diseases on board, he proceeded with the surgeon and first mate to inspect the tween decks and other quarters. Meanwhile, the captain ordered his other officers to get all the passengers and crew on the deck.

While this was being organised, a loud wailing came from the married quarter's tween deck. The captain turned to a group of passengers nearby and asked, "What the deuce is that noise all about? It sounds like the howl of a banshee."

"Aye, that could well be what it is, Captain," replied one of the women.

Another added her voice. "It'll be Margaret Killian, the poor soul. She gave birth to a wee boy two days ago. But she's in such a weak state, what with the lack of good food and then her having such a hard labour that she can't feed the babog. Now, it seems the wee one has passed on to heaven and may he have a better time of it there than we're havin' here."

That's just what we need, another death on board at this point, thought the captain as he grimly went to investigate and placate the medical officer.

But Dr Martin was an understanding man and not a bureaucrat. "I can see from the look of your passengers that they have had a hard time of it. Such a shame that the poor woman had no milk to give her babe and just as they were about to land in their new home."

After inspecting the ship, passengers and crew, Dr Martin announced that there was no contagious disease on board and the ship was free to dock in Hobart Town. The passengers and crew would be allowed to go ashore.

*****

The sun was setting behind the mountains to the west of Hobart Town as the *Erin go Bragh* edged her way alongside the dock. Teddy was with Jane and the rest of his family, trying not to get in the way of the crew as they furled the last of the sails and threw lines to two large rowing boats, which then set to in order to pull the ship towards the dock. Closer in, two other smaller rowing boats were thrown thin messenger lines. These were carried to the dock and thrown to waiting dock workers, who pulled on the messenger lines to bring ashore thick hawsers from the ship, which were then wound around capstans on the dock. Workers then set about winding the capstan and bringing the ship to the dock. Once the *Erin go Bragh* was alongside, the hawsers were unwound from the capstan and tied to bollards on the dock.

Teddy spied the second mate and asked, "Mr Harvey, will we be allowed to go ashore?"

"The captain said you will be allowed ashore once we have secured the ship and met with the harbourmaster. That may take some time, so maybe later tonight or tomorrow morning."

Hobart Town was not much to look at from the dock. There were solid stone houses, from single storey to three storeys, built close together around the dock area, where two other large sailing vessels were also moored. The houses seemed to extend up the low hillsides that surrounded the port. Beyond this, higher up the slopes, it was mainly forest with the odd building seen on land that had been cleared. Quite a number of local residents had come down to the dock to view this ship that had just arrived. Teddy thought them a motley lot – some seemingly well-to-do and well-dressed men, but most were poorly dressed. A few of the latter seemed to be rather under the influence of alcohol, laughing, joking and pointing at what was amusing them.

"It don't seem like much of a town to me," said Andrew as he surveyed the waterfront scene with his parents. "Let's hope we can find somewhere to give us some good food after the shite we've been eating lately."

"Andrew! Watch your mouth with your mother and sisters about. But I agree we all need a good feed, and I'm sure we can find something when they let us ashore."

As Teddy was speaking, a large man dressed all in brown, with a brown patterned waistcoat and a brown bowler hat that crowned a red, fleshy face, made his way up the gangway, which had just been lowered.

Once on deck, he addressed the first mate. "I'm Captain Deering, the harbourmaster. Could I speak with the captain of this here vessel?"

"Certainly, Captain. Please follow me."

Shortly afterwards, the harbourmaster came back to the gangway, accompanied by Captain Borlase.

"Come and see me tomorrow, Captain Borlase. My office is in yonder building by the quay. We can then discuss this dismissal of your storekeeper and whether you wish to lay any charges. As for your provision needs, the agent for the Black Ball Line is Messrs Bright Bros. They'll handle all your food and water requirements, so when you visit me on the morrow, I'll direct you to their office.

"But I'm glad you have made it to Hobart Town. And there's many in Brisbane that are anxious for word of your very existence. They were expecting you back in May. Since then, and particularly lately, we've been getting messages asking if we have seen or heard of you. I will send a message to the Brisbane harbourmaster via Melbourne to inform him of your arrival and condition. When do you expect you'll be able to continue your voyage to Brisbane?"

"Thank you, Captain Deering. We appreciate your assistance. I estimate that about five days should see us adequately provisioned and watered, though I shall have a better idea after talking with the agent. Hopefully, we'll be ready to head out on the 16th."

"Right. Before you proceed, I will ask our Emigration Officer, Mr Haig, to visit the ship to ascertain that you are seaworthy and that the passengers are fit to continue on the voyage."

With that, the harbourmaster slowly made his way down the gangway and the captain turned to the first mate, who was standing nearby. "Let the passengers and crew know they can go ashore, though roster duty crews to remain on board."

Teddy had overheard the captain's instructions to the first mate and whooped for joy. "Are you for going ashore now, Jane? I feel the sooner we go, the better, as there are there's an awful lot of hungry people on board this ship looking for something to eat."

"All right, Teddy. I am with you, and I need to feel some solid ground under my feet. Have we got any money to buy food, husband?"

"Aye, that we have, my love. I still have some of that money we was given in Cork to fend for ourselves and that should be good enough for the likes of them here to get some victuals."

The Ryan family quickly joined others going ashore, with Teddy holding onto Jane as the steep wooden gangway had no railings. Once ashore, they all experienced the sensation of feeling as though they were still on the ship.

"Oh, Pa. I feel like I'm going to fall over!" cried Anne. "This is a really strange feeling. I thought the movement would stop once we had our feet on solid ground, but I still feel like I'm on board a rocking ship."

Other passengers were experiencing the same feeling, and it was an almost comical crowd that made their way up the streets of Hobart Town, exploring and looking for food. There was a sense of gaiety about them, so glad were they to be off the ship that had been their virtual prison for five months.

This lower part of the town consisted of many substantial-looking stone buildings, most at least two stories high and some three. There were also several wooden buildings interspersed between the stone ones. The streets were unpaved dirt but generally in good condition and there were sidewalks for pedestrians. Teddy noted that a number of shops had metal awnings supported by posts that came over the footpaths outside.

It was too late in the day to buy any food provisions, but the Ryan's found an eatery where they ordered a hot meal of steak and kidney puddings. Two earlier attempts to be fed had been met by prices that put the food beyond their reach, the eatery owners inflating their prices when they heard of the plight of the passengers. But further up the hill, John Byrne was not going to let his fellow Irish go hungry and kept his prices affordable.

That night, all the Ryans and many other passengers slept soundly back on board the *Erin go Bragh* with full bellies and no violent seas. The port holes were opened to let in fresh air, and the night was dry, though chilly.

****

During the next few days, most passengers, including the Ryan family, spent much of their time ashore. The Ryans didn't have much money, and with nine in the family, it was spread thinly when it came to buying food and provisions to take with them for the remainder of the voyage. Teddy also wanted to have some cash for when they arrived in Brisbane. They explored the streets and shops and gathered a few items of food to take back to the ship – some fresh pork, a few vegetables, and there were still apples to be had even though they had been picked a month or two earlier.

The weather was chilly, though not as cold as it would have been back in Ireland in mid-winter. It rained and was windy for the first two days, making outdoor activities unpleasant. But as John told Teddy, "If this be winter here, then it's a darn sight better than winter around Tullamore."

When the rain eased Teddy and the boys walked further up the hill from the harbour. At first, they passed rather run-down wooden houses, but further up the hill, there were neat stone houses. Then they were out beyond the town and into the forest.

"Look at them trees, Father! They're so straight and tall. They are amazing. I wonder what they are called?"

Further along a track on which they were walking, they came across a group of men felling one of the giant trees. As they approached, one of the men, dressed in filthy trousers and a jacket with a battered bowler hat, came towards them.

"Best stay back. When this fella comes down, it might not go where we are planning he should go."

As Teddy and his sons backed away, John asked the man, "What are these enormous trees called?"

"Eucalypts. That's what they're called. Though we call these beauties Tasmanian oaks. Beautiful timber, if they don't have a hole up the middle. But hard as anything to cut."

Teddy and his sons watched from a hundred yards away as two men, standing on boards that had been inserted into the trunk of the tree, about three feet up, on each side of the trunk, swung their axes. Every few strokes, a large wedge of reddish wood flew out and dropped to the ground as the back cut was gradually deepened, eating into the tree trunk. Teddy had seen that an undercut had already been made on the opposite side, in the direction the fellers wanted the tree to fall.

Eventually, there was a shout from one of the men near the tree. "She's goin'!" The fellers jumped from their springboards and ran with the others to safety.

At first, the tree seemed just to groan, and then, with almost a scream of tortured wood, it fell in the planned direction, landing with a thumping crash while bringing down a cascade of branches and leaves from surrounding trees. Teddy could see the vibrant red colour of the wood in the fallen trunk. How were they going to get this massive log to town or where it could be sawn into planks? Approaching the massive stump, he asked the question of one of the fellers standing admiring their handiwork.

"Now we cut it into lengths about twenty feet long. Then we use horses to roll these onto a dray, which will take it to a sawmill near town."

Standing by the huge stump, John remarked to Teddy and the others. "Do you smell that smell? It's sort of sweet and sickly but strong."

"That's the smell from the eucalypt leaves," replied one of the fellers. "It's a beautiful smell, and you get it all through the eucalypt forests, particularly when you stand amongst the trees when it's hot. Some take the leaves and boil em to get the oil, which they say is good for colds and the like if you rub it on your chest or inhale it."

The Ryan men stood around for a while, watching as the fellers now proceeded to saw the log. They had a cross-cut saw, about nine feet in length, which two men pulled and pushed, one on either end, as they cut through the massive log. It looked like back-breaking work.

Teddy thought, *Perhaps we might be doing something the same up in Queensland on our new land.*

Teddy and his sons eventually left the tree fellers to it and walked back along the dirt forest road towards the town. Then, suddenly, Andrew grabbed Teddy by the arm and said in a low voice, "Father, look at those animals!"

He pointed to three grey-furred beasts standing some five feet high but with two bent over and grazing on the grass by the side of the road. Becoming aware of the men, the beasts stood tall on strong hind legs, with two small legs out in front and their elongated faces with pointed ears now watching Teddy and his sons. Then, sensing possible danger, they turned and headed off into the surrounding forest, bounding some six feet each time.

The men stared at them, mesmerised. "Bejesus, what were those?" exclaimed Andrew. "They're amazing. Did you see how they leaped so fast away?"

"I've no idea what they are," said Teddy. "Though I have heard that there's some strange animals down here in Australia. We'll ask someone back in the town."

Back at the ship, Teddy and the others related their experiences to Jane and the girls. "Jane, you shoulda seen the size of them trees, and so many through the forest, with beautiful timber. And then there were these strange beasts we saw that stand as tall as you and leap away in great bounds. The publican at the hotel said they are called kangaroos. He said they be good eating, but they can also be dangerous as their strong legs can rip out a man's guts."

"So, you took in the hotel as part of your looking around, did you, Teddy Ryan? I suppose it was just to ask a question about some fanciful beasts, was it, or was there another reason you felt you had to go into the bar?"

"Jane! We was also thirsty as we'd walked some way into the forests exploring. So, I felt we needed some refreshment."

"Oh, did you now! And what's the matter with water to quench your thirst? Here's me and the girls out foraging for some victuals, and you're spending what few shillings we have on drink."

Teddy felt there was no point arguing and asked, "Did you get some good victuals, my love? Maybe something for our tea?"

"Well, if you must know, we got some nice fish at a market they have here. Fresh it is and a good price. So, we can cook that up in a stew. And I seen them loading casks of water and barrels of some other food to get us to Queensland. It can't be long before we sail out of here, although it is going to be hard getting back to sea after this time on land here."

Later that evening, after a good fish stew for tea, Jane and Teddy stood on the deck of the *Erin go Bragh* and looked out across the poorly lit dock and up into the town, which showed a few lights. It was a clear, cold evening with good light from a gibbous moon, only four days after the full moon. In the moonlight, the houses in the town were visible, as was the dark forest on the slopes of what they had learned was Mount Wellington, with the moon's light reflected from the snow on the mountain's summit.

Teddy was in a pensive mood with his arm around Jane's shoulders. "This is a different type of country, Jane. More different than I thought it would be. There's so much land with just forest and not much settlement, but from what I saw with them tree fellers today, it will take hard work to clear any land for farming. Most people seem friendly and helpful, though there's some that don't seem to like us Irish, or maybe it's because we're Catholic, and not many here seem to be Catholic."

"To be sure, you're right, Teddy. There's some here that won't give us the time of day or mark up their prices when they see us coming. I don't know whether it's 'cos we're Catholics or Irish or just fresh off the boat. But I also feel there's much we can do here, and our sons should have a much better chance to make something of themselves than back in Ireland."

****

Next day, the 16th of July, Mr Haig, the Emigration Officer, visited the ship. He came bounding up the gangway mid-morning, a good-looking middle-aged man with a pleasant face, enclosed on each side by prominent mutton-chop whiskers. Mr Green, the third mate, was on watch and moved across the deck to meet the newcomer.

"Can I help you, Sir?"

"You certainly can, my man. My name is Haig, and I'm the Emigration Officer for this here port of Hobart Town. I need to check to see you are all shipshape and healthy before setting sail for Moreton Bay."

"Right, Sir. If you come with me, I shall take you to meet the captain."

With that, Mr Haig was led across the main deck to the quarterdeck, where Captain Borlase was taking the air with his wife and daughter.

"Excuse me, Captain; this is Mr Haig, the Emigration Officer for Hobart Town. He's here to check the vessel is seaworthy and that all are healthy before we sail up to Moreton Bay."

Captain Borlase excused himself from his wife and advanced with an outstretched hand to greet the Emigration Officer.

"Welcome on board the *Erin go Bragh*, Mr Haig. My name is Captain Borlase. So how exactly can we help you to permit us to proceed north up the coast? We had been hoping to have departed today after obtaining all our provisions and water. We are, therefore, looking forward to receiving clearance to depart. You are welcome to go over the ship and talk to all those on board, and I shall ask our ship's surgeon, Mr Long, to join us."

"Oh, I don't feel we have to interview all the passengers and crew, Captain. If I don't see a number lying on their sick beds, I can presume there is no infectious disease, which the surgeon can confirm."

Mr Haig then explained what he needed to do and, accompanied by the captain, made a tour of the ship, including the passengers' tween deck accommodation. He talked with a few passengers and crew and then met with the ship's surgeon, James Long. His conclusion, as he then announced to the captain, was that the *Erin go Bragh* was seaworthy, well provisioned with a healthy crew and passengers, and free to depart for Moreton Bay. The captain had not mentioned the state of their leaking hull, as this might have just complicated matters. A copy of his report and clearance certificate, signed by Andrew Haig, was handed to the captain the following morning, the 17th of July, and they read as follows:

Hobart Town,
17th July 1862.

Sir. I beg to inform you that I visited the ship Erin-go-Bragh yesterday afternoon, having previously seen the necessary supplies of provisions and water despatched from hence. On arrival on board, accompanied by the Captain, I inspected the vessel and found her a first class emigrant ship, in accordance with her tonnage and fittings as prescribed by the Passengers' Act.

I found the passengers and crew very good looking, and as far as I could learn, in a healthy state, which is borne out by the Doctor's certificate as enclosed, and as a full supply of provisions and water have been put on board for thirty-five days, I am of the opinion that she is in a fit state to proceed on her intended voyage to Moreton Bay.
  I have the honor to remain, Sir,
  Your obedient servant,
  ANDREW HAIG.

Emigration Officer.

H. D'Arch, Esq.,
Collector of Customs, &c.
Ship Erin go Bragh,
16th July, 1862
Tide Surveyor, Customs

SIR, On the other side of this paper is the certificate of Clearance, under the Passengers' Act. In handing the same to you, I beg to say you will be fully justified in delivering the ship's Clearance at the Customs to the Master, in conformity with the instructions from H. D'Arch, Esq, the Collector.
    ANDREW HAIG,
    Emigration Officer

16th July, 1862
    I hereby certify that the Emigrant Ship Erin go Bragh is at present free from infectious disease. No recurrence of any disease of an infectious nature having appeared during the last five weeks.,

    J. A. LONG,
    Surgeon

Having been somewhat prepared to leave Hobart Town the previous day, the captain immediately called the first mate. "Mr Meyler, are all the passengers and crew on board?"

"Yes, Captain, including the two crew who absconded the day after we got here. It took some searching, but a couple of the local molls finally gave them away. Seems like they didn't have enough cash to pay for all the pleasures they had experienced."

"Very good, Mr Meyler. Let's get this ship underway and head for Queensland."

The Last Leg and Hope on the Horizon

By early afternoon on the 17th of July, the *Erin go Bragh* was slowly heading down the Derwent River. They had a light north-westerly breeze, enough to fill their topsails, top gallant and the mizzen. By sunset, they had reached the mouth of the Derwent and were approaching Storm Bay with Passage Point to their west and Cape Direction to the east. The captain decided it would be foolhardy to sail through Storm Bay at night. He had been told by a few sailors with whom he had shared an ale or two in Hobart that Storm Bay was aptly named as it was notorious for sudden tempests.

Turning to the first mate, he said, "Mr Meyler, let's drop anchor here for the night and then have daylight to negotiate Storm Bay to the open sea tomorrow."

That being accomplished, the *Erin go Bragh,* with its passengers and crew, settled down for a quiet, though chilly night before heading north to their final destination.

Below, in the dim, lantern-lit tween decks, there was now an excited anticipation. Many were estimating how long it would take to make it to Moreton Bay, while others were exclaiming how it would be heaven on earth to be off "this stinking hulk."

One wag was heard to remark. "*Erin go Bragh,* my arse! Whoever named this tub that was too full of the blarney. No, *Erin go Slow* is what it should have been called!" at which there was much shouted agreement and laughter.

****

The next morning dawned grey and cold, just before eight o'clock, with the clouds hanging low and a drizzling rain adding to the discomfort. Captain Borlase was on deck with the second mate and, after studying the situation, decided they weren't going anywhere for a while.

"I feel we will have to sit it out here till around noon when the tide turns and ebbs. With this breeze from the southeast and the sea coming from the same direction as well as an incoming tide we'll be hard put to move a mile by then."

So they waited, once again, although the mood lifted with the sun coming through mid-morning and the prospect of leaving in an hour or so. The mess captains took advantage of the relatively calm conditions to obtain their mess rations, and an early dinner was prepared by all. The presence of fresh vegetables and meat was also a plus for passengers who had been existing on hard biscuits and salt pork for some weeks before arriving in Tasmania.

By one o'clock in the afternoon the wind had shifted to the southwest and was slightly stronger. Taking advantage of the ebb tide, which would increase in strength over the next three hours, the captain ordered the ship to get underway.

"It is going to be tight for a while, Mr Meyler," he said to the first mate, "but we should have enough room to manoeuvre. I feel we can make it on a close reach to port, but stay well clear of that lighthouse off Cape Direction to our port. I estimate 130 degrees should do it and don't set the mainsails till we're well into Storm Bay. Then we should have a good run through past Cape Raoul, even though it will be dark by then."

Mr Meyler soon had the crew up the ratlines and lowering sails as the *Erin go Bragh* made her way slowly out into Storm Bay. Teddy, his family, and many other passengers watched as the land slid back over the horizon. He felt it was like leaving a safe and comfortable haven before, once again, venturing into the wild ocean. But this time, it was not the start of their voyage. That was behind them. This was the final phase with the hope of a bright future for himself and his family now almost within reach, over the horizon ahead.

The wind continued from the southwest and strengthened as they approached the open sea. But as night fell, the captain felt it better to leave any course changes until daylight and ordered reduced sail while keeping to their present heading, which would see them clear of Storm Bay, but also away from the twin hazards of Cape Raoul and Cape Pillar.

****

It continued to be grey and raining next morning as a course was set roughly north of east. With a strong southwesterly wind, the ship made good progress until around ten that night when the captain ordered a course of east of north to take them up the eastern Australian coast. However, for the subsequent twenty-four hours, the winds were strong and had swung to the east and northeast, making sailing in a northerly direction difficult. Then, the winds lightened, although they were still from the east, resulting in a slow rate of progress until just south of Sydney. At that point, the winds, although still light, changed to south south-easterlies, enabling an easier passage. But the light winds and very little rain meant that life on board was easier for the passengers.

The weather gradually became warmer, and during the day, most passengers spent their time on deck, standing or sitting around as best they could. There was a sense that the voyage was nearing its end, finally, and the mostly clear sunny skies added to the general feeling of well-being. As they progressed up the coast, they could see little of what the land was like, although what struck most of them, including Teddy, was the almost never-ending mass of green-grey forest with only the occasional signs of habitation and settlement, except when they passed by Sydney.

The sorry state of their ship was evident to all gathered on the sunlit deck as there continued to be regular pumping of the bilges during the daylight hours, which a number of the passengers were still willingly rostered to do, including Andrew and John Ryan. The leaks continued and pumping was the only way the *Erin go Bragh* was staying afloat.

During the day, there was much relaxation, something the passengers had not experienced in nearly four months since they had sailed through the tropics southbound in early April, but then sickness and death had haunted the ship. Now, that seemed to be behind them and there was an almost carefree feeling with their destination approaching and reasonable food again available after calling into Hobart Town. However, there was also a nervousness among many like Teddy Ryan, as they considered what future and prospects awaited them on their arrival in Brisbane.

Teddy was lazing with John Gavan and Tony Molloy, sitting on a low hatch cover. "So, how do we go about getting land when we get to Brisbane?" Tony Molloy wanted to know.

"I think we best ask Father Dunne about that," came Teddy's reply as he held his hand up to shade his eyes from what he was finding to be very bright sunlight, particularly as it glinted off the small waves.

"I thought we were supposed to get some grants to help us buy land, but then the father says those were used to pay for our passage. So, are there other grants or something similar we can get to get us some land? None of us have enough money to buy any land," said John Gavan, voicing his concern.

At this point Father Dunne came strolling across the deck, acknowledging greetings from numerous passengers as he came. Seeing Teddy's group, he stopped, saying, "Good morning, gentlemen; I hope you are enjoying this balmy weather."

"Aye, that we are, Father. It's good to be having an easier time of it now after all them months of rough weather, storms, sickness and not enough decent food. To be sure, it was getting to be almost no food at all, weren't it?" exclaimed John Gavan.

"There's no doubt that you've all had a hard time of it on this voyage. And I had no idea the ship was in such a poor state of seaworthiness, with all these leaks we've got, not to mention the ones caused by some bigoted Englishman drilling holes in the hull."

"Aye, may he rot in hell for all eternity for that one, Father," piped up Tony Molloy. "But we was talking just now about how we're gonna get some land once we get to Brisbane. This land grant thing, was it all used to pay for our passages, or do we get some of that to help us get a bit of land? After all, it can't be called a land order for nothing. And do you happen to be knowing where that land might be and what sort of land it might be?"

"Well, now, the way I understand it is that the land orders that the Queensland Immigration Society used to pay for your passages out here from Ireland were eighteen pounds for every statute adult. That's everyone fourteen years and older, and anyone between the ages of four and fourteen is considered half an adult. If you didn't pay anything towards the fares of your family yourselves, then most of the money from your land orders would have been used to pay for the fares. It is then hoped that when you can, you will pay at least some of that back to the Society so more immigrants can be brought to Queensland. But not all the eighteen pounds for each adult was needed for the fare. So, the Society should be able to give you some money to help purchase land and for supplies to get yourselves started. When we get to Brisbane, I shall talk to the Society people and hopefully arrange for you to get sufficient money."

"That doesn't sound too promising," said Teddy. "We come all this way with the idea and the promise we can start a new life and have our own land, and now you're telling us that that's not a sure thing."

"Well, there is a chance that you may be able to get some land orders direct from the government. And they have said that if you settle and farm the land, you'll be entitled to another set of land orders after two years. But, as you say, this isn't much use to you now. So, maybe you can get some of that grant money when you land. It would be worth applying for. As for where the land is and what it is like, I can only assume it will be not too far outside of Brisbane Town, but I don't know its condition. However, if the government is putting up land for sale or auction for farming, it should be quite good, although it will likely need clearing."

The news about obtaining land wasn't what Teddy and the others had expected. But then, nothing much on this voyage had gone as expected, and an air of despondency descended on the group of men, with their future in this new land far from secure.

****

The weather and wind remained favourable until, on the 30th of July, the *Erin go Bragh* was off the southern Queensland coast. Daytime temperatures were warmer now, and with the ship closer to land, the passengers scanned the well-forested countryside that rose steeply to mountain ranges inland. Again, there was very little in the way of habitation apart from a few scattered clearings and houses with some smoke rising in the hinterland. There was much thought given by those among the passengers looking to take to the land as to where and how they were going to farm.

As Teddy, Jane, John, and Andrew gazed at the distant landscape, John voiced what many were thinking, "It's gonna be mighty hard work establishing a farm in country like this. Maybe it's better closer to Brisbane. I wonder how far we are from there now?"

"We'd be some sixty miles from the mouth of the Brisbane River," said a voice behind them, and they turned to find the second mate. "Yes, I reckon we should reach the north of Moreton Island tomorrow morning. Then we turn back into Moreton Bay and head for the mouth of the Brisbane River, where we'll be anchoring."

"Well, thank God for that!" stated Teddy. "Then we can get off this feckin' ship forever!"

The next minute there was a shout from the other side of the ship as some passengers spied a pod of humpback whales breaching in the dark blue, sunlit waters. Although they had seen whales off South America, these were closer and seemed bigger. Teddy and the others stared as the mammals made their graceful way north, seemingly in no hurry.

****

On the quarterdeck the next morning, Captain Borlase was eying the northern end of Moreton Island through his glass while one of the crew threw the lead line overboard at the bow to check on the water depth. "By the mark, twenty fathoms," came his cry as he prepared to throw the lead line in again.

"From what they told me in Hobart," said the captain to the first mate, "they marked out a passage into Moreton Bay from the north with buoys back about 1830. But they also said there's a pilot we can pick up from Moreton Island, who will guide us in."

"From the charts, we should get north of Moreton Island first, then see what our situation is and maybe pick up the pilot," suggested the first mate.

"Aye, we'll do that, Mr Meyler. Just keep your eye on these sandbanks and shallows. I don't want us running aground after all we've been through. That would be the last straw and we'd probably have a mutiny."

All morning, the passengers had stared in wonder at an endless white sandy beach that bordered the east coast of Moreton Island. Behind the beach sand dunes were clothed in a mixture of scrub and treed vegetation, with great gashes of sand exposed every now and again. At the same time, looking over the ship's side, the water was so clear they could see deep into its depths and where it was shallower, to the very bottom. Exclamations were made as different sea life was observed.

"Will you look at them things, like some unnatural creature with a shield on its back," cried Andrew as he viewed some green turtles swimming nearby.

"And what are those large, sleek fish gliding about like they're hunting?" asked John as he eyed some sharks cruising nearby.

"To be sure," said Teddy, "Tis indeed a wondrous sight. And so many fish, one could just dip in one of your poaching nets, Andrew, and take out two or three or more at a time."

"That I could, Father, and it certainly beats avoiding the gamekeeper and freezing half to death while waiting to snare one of his lordships trouts."

Just before midday, the captain decided that having left Cape Moreton behind on the port quarter by a safe distance and with thirty fathoms under the keel, it was time to head west.

"Bring her around to due west, Mr Meyler. With that breeze on our port beam, we'll take her on a beam reach to a good position at the mouth of the bay to make a straight run in tomorrow morning if the winds are favourable after anchoring for the night. But we need to keep a close eye on the soundings as the charts show much shallow water with sand banks all over the place around the entrance to the bay."

Later that afternoon, the ship reached a point roughly midway between Cape Moreton and the mainland. It had been a slow passage as shallow sand banks meant there needed to be some expert handling of the vessel to avoid running aground. They eventually anchored in about four fathoms, which the captain estimated should be enough to take care of the tides and still allow the ship to have sufficient water below the keel.

Although the day had been comfortably warm, there was a chill in the air as the sun sank over the land to the west, providing a brilliant red sunset that spread across half the sky. The sea was calm, and most of the passengers had gathered on the deck for what was expected would be their last night on board their home for the last six months. A few had produced jugs of whiskey that had been hoarded from when they left Ireland, and there was a carefree party atmosphere. Captain Borlase and a number of the crew joined the passengers, with the captain providing a couple of jugs of rum. And as the liquor was consumed, the noise and laughter rose, with the sound of fiddles adding to the noise prompting a number of passengers to start dancing jigs with great gusto.

Teddy had helped himself to a tot of whiskey, and he and Jane were joined by the Molloys and Gavans.

"Thank God in heaven, but we seem to have finally made it!" exclaimed Teddy, as his arm tightened around Jane's shoulders.

"There were times when I wondered if I had led us all on some disaster the way them deaths and storms were early on. Then we lost our Peter. Then we seemed to drift along, taking forever to get anywhere, and all the time there was this leak threatening to sink the ship. I tell you, this must be a voyage from hell and there's no way I will set out on another!"

"But we did make it, Teddy. And you had more faith that we would than I," replied Jane. "There was times early on when I was so sick and scared. And I was so heartbroken I couldn't feed Peter properly. Then, you, Mary, offers to help feed him; God bless you from the bottom of my heart. But then you goes and loses one of your own. It just seems so unfair."

"It's been a sad voyage that it has," replied Mary Gavan. "But now we've arrived, Jane, and I gotta be thinking there's a better life here. I understand we can be owning our own land, something that them English would never let us do back in Ireland."

And so the talk proceeded until it became too chilly and the families drifted below to the tween decks for what they hoped would be their last night in such conditions.

****

The next morning, the 1st of August, produced a partly cloudy sky with a chilly westerly wind blowing. The captain and crew were active at first light and preparing to raise the anchor and sail into Moreton Bay through what was known as the Northern Passage.

After studying the charts with the first mate and, as yet, no sign of a pilot, Captain Borlase ordered that they proceed on a southerly course.

"If this wind holds as it is, we should be able to come close to the mouth of the Brisbane River. Perhaps we'll pick up the pilot on the way. But I want a man in the round top and one in the bow with the lead man to watch these sand shoals."

So, the *Erin go Bragh* set sail for its final destination as the passengers once again crowded the deck. But the land they saw from the vessel was not inspiring. Across the relatively calm waters of Moreton Bay, ruffled by the offshore wind, the shoreline seemed composed mainly of low trees, right down to mangroves at the water's edge, with mud flats extending out as the tide dropped.

"It doesn't look too inviting here," ventured Tony Molloy to Teddy. "I mean, that almost looks sorta swampy."

"Ah, don't get your pants in a twist, Tony. We seen a lot of other good land further south as we was coming here. This is just gotta be what the shore is like here."

At this point, as the ship was almost due west of Comboyuro Point on Moreton Island, the lookout yelled down to the deck "Boat approaching on the port bow."

The captain and first mate turned their gaze and telescopes to try and make out the vessel. It was a pinnace making its way from the northwest of Moreton Island[6]. The small vessel had a single sail and was heading directly towards the *Erin go Bragh,* close hauled on a port tack.

"I think that will be our pilot,' said the first mate."

Sure enough, within twenty minutes the pinnace had come within hailing distance and a lean, poorly dressed man yelled over to the *Erin go Bragh.* "Ahoy there. You are going to need a pilot to find your way safely through Moreton Bay. So, if you will allow me on board, I will direct you."

The *Erin go Bragh* hove to, while the pilot's vessel came alongside. He clambered up the rope ladder that had been lowered and advanced to the quarterdeck, where he was greeting by the captain and first mate.

The pilot, an older gentleman, was dressed shabbily in old dark blue trousers and a duffle coat that looked like he had slept in them, which he probably had. A dark-blue peaked cap on his none-too-clean-looking long hair completed his attire. But as the captain discovered, despite his appearance, he knew his seamanship and the treacheries of Moreton Bay.

By about ten a.m., the ship was approaching the Brisbane River, which was now apparent from the grey colour of the outflowing stream. Those on board the *Erin go Bragh* could see four other ships already at anchor not far from the mouth of the river and opposite a low island.

---

[6] A pilot station was established at Cowan Cowan on the north-west of Moreton Island in 1848 to cover the North Passage into Moreton Bay. Prior to this, the pilot station was at Amity on Stradbroke Island to cover the South Passage, until a disastrous shipwreck in 1847, meant that the North Passage was the preferred entrance to the bay.

Selecting a suitable location just northeast of a low mud island, the *Erin go Bragh* dropped her anchor in about four fathoms of water.

As the crew and passengers watched, a two-masted workboat, some fifty feet long, made its way from one of the other anchored vessels and came within hailing distance of the *Erin go Bragh*. Those on board could clearly see a rather short, hatless man in a dark-grey suit standing by the nearside ship's railings. Cupping his hands around his mouth, he hailed the *Erin go Bragh*.

"Ahoy there. Would you be the *Erin go Bragh*?"

The first mate yelled back. "Aye, that we are. Out of Liverpool via Queenstown."

"We've been expecting you since sometime in May and were thinking the worst when there was no sign or word of you until we had a message that you had called into Hobart Town."

"It's been a long and hard voyage, and the winds have not been kind to us. But now we're here and have some three hundred and eighty passengers anxious to get ashore and steady their legs on dry land."

"Well, we'll see about that. My name is Dr Hobbs, and I am the medical officer for the Port of Brisbane. I need to determine if you have any infectious diseases on board. So, could I talk with your doctor or surgeon?"

The first mate sent a crew member to find the surgeon and turned back to the workboat. "The surgeon, Mr Long, will be here presently. In the meantime, if you would like to come aboard and inspect the ship, passengers and crew, you are welcome. We will put down a ladder for yer."

"No, first I would like to determine if you have any infectious disease on board by talking to your surgeon. Then, if all seems clear, I can come on board."

"Have it your own way, Dr Hobbs, but we ain't got any infectious diseases on board and haven't had for some weeks."

A few minutes later, James Long, the surgeon, came to the rail and, having been informed by the first mate of the situation, called across. "Dr Hobbs, my name is James Long and I am the surgeon on this vessel. How can I help you?"

"Mr Long, do you have any passengers or crew on board who have currently got a fever or any other signs of a contagious disease?"

"No, Dr Hobbs, we have nobody on board who has any symptoms of an infectious disease. We do have one woman who is poorly after childbirth and a lack of good food, but otherwise, all passengers and crew are in good shape."

"I understand from reports that you have had some serious incidents of disease such as typhoid and maybe others?"

"That we have had. It was bad during the first couple of months of the voyage, with many, mainly small children, dying of cholera or scarlatina. But, after we stopped in Cape Town, we have had very little sickness, though many were suffering from poor food or a lack of food by the time we put into Hobart Town. We did have one death from a fever on the 10th of July, though, that was likely from eating bad food. Then another death of a child who had earlier had scarlatina but, with lack of good food, was unable to recover. That was just before arriving in Hobart Town on 11th July."

"Ah, that's not good, Mr Long. Having had fever only three weeks ago on the ship, you still could have some disease like typhoid or scarlatina on board. I am going to have to declare that this ship is now under quarantine for a week in order to ensure there is no infectious disease on board. If there is no sign of any infection at the end of the week, then you shall all be free to land."

"But how can you put us under quarantine when the health officer in Hobart Town cleared us as free of disease?" This was the captain's strident voice, having joined others by the ship's side.

"Well, this is Brisbane and not Hobart Town, and I am the medical officer here, and I say you are under quarantine until I say you are not. You can allow your passengers and crew to go ashore onto St Helena Island, which is just beyond this mud island. And I recommend that you get them off the ship and then fumigate the quarters and bedding and wash all their clothes."

Captain Borlase's face had now turned quite red and he seemed to have difficulty in forming his words as his temper rose. The passengers on the deck who had been listening to this exchange had also gone into a shocked silence.

"Damn it, man, you can't be serious! You might call yourself the medical officer for Brisbane, but you haven't got the balls to come on board and inspect the ship or its passengers and crew as the medical officer in Hobart Town did. Then you make these bloody proclamations like you were God Himself. And as for getting the passengers and crew to wash all their clothing and bedding after the voyage they have been on, and having been half-starved for part of it, well, I don't think you'll get many takers."

"Yeah, you feckin' arsehole," was one of many similar retorts from the passengers lining the ship's side. "Neither I nor my missus are gonna be washing any bedding or cloths, just 'cos you tell us."

Dr Hobbs might have taken what he regarded as his important position as port medical officer very seriously, but he was not without any compassion or understanding of the plight of the passengers.

"I understand your frustration, but it is my job to protect the good people of Brisbane from contagion that may be carried in on ships. So, if no signs of infectious disease are present in a week, you will all be free to land. I also suggest that before you do, you burn your bedding, just to be sure it does not contain any infection from being on the ship when there was infectious disease. However, I will make sure that you have sufficient good food and water for the week's quarantine. I shall have a boat bring down supplies tomorrow or the next day." With that, Dr Hobbs ordered the customs boat to proceed back up the Brisbane River.

On the deck of the *Erin go Bragh* the captain turned and faced the bewildered, disappointed, and angry passengers. "You probably all heard what that man, who calls himself a medical officer, said. It looks like we shall be anchored around here for at least a week, so don't any of you go and get some serious disease, or it will be longer. We'll move the ship down next to this St Helena Island and arrange for boats to take those of you ashore who wish to go. Also, despite what your feelings are, I suggest you wash your bedding and clothes as Dr Hobbs recommended just so we can be sure there's nothing that will cause disease and stop us from getting out of quarantine. You've got a week to do it."

Teddy, Jane and the rest of their family had been listening, in disbelief, to the exchange between the medical officer and the ship, and now Jane turned to her husband.

"Teddy, when is this hell going to end? I thought we'd be getting off the ship today, but now we have to wait another week. And that medical man doesn't seem to care that some on board here are just about at their wit's end. He's just a pompous old government man and an Englishman as well."

"It's a crying shame, Father," put in Anne. "It's like this man is taunting us. We've come so far and had so many delays, and now he's making us wait again before we can go ashore."

Teddy looked at his disconsolate family. He too felt let down and disheartened, but he needed to try and get their spirits up.

"I know it is hard to take on top of everything else we have been through but look at it this way; we have arrived. There's no more need to be tossed around at sea, and we can go ashore, though what this island is like, I don't know. And we should have enough food. Like I said, it's hard, but let's be patient just a bit longer."

The *Erin go Brah* was moved a few miles south and anchored in some five fathoms of water opposite a small island with a few trees and low scrub emerging from mud flats that stretched out from its shore at low tide. Part of the island had been cleared and there were signs that it was occasionally used for some purpose. There were a few small huts to be seen from the ship, but no inhabitants.

There was palpable disappointment among the passengers that their time on the ship would not end today or even the next day. But at least a number took the chance to get off the ship onto St. Helena Island when two of the ship's boats were lowered over the side and a rope ladder set up. Teddy and his sons were among them. Jane declined to go at this point, saying she might go the following day; her depression at being unable to land made her feel listless. Tessie, however, did want to go ashore. To her, there was always some excitement in exploring new surroundings.

As the boat with Teddy and the others was being rowed by four crewmen across the increasingly shallow depths towards a landing on the island, Andrew and Tessie looked over the side. The bottom was visible but appeared covered to a large extent with some sort of long grass that waved in the current. Then they spied a movement amongst the seagrass and Tessie exclaimed. "Father! Will you look at those creatures. What are they?"

Teddy, who was seated in the middle of the boat tried to see over the edge without upsetting the boat but was not able to help Tessie. Then one of the seamen piped up.

"They'd be sea cows. There's plenty of them around here, and they seem to like to graze on that grass under the water. They call them dugongs here. Don't know why."

"They are really strange beasts," chimed in Andrew.

"And they don't look like cows at all," said Tessie, who continued to gaze attentively at the slowly swimming mammals.

One of the other seamen then volunteered, "I heard they use this island to slaughter the beasts and melt down their fat or blubber to get the oil."

And sure enough, when the group waded ashore, through glutinous, black mud, onto St Helena, they could see large iron pots with the remains of fires that had been lit beneath them to render down the blubber. There was no other sign of activity on the island except where trees and bushes had been cut to clear a work area and provide fuel for rendering the blubber. Once ashore, the passengers took advantage of being able to wander and explore. A few had brought some food, and those found a comfortable location to sit and eat their repast, though the chilly wind from the west made the experience less than comfortable.

Back on board the *Erin go Bragh,* Teddy explained to Jane and his other daughters what they had found, with Tessie butting in to give her version of seeing the dugongs and their potential fate on the island.

"I think we should all go ashore tomorrow, if it isn't raining, and have a picnic. If we are going to be stuck here for at least a week, let's make the best of it," Teddy suggested.

****

The sun shone the next day, although the wind was still a chilly south-westerly. The crew were hard put to transfer the number of passengers and crew who wished to spend time on St Helena. Someone found a small tank holding rainwater, and several buckets were brought from the ship so passengers could wash clothes. But there wasn't enough fresh water to wash the clothes or bedding of all the passengers who wished to do so. Several passengers resorted to seawater to at least rinse some of their clothes being unable to get a lather with the soap they had. However, this left the clothes with a residue of salt that kept them damp and irritated the skin.

On the day after their arrival, a small paddle-wheel steamboat, the *Hotham,* brought out supplies to the *Erin go Bragh*, which meant the passengers had ample food for their messes, including fresh vegetables and meat. Some of the meat was extremely lean, and when Teddy asked the storekeeper what it was, thinking it might be horse meat, he was told it was kangaroo meat. Undeterred, he and the rest of his mess found the meat much to their liking in a stew.

The second day after their arrival was a Sunday, and Father Dunne organised for a special mass to be said on board. As he explained to the crowded congregation, it was a time to celebrate and give thanks for their arrival. They might not have landed in Brisbane, but they had survived the six-month voyage and were on the edge of a new beginning, which he prayed would be beneficial and fruitful for them all in their new home.

And so, the week of quarantine progressed with most passengers stoically accepting their fate and making the best of the conditions. Another shipment of food was brought down by the *Hotham* on the 5th of August and, with it, a letter for Father Dunne from Bishop Quinn. Later that evening, he came down to the tween deck and addressed the passengers there.

"I have had a letter from Bishop Quinn in Brisbane. He informs me that he has approached the government in Brisbane and requested that additional land orders be made available to immigrants on this ship so that they may purchase land once they land in Brisbane. He is hopeful that the government will agree. Apart from the eighteen pounds per adult that the government has given to the Queensland Immigration Society to pay for your passage, you would also be entitled to a further twelve pounds per adult after you have farmed the land you have purchased for two years. He is hoping that this future payment could be advanced, at least in part, so that you can make a start. He said that last year the government opened two tracts of land for agricultural development south of Brisbane and that sales of that land are proceeding."

"What if we don't get no land orders as you are hoping, Father? What can we do then?" asked one of the male passengers.

"Well, I understand that there is no shortage of jobs available in and around Brisbane. In fact, they are sorely short of labour. So, you won't be going without. In the meantime, the bishop has said that he is arranging accommodation for all those that need it, and the Immigration Society will also ensure that sufficient funds are provided to all passengers who need them to get by."

Tony Molloy then asked, "Father, how do we go about using these land orders, if we get them, to buy land? None of us has ever bought land back in Ireland. So, who do we buy it from?"

"I understand that land auctions are held every few weeks, and that's probably how you could buy land. But you may also be able to buy it from another person who wishes to sell his land. We'll have to find out more once we get to Brisbane."

There was much more discussion and questions about the land grants and what would happen when they landed in Brisbane, until Father Dunne finally bade them all good night and retired to his second-class cabin.

In the dim light from a few lanterns, Teddy lay on his bunk, his mind in a turmoil. This was a whole new experience. There was excitement at the thought that he and maybe his sons would actually own their own land.

But what did that mean? Where was this land south of Brisbane, and what was it like? What would they grow there? Surely, they could at least grow vegetables and maybe some fruit? Could they get cows and horses, but how would they pay for such? And how much land would they get if they were able to get some land grants? It could be mighty expensive. Then, it was likely that they would have to clear the land of trees to make it into a farm. It wouldn't be like the open fields in Ireland that had been farmed for ages past with crofter houses and all. They would need money for tools and seeds. Teddy had discussed some of this with his son John, who was keen on acquiring some land, as were John Gavan and Tony Molloy. Although they weren't sure what they might plant and how they would manage any land they acquired, they all felt excited at the potential this offered them. Teddy lay awake for some time thinking about these things until, finally, tiredness and the lapping of the waves against the ship's hull overcame his thoughts and lulled him into a deep sleep.

Landed at Last

Three days later, on the 8th of August, Dr Hobbs again turned up alongside the *Erin go Bragh*. Mr Long and the captain came to the ship's railing as the boat carrying Dr Hobbs came alongside and he called up.

"Mr Long and Captain Borlase, how are we this morning and have you had any cases of fever or contagious disease in this last week?"

"No, Dr Hobbs. Apart from a few sniffles, we have no illness on board," replied Mr Long.

"I and my passengers would now appreciate it if we could have clearance for them to disembark and for arrangements to be made for them to do this," put in the captain.

"First, I would like to inspect the ship, if you please. Then, if I am satisfied with the situation, I can authorise the passengers to disembark."

"Bureaucratic, officious nincompoop!" was Captain Borlase's quiet aside to Mr Long. But, frustrated though he was, he tried not to let this show, as, given the nature of the man, it might not go down well. "If you insist, Dr Hobbs, you are welcome to come on board."

The doctor made his way up the rope ladder to the deck. "I would like to see your passengers' and crew quarters, if you please, Captain Borlase."

And, so, the captain and surgeon escorted the doctor through the tween decks, which had been aired and cleaned, as far as possible, over the last few days. The crew quarters were also inspected. The ship's surgeon was glad to see that no passengers were lying ill on the beds in the tween deck, though he knew at least one person, a woman, was feeling poorly. But the sunshine and comparative warmth of the main deck kept the majority of the passengers either on deck or over on St Helena Island.

Back on the deck, Dr Hobbs addressed the captain and surgeon, with many passengers and crew standing nearby.

"I see no reason this ship should continue in quarantine, so I am releasing it and allowing passengers to disembark. On my return to Brisbane later today, I shall inform the harbourmaster and the ship's agent, and they will organise for a boat to transfer the passengers up to Brisbane."

This announcement was greeted by loud whoops and cheers from the passengers on deck, with many smiling faces and much back-slapping by the men. And it was a relieved Captain Borlase who escorted Dr Hobbs back to the ship's side to board his boat.

That afternoon, Teddy and his family were among the passengers who arrived back from St Helena. As soon as they stepped aboard the *Erin go Bragh,* Teddy could sense that something had happened, and it wasn't long before he heard the good news. He grabbed Jane in his arms and swung her around before her protests forced him to let her down.

"This is finally it, Jane! We are going ashore! Can you believe it? Oh, thank God and the Blessed Virgin and all the saints!"

"Aye, it's hard to believe after all this time and all the delays; but it seems that, finally, our prayers have been answered. So, when do you think we can get ashore?"

"Hopefully, they can get a boat down from Brisbane tomorrow to start taking us off, although it may take some time and more than one trip with so many of us; and then there's our baggage and belongings that have to be taken up."

That night there were more celebrations, with a few remaining jugs of whiskey now being consumed.

****

By morning, a few sore heads came on deck to see what might be happening and when they might be disembarking. As they waited, the first officer and Father Dunne decided they needed to establish a priority for disembarking, as any boat taking them ashore would not be able to carry more than half the passengers and probably much less on one trip. It was agreed that families with children should be given priority after the particular hardships many of those families had suffered.

Father Dunne pointed out. "There are forty families with children, and these had sixty-one children under fourteen when they boarded at Queenstown. Thirty-six of these children have died on the voyage as well as six adults within those families. That leaves one hundred and ninety-one persons in the family category, plus six married couples without children.

"The next priority would be the single females, of whom fifty-one boarded, with four dying on the voyage, leaving forty-seven to disembark. Finally, there would be the single males, of whom there would be one hundred and twenty, with three having died on the trip."

Then they all waited, with hope and anticipation, as the sun rose to its zenith and then started dropping towards the western horizon. Any boat that was seen coming out from the Brisbane River mouth was eagerly eyed until it went in another direction than the *Erin go Bragh*. By late afternoon there had been no sight of a boat to take them ashore and no word as to when such a boat may come. Captain Borlase and his officers continually explained to the passengers that it might take a day to organise a boat to transport them. However, these explanations did little to ease the disappointment among the men, women and children who had endured nearly six months of hardship and death on the ship and now only sought to leave it and start their new lives ashore.

****

Next morning, as the passengers settled down to endure another wait, a sturdy steam-powered paddle wheeler was seen heading towards them. As it got closer, those near the rail could see the name *Samson* printed on the bow. The excitement grew as it came alongside and hailed the *Erin go Bragh*.

"Ahoy, there! We've come to start taking your passengers ashore now that you've been cleared for them to land."

The first mate yelled back. "You are most welcome, I am sure. But how many can you take?"

"We can fit about a hundred on board, so we need to make several trips. You go ahead and organise what passengers should come first. But don't be too long, as we would like to get another trip in today, and it takes a few hours to get up the river to Brisbane, depending on the tide."

"We've already decided on the order of disembarking and have told the passengers. Families will be going first, and then the single women and lastly the single men." Then, turning to the passengers, he announced. "As there are one hundred and ninety-one persons in the family group, these will be roughly divided in half, and the six married but childless couples added to make up the first two boatloads."

The families were divided alphabetically, which meant that the Ryans and their friends, the Molloys had to wait for the second trip. For those leaving on the first trip, there was a mad scramble to get their belongings from the tween deck. The other passengers watched as they negotiated their way down the rather precarious wooden gangway between the two vessels, clutching bundles and bags. The women shepherded their small children and held their babies tight while their menfolk steadied them as they slowly boarded the *Samson*. Some men threw bundles over to be caught by those already on board. There was a sense of gaiety as if they were heading for a picnic as the relief at leaving the *Erin go Bragh* washed over them.

Shortly after that, the *Samson* departed and headed towards the mouth of the Brisbane River, belching smoke from its tall funnel and leaving those on board wondering when it would return. But by early afternoon, the steamer could be seen heading their way again.

Teddy had organised for all their belongings from the tween deck to be ready with them on the main deck. As soon as the *Samson* had tied up alongside, he and John helped Jane, William and the girls down the none-too-stable gangway between the two ships, carrying what belongings they could. Then Andrew threw down the rest of their belongings, and, as a family, they found a position near the far side of the ship's rail.

When the *Samson* eased away from the *Erin go Bragh*, Teddy felt an overwhelming relief that their ordeal on that ship was over. He could barely contain his excitement. At last, they were about to land and take hold of their future, and he sensed that that future was more under his control than it had been in Ireland. Sensing that Jane was having similar thoughts, he put his arm around her thin shoulders without speaking as the *Samson* now made its way, quite rapidly through a light chop, towards the mouth of the river.

As they advanced upstream on what was initially a broad brown river, perhaps six hundred yards wide, the land changed from flat with mud flats extending out from the shores to low hills. These were mostly forested with tall trees, similar to those they had seen in Tasmania, though smaller. Here and there, trees had been cleared and either single houses or small groups of houses had been built. They seemed to be made mainly of wood.

The day was sunny and warm with the afternoon sun glinting off the river and a southerly breeze bringing the smell of the eucalypt forests south of the river.

Jane commented, "Tis really so different to Ireland, Teddy. The trees are green but not so green as in Ireland. Like a dull grey-green."

"You're right, my love. And the light here is something fierce, not like the softer light we had at home, though, I can't be saying that Ireland is home anymore, now that we have arrived here. And they tell me this is winter here still. Well, what's summer gonna be like then?"

Some two hours later, after negotiating a couple of bends in the river, the Samson was approaching considerably more buildings, particularly on the south side. There were also many buildings, some smaller and some larger in various stages of construction to be seen on both sides of the river.

"It don't seem like much of a town," observed Andrew. "I don't see a lot of buildings like one would see in a big town. Most of the ones here seem like they were only built in the last couple of years, and they're mainly just built from wood."

One of the *Samson's* crew, who was making his way aft, on hearing Andrew's comment, volunteered. "Aye, this here Brisbane Town is mostly new. Four years ago, there weren't so many buildings here. But since they made Queensland a separate colony from New South Wales, there's been all sorts of building going on. And, then, from about three years ago we started getting all sorts of people coming, mostly from England. Yous will be some of the first comin' from Ireland. Mind you, there's some here that aren't too happy about that, thinkin' the local bishop is just trying to ship in boatloads of Catholics. His name is Bishop Quinn, and there's some are saying that instead of Queensland he wants to make it Quinnsland. I, myself, don't much care. We're short of labourers here, and there's much work to do, and we're short of farmers too. So, you are all most welcome." With that, the crewman continued on his way to the stern, where he proceeded to prepare ropes for mooring.

"Well, that was interesting," said John. "Particularly the bit about Catholics or Irish not being welcome."

"Oh, don't you go worryin' about such stuff," chided Teddy. "There might be a lot of English here, but I don't feel they're the kind of overlording landlord and pompous arses such as we had to live with in Ireland, and, you heard the man. They're short of labourers and need people to farm the land. And that's us, my son, though first, we must get us some land."

****

It was a somewhat bedraggled collection of passengers that disembarked onto a wooden jetty at Kangaroo Point. After six months at sea their clothes hung on their bodies more like rags than clothes and many were still malnourished after weeks without proper food. But, being on solid ground was a blessing for them all, although most wandered about, seemingly in a daze, not sure what to do next.

Coming ashore from the *Samson*, Teddy was anxious to find out where they might find lodgings and obtain food, at least in the short term, particularly as it was getting late in the afternoon. He was also filled with gratitude and relief to have finally arrived. The burden of gambling with Jane and his children on undertaking the voyage and then enduring and supporting his family through all the hardships on the voyage seemed to lift from his shoulders. Once all the family were ashore, he turned to Jane with tears in his eyes and, looking at her, said, in a low voice. "We made it, my love. We made it at last!"

Jane knew Teddy for the strong but sentimental man he was and, smiling, grasped his hand. "That we did, Teddy Ryan. That we did. Thank you." Though always the practical and no-nonsense woman, she added, "but now we'd best be seeing about findin' a place to sleep and some food to eat."

It was Father Dunne who once again came to their rescue. He met the disembarking passengers, having arrived with the first load. While waiting for the second boatload of passengers, he had been busy meeting with Bishop Quinn and others to sort out accommodation and board. Having gathered the passengers together, he announced in a loud voice while several passers-by looked on.

"My fellow passengers, I have been talking with Bishop Quinn and have some news regarding where you might find a place to stay for a while. There are a number of boarding houses that are prepared to take some of you, preferably families. Others will find shelter and beds in the local hall. Then there is a wooden store called 'Petreos' nearby, and another, on the Ipswich main road called 'Cassim's, where you can find shelter.

"I am also told that the government has agreed to give each of you rations until such time as you can find work and support yourselves. The bishop has also instructed me to tell you that the Queensland Immigration Society will give you an allowance to help in these early days after your arrival; the amount will depend on the size of the family. Arrangements will be made to get this allowance tomorrow."

At this point, one of the male passengers interjected. "What about work? How do we find that?"

Another spoke up. "So, how do we go about getting this land that we've been told we can get, or the grants to get the land?"

To both of these queries, there was loud approval from the passengers. Father Dunne held up his hands for silence.

"I've been told there is plenty of work for both men and single women. I believe there is a central labour bureau that has notices for all the jobs available. I also know that there are many opportunities for work in other towns in Queensland, such as Rockhampton. A passage can be arranged for people wishing to travel to these towns. As for land, I am hoping that the government will agree with Bishop Quinn's request that an additional land grant be provided for immigrants coming out with the Queensland Immigration Society who wish to be farmers. Hopefully, we will have word on that in the next day or two."

Teddy gathered his family and suggested they try walking to the Petreos store, as that seemed the closest and they had little money to spare for a boarding house. He asked some locals standing around observing the arrival of the passengers where and how far the store was. Then, he directed Andrew and John to look after the bulk of their belongings, and told the rest of the family to follow him as he set off up a hard-packed dirt road. There was a combination of wooden and stone buildings close to the river on both sides. But as they walked up a slight incline, gaps were occurring and in the near distance, quite a few tall trees were still standing.

Some fifteen minutes later they had reached the Petreos store, a sign painted on the front of the wooden single-storey building proclaiming it to be so. Inside, it was well-lit from windows letting in the afternoon sun, but there were only bare floorboards and little else; no beds and only a few chairs and tables scattered about. Tired and now downhearted at having, once again, to set up the family in rough conditions, Teddy looked at Jane and suggested that they would just have to make the most of it.

"Hopefully, we can find something better in a day or three."

Jane, grim-faced and also tired, set about arranging places for themselves, as by now, other passengers were also entering the store and looking for places to squat. She picked a position under one of the windows. Teddy, meanwhile, set off back down to the jetty and, over the next hour, moved the rest of their belongings, including their bedding, up to the store. Having deposited the last of it, he informed Jane.

"I can't see us eating tonight or in the morning. Not till I get to the government office to get us some rations or we get this allowance."

And so, the Ryan family and most of the other passengers from the *Erin go Bragh* prepared to sleep hungry that night. For many, including Teddy, it was a strange sensation, not having the almost continual motion of the ship. Instead, they had a cool light southerly breeze and a solid wood floor under their bedding, which, fortunately, and against Dr Hobbs's directive to burn it, they still possessed. In fact, it was much the same bedding that they had brought from Teddy's mother's cottage in Kilclonfert, though now in a rather tatty condition.

****

Teddy was awakened by a raucous bird chorus. It seemed there were many different types of birds in the nearby trees and bushes and several of each kind, all vying with the other to be heard. He had never heard such a bird song, with it varying from the raucous to the melodious. He lay there listening with some wonder and amazement until he noticed that Jane was also awake and listening, as were several others. Jane looked across at Teddy and smiled thinly.

"Mother of Mercy, are we gonna have that to wake us each morning from now on? Couldn't they be a little quieter? It's enough to wake the dead."

"Aye, it is somewhat noisy. But sounds like they're happy." And with that, Teddy rose and prepared to go searching for food and money. He took John with him, and John Gavan came along as well; he having also decided to opt for the Petreos store as a temporary place to stay.

Few people were about so early, but not far down the dirt road they came across an eating establishment. It was a small wooden house with wide open shutters in the front, allowing one to see several benches and tables. At the back was a kitchen of sorts from where the delicious smell of bacon and sausages filled the air. Teddy and the others stood just outside salivating, but with very little money they were unable to buy anything. As they stood mesmerised, a female voice hailed them.

"Oi. If you want some breakfast you'd better get in fast before the herd arrives." She was referring to the labourers and others on their way to work, some of whom were drifting in for a meal.

Teddy and the others turned to see a well-rounded woman of middle age wearing a long grey dress covered in a rather dirty white apron. Her round, reddish face looked as though it would not take any nonsense, although there was a softness to her eyes.

Teddy said, "I'm afraid we can't partake of your breakfast this morning, ma'am, as we don't have enough money, having just got off the boat from Ireland yesterday afternoon."

"Have you now," she replied, standing with her solid arms on her equally solid hips. "You must be starving, you poor bastards. Look, I tell you what. Come in and get some tucker and you can pay me tomorrow or the next day when you gets some coin. You look sort of honest, you do."

"We are honest, as the day is long, mistress," volunteered John. "But we ain't no bastards, us being born wholly within wedlock, and I don't think you should be insulting my father by thinking that we weren't."

"I meant no disrespect, young man. No. You'll find that bastard is a word used for many people, most of whom were born in wedlock. When someone is down on their luck, they could be called poor bastards, a sort of term of commiseration. Then when someone does the dirty on you, that person could be called a rotten thieving bastard."

"I think we are gonna have to learn some new words out here as I didn't understand a couple of others you said," said John Gavan. "But we would love to accept your offer of some breakfast."

The three men then devoured a good breakfast, though they each saved a sausage and some toast to take back to the families at the warehouse. They wrapped these in a somewhat clean cloth provided by the owner, to which she added some extra bacon and bread. Her name, they discovered from other patrons, who now filled the eatery, was Val Porter.

After taking the breakfast offerings back to Jane and the families, with many envious looks from others in the warehouse, they headed back down the road. The town was coming to life; shops were opening and people were starting their businesses for the day. Having asked directions to the Catholic church, they found Father Dunne about to set out to meet more passengers due to arrive that morning from the *Erin go Bragh*. He directed them to the office of the Queensland Immigration Society, next door to the church.

It was a single, rather dingy room on the second floor of a two-storey wooden building. There was a large desk, one of only four furniture items in the room, the others being two wooden, straight-back chairs and a bookcase, filled haphazardly with books and files. Behind the desk sat a man who was straight-backed as well, being of slight build but well-groomed with an intelligent face, a moustache and slicked-back black hair.

As Teddy and the others entered, he glanced towards them and said, "Ah. You're the first of what I expect will be many coming to see me today. I imagine you are looking for some cash to help you out till you get work or a farm, am I right?"

This was said in a not unpleasant manner, and Teddy answered for them all. "Yes. You are right. I and my family would like to buy some land, which I understand we can do if we get a land grant from the government. And we are prepared to work hard to make any farm we have prosper. But first, we need to survive and also purchase tools and other things we'll need to live here. Father Dunne said something about the Society being able to give us some allowances."

"That's right. I can give you an allowance based on the number of adults and children in your family. As far as getting land. Well, there's all sorts of land available now down south of here at Eight-Mile Plains and Logan agricultural reserves that the government has set up. How you are going to acquire such land is another question. A lot of immigrants have got and used them land orders the government is issuing to get some land. Now, the Society has used most of the land orders to which you were entitled to pay for your passage out here. But I understand that the bishop, God bless him, is trying to get the government to give those of you who want land an additional grant.

"Once you have a order, there are land auctions that take place quite frequently. In fact, there may be one in the next couple of weeks. Usually, this land down at Logan or Eight Mile Plains goes for about a pound an acre, though sometimes it goes up to thirty shillings or two pounds an acre, and often it's less than a pound. Of course, you can also purchase land from those who already have it."

"It all sounds sort of complicated," said Teddy. "And how do we know what this land is like? Is it any good for growin' crops, and how much clearin' of trees is needed, 'cos we've seen much of the land has trees on it, and not so open or with just heather like back in Ireland?"

"Ah, you're thinking like a farmer, you are," replied the clerk. "What I suggest you do in the next few days is acquaint yourselves with the land by going down to the

Logan and Eight Mile Plains agricultural reserves and having a look. It's about twenty miles on a rather indifferent road called Slack's Track. First, though, you have to cross the river by ferry near where the boat landed you. It will take you a good part of a day to get to the Logan River by walking, so you'll need to be prepared to look after yourselves for a couple of days. There's also a boat that goes down there and up the Logan River, but it only runs about every week and it will cost you a bit of money. No, going down Slack's Track to have a look is the best way of doin' it."

Teddy and his family received ten pounds from the clerk to assist with expenses, with the proviso that they would repay the money when they could. The men's first call after leaving the Immigration Society office was to the government store, where they received rations for the next two days. They then found a grocery shop to get further provisions to supplement the rather meagre rations supplied. Preparing meals would be difficult, with cooking facilities being limited to a couple of open fireplaces. Luckily, the Ryans still had some pots and cooking utensils and, with luck, they would have more of their belongings in the next day or two when they were transported up from the *Erin go Bragh*.

Back at the Petreos warehouse, Teddy, Jane, the two elder sons, and John and Mary Gavan set about planning what they would do over the next few days. It was agreed that Teddy, John, and John Gavan would head to the Logan area in a day or two.

"I feel we should not waste too much time," explained Teddy. "There's bound to be many others looking for land with all these ships that have just arrived, and we want to get something that is good farming land, not some leftover rubbish."

"To be sure," replied John Gavan, "but we'd better make sure we get some food and maybe even something to give us some shelter, as it will be two or three days we'll be away."

It was thought best that Andrew would stay behind to see to their goods that were being offloaded from the ship's hold and to help Jane, the girls and Willie. The latter was downhearted that he could not accompany the men on their trek.

"There's too much we don't know, Willie," explained Teddy. "And it could be dangerous. I heard there's some local savages have been causing trouble to people going back and forth down there. Maybe because they feel we might be taking their land from them."

"Well, you'd best be lookin' after yourself, Teddy Ryan," exclaimed Jane. "All this talk about savages and such. You had better get back here to help set up this new home we be planning."

Land to Call Their Own

Two days later, Teddy was feeling slightly more at ease with the world now that the family had some money and food. The knowledge that there was some prospect of getting some land also helped to raise his spirits. He slept more soundly that night, at least until just before dawn. Then he was awakened by a most unusual sound - a sort of raucous laughing-like cry that was started with one individual and was then picked up by several others, causing a loud chorus that lasted about a minute.

"What was that!" demanded Andrew.

"I've no idea," replied Teddy, "but I think they are birds."

Later, down at Val Porter's, where they devoured a hearty breakfast before setting off, Teddy learned that the birds were called Kookaburras.

"Or, as some calls them, laughing jackasses," Mrs Porter informed them. "So, what are you gentlemen up to today? You looks as if yous are goin' some place."

"We're going to see what the land is like down at Eight-Mile-Plains and Logan," replied Teddy. "We're after thinking that we'd like to get some land and start some farming, and we are hearing there's land available down that way, though, at this point, we ain't sure how we're gonna pay for it."

"Are you now. And how are yous gonna get there?"

"We're gonna walk. We've been told to take the ferry across the river and head down Slack's Track," volunteered John Gavan. "Do you have a better way to get there?"

"You could get the boat that goes sort of regularly from here to up the Logan River. But that'll cost you something, and I ain't sure when the next one is leaving from here or when it's coming back. No, Slack's Track is the only other way to get there. But you might do better than walking.

See that fella over by the window with that enormous hat and bushy beard? Well, that's Don Nettles, and he's got a property down near Logan River. He's up here gettin' some supplies. But he's headin' back today, and he has a horse and cart. For a small fee, he might be prepared to give you a lift."

"Why not," said Teddy after getting eager nods from his two companions. "Could you introduce us, Mrs Porter? By the way, my name is Teddy Ryan, and this here is my son, John, while this other gent here is John Gavan, a good friend."

Val Porter duly obliged, and after the introductions, Teddy and the two Johns found themselves a ride in exchange for helping with the carrying and loading of Don Nettles' purchases. By late morning they were on the south side of the Brisbane River and ready to depart. Teddy was sitting up with Don on the front wooden seat while the other two were perching where they could on the loaded, high-sided cart.

As they slowly travelled south along the rough and rutted dirt track, Teddy and his two companions acquired much useful information from Don. He spoke in a quiet voice for such a big man, but it was apparent he had experienced much in the two years since he had bought his land on the north side of the Logan River.

"You see them high sides on me wagon. Well, that's for protection against the blacks. They were a real nuisance when we got our land down Logan way. They don't seem to like us moving in down there. So, they attacked with spears and also harassed the women. There's been a few settlers killed, but more cattle have been lost, maybe 'cos they don't know how to dodge the spears or shoot back. But it ain't so much of a problem now, with more settlers moving in."

"What's the land like down at Logan?" asked Teddy.

"Oh, it's beautiful farmland. Mainly flat and fertile. But you have to cut down a fair number of trees and uproot the stumps, which can be extra hard work. Some try and burn the stumps out, but it don't always work well. Still, it's worth it in the end to get rid of the stumps so's you can plough and plant more easily. If you don't need to get rid of the stumps to plant, like if you have cattle, which some do, then you can ringbark and kill the trees and just leave a lot of them standing. They was plantin' cotton down there until a year or so ago but couldn't make a go of it. Now, it's sugar cane."

After leaving the houses and other buildings that made up the southern outskirts of Brisbane, Teddy found they were now plodding through thickly forested, undulating country. The tall trees were of varying types, some with whitish, smooth bark, while others had rough fibrous bark, sometimes deeply furrowed. In some areas, the forest was thick with understorey vegetation, which often included curious plants on blackened stems with thin leaves hanging down like a dress and then a tall woody pole with minute flowers over the top half. In other places, the forest was more open with grass undergrowth and a scattering of trees that looked like pines, with long, thin needle-like grey-green foliage. There were also bursts of yellow blossoms lighting up the understory on what Don called wattles.

"It's weird the way some of the plants flower in the winter, like now or even earlier. Don't know why, but I guess they've got a reason for it."

Now and then, they would come across cleared forest, usually with rough dwellings, most of which were no more than slab-sided, bark-roofed huts. The cleared land was in various stages of cultivation and in some cases, crops of vegetables seemed to be doing well. By late afternoon, they had moved onto a flat flood plain with dense forest, though this, too, had been cleared in many places by recently established landowner farmers.

Teddy and the two Johns eyed the land and forest as they made their way to Don's plot close to the Logan River. They were able to get some idea of what would be in store for them as farmers in this new environment. Teddy looked at the land and the future with a certain amount of dismay as well as hope. From what they saw, it was very good farming land, much better than they had been used to in Ireland. The potential to make something of their future was there, but there would be a mountain of hard work to achieve that end and Teddy wasn't sure he had it in him. But then he looked at John, saw his enthusiasm, and reckoned that with his sons' help, they would make it, After all, it was their future, even more than his own about which he was concerned.

Don Nettles showed them how the plots of land were marked by stakes and blazed tree trunks, with numbers etched in the tree blazes and painted on the stakes.

"Best you wander around and see for yourselves what there is to offer. This Slacks Track goes down to the river, not far from here. There are also a few tracks that lead off into the bush you can follow. Get the lie of the land so when you see the sketch map for the land on offer by the government, you'll have an idea of where it is and how good it is. You're welcome to stay a couple of nights with me and the missus. It mightn't be much, but at least you'd have a roof over your heads if it rains or the possums piss on you while you're asleep."

Teddy and the other two spent two days roaming as far as they could, even taking a ferry to see what the land was like on the south side of the river. They returned each evening to share their food with Don and his wife, Virginia or Gini as Don affectionately called her. Don regaled their guests with stories of both life as a settler and the history of the Logan River area, including that of the notorious

Captain Logan, the convicts under him and his death at the hands of the local aboriginals.

"Then there's been those who came in to log the red cedar trees that grow in these parts. You can see the enormous stumps they've left behind. Beautiful timber it is for making furniture and it won't rot. A lot of the wood here gets eaten up by these white ants, but not red cedar. The white ants don't like the ironbarks much either; too hard for them."

****

On the third day, the three of them set out to walk back to Brisbane. It was going to be a long trek, but they felt they could make the twenty-odd miles in a day. And they did, arriving back on the Brisbane River's south bank late in the afternoon, only to find that there were no more ferries crossing that day. So, they found a boarding house near the ferry and, with money in their pockets, were able to get a room for all three to share and a good supper.

Next morning, they were on the first ferry after an early breakfast, and soon after that, they walked into the warehouse to find Jane and the rest of the family preparing to wash some clothes.

As soon as Jane saw Teddy, she came up to him, eyes shining, and hugging him and said, "You won't believe it, Teddy, but Father Dunne came yesterday and told us that the government has agreed to give families who want some land one land grant of eighteen pounds!"

"Praise be to God, but that's marvellous news, my love, though it's less than I thought we might get, given what others who have paid their own way have got, but let's be thankful for that. So, how and when do we get this order?"

"Father Dunne said that you have to present yourself at the government offices as soon as you can to claim our order. I don't think you should waste any time in doing that and getting the order so we can get us some land. But first, tell us how your trip was and what did you find? Is there any good land to be had?"

"Oh, aye, it's great farming country, Jane. Good soil and flat or only low hills. But there's so much work to do in clearing the land as most of it is covered in trees, many of them bigger than you've ever seen. It's going to be hard work, but thank the Lord we have John and Andrew to help. And we was lucky, or the angels were smiling on us 'cos we got a lift on a cart down there and the man, a Don Nettles, gave us much good information. In fact, we stayed in his house, if you can call it that."

"And what about them black savages we've been hearing about?" asked Maria with concern on her face. "Did you see any, or was there any danger?"

"We saw some black men that were working on some of the farms down there, but we didn't have any trouble. Don Nettles was telling us that them blacks have caused all sorts of trouble in the past, killing cattle and even attacking some of the settlers. But they don't seem to be causing many problems now."

After satisfying Jane and the rest of the family with his tales of their trip to the Logan Reserve, Teddy and John Gavan, with John, went in search of the government offices. Some two hours later, they were back, in possession of a land order for each family worth eighteen pounds. Teddy had also learned there would be a land auction the following week.

****

With great excitement, Teddy and Jane, with their two elder sons, made their way to the police station early on a morning towards the end of August. They wanted to view the map and the list with the lots to be auctioned first. Of course, so did about forty other prospective land buyers, and it was a while before Teddy could get close. He wasn't that literate, but he and John could read and write sufficiently in a simple way. They chose several lots they felt would be suitable with an acreage they could afford to buy with their eighteen-pound land order.

The auction was a fast and furious affair, with the auctioneer, an average-looking man in a brown check suit with a waistcoat and brown bowler hat, yelling the price in a rapid voice. Initially, Teddy found it hard to understand him and how the process was supposed to work. Then, having seen a few properties sold off, including one in which he was interested, he got the hang of it. He was outbid for the next of his favoured properties, with Andrew having told him he shouldn't bid more than one pound and one shilling an acre.

Finally, after wondering if he would actually be successful, he managed to purchase twenty-two acres for seventeen pounds, twelve shillings, or sixteen shillings an acre on the south side of the Logan River. He made his way to the auction clerk and paid over the land order and received his change. He was told to present himself at the government offices the following day to receive his land title certificate and a map of his property. He would then be free to set about farming the land. In fact, because he had received a land order, he was obliged to start developing the land within the next six months. Also, as the land was now his, he could sell it to whomever and whenever he pleased.

Teddy, Jane, John, and Andrew left the police station in something of a daze. For Teddy, in particular, this seemed an unreal situation. Here was he, a poor crofter who, in Ireland, had struggled for years to feed his family and maybe make a bit of extra money from the sale of surplus produce. And this was done while farming a leased crofter's plot of a few acres, for which he could not afford to pay the full rent. Then he and his family had been evicted, leaving him with no land and no real prospects except for occasional work as a labourer. Now, he had bought and owned twenty-two acres of good farmland.

Although much work was needed to make a farm a reality, nevertheless, he felt he now had his, Jane's and his children's destiny more in his hands. It was both an amazing, but also something of a daunting feeling with so many unknowns and so much to learn in this new land.

"Jane, can you believe it? We now own twenty-two acres of farmland!" exclaimed Teddy, feeling so exhilarated he could have danced a jib as they walked along the dirt road, passing some shops with a two-storey hotel further along.

"Aye, Teddy, we do. The saints be praised. Who would have thought it? Tis something I would have never thought possible last year when there we were trying to find enough food to feed the family while with your mother; God bless and keep her."

"Why don't we celebrate a bit, Father, and have us a meal at the hotel or some chop shop?" suggested Andrew.

"Why not?" said Teddy. "Let's try that hotel up ahead," which they did.

Over a good lunch of steak and kidney pudding, they discussed their next moves and what needed to be done to turn their newly acquired land into a worthwhile farm. There were tools to purchase to remove the trees that would be present and then to build some sort of house. Then they'd need tools to farm the land. But it wasn't going to be easy as their funds for buying these were limited.

Having drawn up a list of items to purchase, they started to discuss how they would go about moving themselves and their belongings down to the Logan Reserve and when.

"I feel the best way to get down there is by boat up the Logan River," volunteered John. "I've been asking around, and there's a boat going down that way every few days now, and the fare isn't that expensive. It'll be much easier to get ourselves and our tools and belongings down there than by hiring a cart or walking down with a wheelbarrow."

Teddy agreed and suggested that John find out what boats might be leaving over the next few weeks.

"Do you and the girls want to come with us when we first go down to the land, Jane? Or we can leave you and them here while we set up a house of some sort, and then you can all join us."

"I'd like to be with you from the start, Teddy, but it'll be hard on the girls. So, perhaps it's best if we stay until you have built some sort of house for us. But how will you manage to do that?"

'We'll use some of the wood from the trees we cut down. One of our purchases will be a cross-cut saw and a good file, and with that, we can make us some boards. I seen how they did it when we went down to Logan earlier. Or, perhaps, we can make it with wattle and daub, like they do back in Ireland, which might be quicker, though the floor will just be dirt, which we'll tamp down and keep dry.'

"That sounds rough, Teddy. And it'll be a tight fit to get us all into this hovel you are planning on building?" replied Jane.

"We'll make it big enough. Then as we get some more money, we can expand or build ourselves a better house."

"You're right, Father," said John. "I feel there's so much potential to make an honest living here. If only we can set ourselves up and get some income, then we can go places; not just you, but the rest of us also."

****

Over the next two weeks, Teddy and his elder sons visited stores and purchased what they would need to get their new life underway. This included axes, hammers, nails, two cross-cut saws, some files and an adze. They also managed to get themselves a second-hand wheelbarrow and a couple of canvas tent flies when they answered a notice pinned to the wall of the hardware store.

Teddy needed to return to the Immigration Society office to obtain some more funds from the helpful clerk, who expressed his satisfaction that they had managed to purchase some land. The pots and pans and eating utensils they had brought from Ireland would stand them in good stead until they got something else, as would their bedding, although the milder climate in Queensland meant they didn't need so much of the heavy, woollen covers.

By the second week in September, they were ready, having also acquired some basic foodstuffs – flour, salt, sugar, tea, dried fruit, onions, potatoes and some fresh mutton. After talking with the locals, they had learned they should be able to get fresh meat locally, either kangaroo from the aborigines or from farmers who had guns. And there was mutton to be had from the local farmers who kept sheep. There was also plenty of fish in the local streams, particularly the Logan River, and Teddy managed to get some fishing line and hooks to add to their pile of goods to be transported down to Logan Agricultural Reserve.

On the day of their departure, Jane and the rest of the family joined Teddy, John and Andrew as they made their way to the bank of the Brisbane River. Everyone carried something to ease the load, though the heaviest items were in the wheelbarrow. At the solid timber wharf was the small steamer that would take them down the Brisbane River, then up the Logan River. It was about ninety feet long with a wooden hull and a low, covered structure at the stern. A solid derrick on the ship was loading cargo into the centrally placed hold, and at the bow was an area covered by canvas. From a narrow funnel, some twelve feet high towards the stern, black coal smoke billowed as if the vessel was impatient to leave.

After paying for their passage and arranging for their goods to be loaded onto the ship, Teddy turned to Jane.

"I don't know how long it will be before we get back to fetch you and the girls, but hopefully, we can have enough land cleared and some sort of a house built in a few weeks."

Then, Teddy, John and Andrew boarded the broad-beamed vessel and found themselves a comfortable spot to sit. As the sun rose in a clear blue sky, the ship's engine came to life with a loud thumping noise, with even more smoke billowing from the funnel. As the vessel eased out into midstream and started down the river, Teddy and his sons watched and waved at Jane, the girls and William, standing watching on the dock.

It took about an hour and a half to reach the mouth of the Brisbane River, where they turned and headed across a choppy Moreton Bay to the mouth of the Logan River, located amidst a series of low islands and mud flats, some twenty miles to the south. It was then a slow and winding journey up the Logan until they arrived at a makeshift jetty by mid-afternoon.

As their tools and supplies were being unloaded, Teddy and his sons were startled to hear a loud voice yelling, "Oi! Is that Teddy Ryan with all that paraphernalia?"

They turned to see the smiling, heavily-bearded face of Don Nettles. "Good afternoon to you, Don. What would you be doing here on this side of the river?"

"I'm here to pick up a new plough and some iron sheets I had sent down from Brisbane. Ordered them when I was up there some time ago. Always needing something. So, you've got yourselves quite a load there, which likely means you've got yourself some land. I think I'd best give you a hand afore I head back home."

Teddy was very grateful to Don for turning up, just as he realised they would have to somehow carry their possessions the mile or so to their new property. They loaded their gear and climbed aboard Don's substantial wagon that already had the plough and iron sheets on board.

Up next to Don, Teddy explained how they had acquired twenty-two acres of land not far from the Logan River and were now intent on starting their life there.

"Best build yourselves a hut to start with," suggested Don. "Of course, you're gonna have to start cutting down some trees even to get room for a house, but then you can use the timber from those to build your hut. And strip the bark off to use for the roof, overlapping it like tiles to seal it off, then nailing it down."

"I was thinking of making the walls from wattle and daub like they do in some places back in Ireland," said Teddy. "Do you think that might work, Don?"

"Well, you can try that, and a few have built huts like that around here. But the rain here is something fierce. It ain't anything like you would have seen in Ireland. Comes down in torrents, it can, and that will quickly wash your daub away. No, you'd best make yourselves a slab hut."

"A slab hut! Now, what would that be?" asked a puzzled Andrew.

"It's pretty easy, really. When you've cut down some trees, cut them into lengths about ten feet long. Next, you want to take the bark off, and it's best to do that as soon after you fell the tree as possible. You use the back of your axe and go along the trunk, hitting the bark all over. Then using the axe, cut into the bark and strip it off. It's probably best, though, to cut lines along the bark with your axe where you want the bark to come off. I'll show you what I mean when you cut your first tree. Then, once the bark is off, use your axe, or a maul is better, with some wedges and split off flitches as wide as you like. A lot of these eucalypts split pretty easy. Again, I can show you when you cut a tree down. These flitches or slabs will be the walls of the hut that you can nail to longer posts or flitches you've set in the ground. Of course, you could always use your crosscut saw to make planks, but that will take you forever by pit-sawing."

Teddy and the boys had more questions for Don as they slowly made their way along the dusty track. Don invited them to stay the night with him and his missus before setting out to establish their own farm, for which they were again grateful.

They arrived late afternoon at Don's dwelling to be greeted by Gini.

"I found these three blokes just off the boat from Brisbane and so gave them a lift. They now have a plot of land down here and are anxious to get to work on it. Anyway, I said they could have a meal and stay the night with us, maybe even stay here until they get their own shelter if their place isn't too far away."

Gini smiled at the three Ryan men. "Of course, you are very welcome."

"We're most grateful for your offer, and, of course, we'll contribute to your larder with some of our own food that we've brought down. We have got a tent we can put up, and, hopefully, we can get something of a house up before too long on our own place," replied Teddy. "Could we decide on whether to accept your offer to stay with you until after we've seen our plot and how far away it is?"

"To be sure, that would be fine. You'd always be welcome."

Settling In

Early next morning, the three Ryan men joined Don on his wagon, which still had their tools on board. They headed down the track to the river, waiting for a pontoon ferry to carry them across to the south side. Don had offered to carry them and their belongings to their plot as well as to give some advice on how they should proceed with clearing the land and demonstrate a few techniques. It was a cool morning, although with the sunlight filtering through the overhead canopy and with only a few clouds, it looked like a warmer day ahead. The birds were in full chorus in the surrounding bush, making such a noise it was difficult at times to hear each other talking.

After landing on the south bank, they consulted the crude map they had got from the government office when Teddy obtained his land title. The men then set off to find their plot of land. At first, the dirt track took them through tall forest with stands of straight, white-barked flooded gum mixed with other rainforest species. Further along the track, the forest became more open with gum-barked eucalypts, like blackbutt and grey gum, but also thick-barked stringybarks and ironbarks, mixed with lower acacia bushes. There was evidence that many other plots along the way were being prepared for farming, with trees cleared and the rudiments of houses taking shape.

About a mile from the river, they found one of their property's corner markers, emblazoned with the number of their plot and arrows showing the direction of the property boundaries. The three Ryan men stood looking at the land enclosed within the boundary. From where they stood, masses of tall trees lay across the land, except where some had been felled earlier, as evidenced by large tree stumps.

Andrew voiced their mutual thoughts. "It's wonderful looking land, Father, but, oh, what a job to clear this lot and make something of it."

"It's gonna be a mighty task to clear these trees, though maybe it's not all like this," said Teddy. "The sooner we get started, though, the sooner we'll get us a house and put some crops in."

The men first walked around the plot's perimeter and established the boundary as they found more tree blazes. Then they meandered through the centre of it, gaining an impression of the lie of the land and also of the vegetation that was present. Being on a river floodplain, it was quite flat, with shallow swales and a creek traversing the land that would provide water for the household. The vegetation was mainly tall eucalypts, with some scattered large figs, including several strangler figs with their whitish roots twined around a large tree that was succumbing to the fig's embrace. There was also the odd hoop and bunya pine with their sharp leaves. Along the creek were tree ferns and several rainforest tree species, including red cedar and pencil cedar.

The soil, where they could see it, was a deep, dark loam, and John voiced what the others were thinking. "Would you look at that soil, Father! It looks so rich that any crops we planted would give a really good yield."

A site for their house was selected on a slight rise to one side of the plot, and it was here that they commenced to fell the trees. Don showed how this could best be done, first with an undercut on the side to which they wished the tree to fall. Andrew and John used axes to cut out large chunks of wood for the undercut, pale on the outside of the trunk but dark red or brown when they reached the heartwood.

None of the Ryan men had been faced with felling such large trees with wood much harder than any in Ireland, and six months on the ship had weakened what condition they had. So, although both young men went to work with gusto, they were soon sweating profusely and their arms and backs were feeling the strain.

Once the undercut was through about a third of the trunk, Teddy and Don used the large crosscut saw to cut the tree from the opposite side until John yelled that the top was starting to move. Pulling the saw out, the men ran back a safe distance and watched as, with a tearing crash, the forest giant fell, scaring trees and ripping off branches from other trees in its path until finally shaking the ground as it hit.

Teddy, Andrew and John stood back with Don and surveyed the tree now lying on the ground, with the trunk as high as the men's chests. They had made a start on their future.

"That took some doing, Father," was John's comment. "I dare say we will get better at it over time."

"Aye, that we will. But will you look at that beautiful timber," said Teddy as he ran his hand over the red heartwood of the felled forest giant.

On that first day, they managed to fell seven trees, but they were all exhausted in the end. Their hands were raw from blisters, their arms ached, and their backs felt as if they had been on the rack. But a quick dip in the river and a good meal that night at Don and Gini's prepared them for the next day's work. Don suggested that they piss on their hands to toughen them. In the meantime, they would need to wind cloths around their hands to try and stop more blistering.

He also instructed them on how to burn out the stumps to at least get level ground for their house. This took about ten days. During that time, they had set about cutting up some of the felled logs into suitable lengths using the cross-cut saw. It was dangerous work as the section that had been cut could roll and trap one of them beneath it unless they wedged small logs under the trunk to stabilise it. On one occasion, Teddy had a narrow escape from serious injury or death when a tree bounced back towards him as it fell before he could get out of its way.

Following Don's advice, they set about removing some bark from the cut sections. Then, using axes, mauls, and wedges, the men began splitting off slabs, each about a foot wide. Having erected a series of posts in the ground to form the framework for the house, they used the slabs to enclose the walls and the bark as roofing material. A few windows were cut, and a fireplace with a chimney was built using wood; they would later parge with mortar obtained on a trip to Brisbane.

After spending the first two nights with Don and Gini, Teddy felt they would be better off camping under their tent on their selection. However, they would head up to Don's place every few days to enjoy Gini's cooking and spend the night. The Ryan men contributed some of their food supplies to these meals. But with that and their own food consumption, fuelling a day's hard work, they found they had underestimated how much food would be needed with such manual labour. Luckily, Don was able to help them out by shooting kangaroos or wallabies, of which there was an abundant supply in the surrounding bush. There was also plenty of good fish in the Logan River, and when they could, one of the Ryan men would try his luck with the fishing tackle they had purchased, usually with success. A grilled, freshly caught bream, bass or mullet with potatoes roasted in the coals of the fire was a treat they had not experienced before.

Occasionally, one of the aboriginal men would come by with a freshly speared kangaroo and some local bush food such as purple quandong berries or even honey from native bee hives. Teddy, Andrew, and John had been fascinated by these nearly naked black men with unkempt hair and beards. They all looked like they could do with a good meal, but there was a tough wiriness about their physiques that indicated a life used to hard physical work and an adequate diet. These aboriginals were friendly, though somewhat shy and wary of the white settlers. But they had come to realise the value of money to purchase goods and so were keen to obtain some currency.

It took a further two weeks to complete the house to a state where, at least, it was habitable, although the floor was beaten earth. At John's suggestion, a ditch had been dug around the outside to stop rainwater from flowing in. Another ten days were spent making some furniture by sawing some of the logs and using slabs. This meant that a pit had first to be dug, deep enough for a man to stand in and pull down the crosscut saw. Don then instructed the Ryan men on how to set up the log and saw straight planks, which was not an easy task and required more back-breaking work by both the sawyer balanced on the log and the man underneath. Ultimately, they managed to produce a rudimentary table, a bench, stools and some bedsteads.

After the first three weeks, although the land was only partially cleared and a number of trees ringbarked, Teddy decided to start planting some vegetables. Once these were growing but protected against browsing kangaroos or wallabies, he felt it was time to fetch the rest of the family down from Brisbane. It was nearly two months since he had left Jane in Brisbane and headed down to start their farm.

Over the last few weeks, Teddy and his sons had also been busy cutting boards, which they hoped to sell in Brisbane to get cash for further purchases. Don happily agreed to take Teddy and his boards up to Brisbane and bring back Jane, Teddy's four daughters and William, together with the goods and chattels they had brought from Ireland. He said he would also take the opportunity to get a few supplies for himself and the missus.

****

The following day, in early November, Teddy joined Don, leaving John and Andrew to continue with the land clearing and tending to the vegetables, and headed up the track to Brisbane. Arriving about mid-afternoon, he went in search of Jane at their lodgings. It was a happy family reunion, with the girls and William all eager to hear of what had happened down at their new home.

"Have you built us a house yet, Father?" asked Tessie solemnly.

"That we've done, my little one. It may not be too grand at the moment, but it will do, and we can build more on to it in the months ahead. There's no shortage of timber to build with," he said, looking also at Jane. "Ah, love, I hope you will like it for what it is. Rough and ready it may be, but it's our own home."

Jane, who could not but be infected with her children's enthusiasm, eyed Teddy tenderly. "I am sure you have done us proud, Teddy Ryan, but now it's gonna need a woman's hand to finish it off."

"Aye, it could certainly do with a woman's touch, and you're very welcome to add those touches."

Teddy had no trouble selling the lumber he had brought up, and he obtained an order for more of the solid eucalypt timber needed for the expanding town of Brisbane. The money he received added to their limited supply of cash, which they then used to purchase a few more tools, some more fishing tackle, plus a good quantity of foodstuffs. Anne suggested they should get some chickens. Teddy and Jane agreed, and with Maria's help, the two sisters managed to buy four hens and a rooster.

Later that day, as Don surveyed all the belongings, tools and foodstuffs to be moved down to Logan, he announced that it would take two trips to move it all, as he also had several items to take back. So, it was agreed that Jane, Maria, and Tessie would remain behind, with Don promising to come back in a day or two to collect them and the rest of their belongings.

The following day, with Don's help, they moved their belongings and purchases over on the ferry and loaded them onto the cart. Don and Teddy arranged things to give Anne and the others somewhere to sit, and off they set, south along Slacks Track. True to his word, Don returned with Teddy the next day to collect Jane, Maria and Tessie and the rest of their belongings. By this time, Jane was very glad to be leaving the depot that had been their home for some two and a half months. Very few *Erin go Bragh* passengers remained in the depot as the great majority had found alternative accommodation and employment. Passengers from other miorder ships had moved in, although most of these were now elsewhere.

Unfortunately, the detritus left behind by the departing passengers had made the depot a stinking mess.

It was late spring. The day was bright and sunny and their future also seemed bright as the cart slowly trundled along the dusty track. The sun's heat and brilliance were more intense than they were used to in Ireland and Jane found it particularly severe, dressed as she was in heavy woollen clothes, more suitable to the wet and chilly Irish climate. Now and then, they would spy a group of kangaroos browsing in the forest's shade or a large goanna or lace monitor slowly making its way up a tree. The younger ones were fascinated by these strange animals, yelling excitedly with each new discovery.

At one point, Don stopped the wagon and pointed to a large brown snake crossing the track ahead.

"You see that snake? Well, you be careful to stay well clear if you see one, as they can make you very sick or even kill you if they bite you."

The children sat mesmerised as they watched the Eastern Brown Snake slither into the grass on the road's edge.

At last, they made it to their plot, with Don bringing the cart up to the new house with the sons and Anne there to greet them and help unload the wagon. Teddy turned to watch Jane's reaction; as usual, it was straightforward and to the point.

"Well, this is certainly a different dwelling to what we're used to. But you've certainly done a fine job making us a home, Teddy. It might be a mite small for all of us. However, I dare say it will do, for now."

The children all helped to unload the cart and move their belongings, tools and food into the hut. As they were still organising themselves and the younger children exploring their surroundings later in the afternoon, Don returned with his wife, bearing a hamper containing a hot kangaroo stew and damper.

"I thought you might like something to eat on your first night here as we thought you may not have set yourselves up to cook," explained Gini.

"Ah, that's most kind of you, and God bless you for that," exclaimed Jane. "Well, you'd best stay and we can share the meal together. It's a good chance to get to know each other as it seems like we're to be sort of neighbours. And you'd best be telling me how you make this bread thing. What did you call it?"

'Damper, and it is easy to make. But I'll show you. Come up to our place tomorra."

After supper, the adults sat and talked around the fire that had been built in the outdoor fireplace. It was here that their food would be cooked until the indoor fireplace and chimney had been parged with the mortar obtained in Brisbane and properly finished. After Don and Gini left, the family prepared to sleep, the bedding having already been set up.

Lying next to Jane in their rudimentary bed in the still of the dark night, Teddy felt a deep sense of gratitude and satisfaction that they had finally arrived at their destination. The occasional sound of some alien bird or creature from the surrounding forest seemed to only add to the tranquility he felt, surrounded by his beloved wife and family in contrast to the months spent in the overcrowded and fetid tween deck of the *Erin go Bragh*.

Jane turned, put her arm over Teddy's chest, and murmured, "This is a might strange experience and so different from what we've known all our lives till a few months ago. We aren't sleeping in some freezing stone house in a town surrounded by all sorts of other people that we've known most of our lives. We also didn't have any land to call our own, and half the time, particularly after we were evicted from our crofter plot, we weren't sure where the next pratie was coming from. Here we are, sleeping in this strange forest, in our own home, such as it is, and on our own land, with the nearest neighbour out of sight. It's so warm that we don't need any of this bedding to cover us. And instead of Patrick O'Farrell's drunken voice, as he makes his way home from the pub, we have these other night noises from the forest that are sort of comforting."

"Ah, to be sure, my love. It is so different. I never imagined it would be like this when Father Dunne told us about getting passage on that ship and coming out to a new start in Queensland. Nobody could have explained what it would really be like. You wait till you hear the birds singing as the sun comes up. It is deafening. But there are things that I miss from Ireland, like the soft green hills and mist rising in the chill of early morning. And I keep thinking about my mother and wondering how she is faring, knowing that I shan't see her again in this life. There's also friends that I miss, though, I daresay we'll make new friends here."

John and Andrew were up early and headed out to clear more land for their main agricultural crop, which they had decided would be sugar cane. They would also plant more vegetables for their own use and to sell to gain income. With orders for more lumber in Brisbane, they also needed to produce more of this from the felled trees. John suggested that because their land was not far from the Logan River, it would be best to ship lumber to Brisbane by boat on the river. The elder girls were helping to organise things in their new house while Tessie and William had set about exploring more of the bush near the house, with a warning from their father to watch for snakes.

Jane and Teddy had walked some way from the house so that Teddy could show her *their* land. Yes, *their* land. This was something he was still learning to appreciate fully. Returning to the house, Jane looked at their dwelling in a different light.

"Teddy, I can hardly believe that this land with these magnificent trees and good soil is truly ours, that we actually own it! And that that there weird-looking hut is our house. I sometimes doubted, thinking that the dream you had for us would come true, particularly with all those hard times on the ship that I didn't think would end. But now I'm looking at your dream for us. You're right, Teddy; this is truly a new start!"

"There's still a lot of hard work, but we now have our destinies more in our hands and not in the hands of some pesky English landlord. And it isn't just you and me, Jane; it's our children's destiny as well. The boys can go on and get their own land in time and there are other good ways of earning money. In fact, John seems to be already thinking of making something of himself. He's been talking about ways of making more lumber and saying how he could help make some of the roads, like Slack's Track, much better. The girls also have better prospects for their future."

Then turning to Jane, he looked into her eyes with love in his. "But I could not have done it without your help and strength, my love, despite your doubts. Thank you."

Jane looked up at Teddy and with a twinkle in her eye said, "Now, don't you be goin' all soft and sentimental on me, Teddy Ryan. There's work that needs doing, but firstly, could we make our house a bit bigger and put in some separate rooms for sleeping."

"Of course we can, Jane. Anything is possible."

Epilogue

The year was 1878 and Teddy was resting comfortably on the veranda of the house he and his son John had built at Tambourine some fourteen miles south of Waterford where he had acquired that first twenty-two acres of land in 1862. It was late afternoon, although it was still possible to be enjoying the winter sunshine. That enjoyment had been boosted by the presence of John Gavan. They had known and helped each other in Ireland as well as on the journey out to Queensland. John's wife, Mary, had helped to suckle Teddy and Jane's son, Peter when Jane was short of breast milk. John and Mary, with their six children, had also obtained land in the Logan Agricultural Reserve – ninety-seven acres across the Logan River from the land that John Ryan had subsequently acquired.

John Gavan had managed to buy a jug of half-decent Irish whiskey, which the two men were now sharing as the sun moved towards the horizon and the shadows lengthened. Teddy looked across at the sun sparkling on the smooth surface of the Albert River that flowed just below his property, and his thoughts reflected on the journey that had led to his family being where they were now.

"You know, John, after we'd been evicted from our crofter's lot and were living with my mother in Kilclonfert, I would never have dreamed that one day I'd be sitting on the veranda of my own home, with my own land in such glorious countryside."

"You're right, Teddy. Aye, it was a brave move to come out from Ireland all those years ago, but I felt we had to seize the opportunity, particularly for you, as your prospects weren't looking good in Ireland. It proved to be a good decision as your family has gone on to prosper here, though it was difficult for us all when we first got here."

"To be sure, it was backbreaking work and I thank God we had John and Andrew, who did much of the hard, manual work, particularly down near the Logan River. They certainly helped make a success of farming our land there," mused Teddy. "Apart from some vegetables, we mainly grew sugar cane, and there was a growing market for sugar, including for the making of that rum at Beenleigh."

"So, what made you move from the Logan to here?" asked John.

"Well, we'd seen what the country was like up this way, and it was getting sort of crowded down around the Logan. So, in 1867, with money earned from farming our land at Logan and selling lumber, I and others in the family were able to purchase more land around the Tambourine area. Jane and I, together with Kate, William and Tessie, moved to this house before that year was out. I also decided to get into grazing some cattle for beef, which has been quite successful, so I don't regret the move at all."

"But it was your John who has done very well for himself, Teddy. You must be right proud of him."

"Yes, that I am. He always was one for finding a way of making some money. Back in Ireland, he was out working on them roads and building bridges, which taught him a lot that he's been using here. Only a couple of years after we got here, he applied for and got that order to purchase a further fifty-six acres of land on the bank of the Logan River, plus a lease over a further sixty-two acres of adjacent land on the river.

"John also had other ideas besides farming. He saw how we could sell the lumber from the trees we cut down on our property for all them new buildings up in Brisbane. Then using his share of the money from that, he managed to establish a sawmill in the Albert River area. Then he started using his experience in building roads and bridges in Ireland to do the same around here. And there was much need for such work with so much development in and around Brisbane and the other towns. It looks like he has done very well at it.

"Never one for standing still, John also managed to purchase land at Tambourine, and then he married a nice colleen from Baillybrian, Kings County. He was the first of our children to marry, and the whole family attended the wedding in 1864 at St Patrick's down on 'Spiddle', Michael Yore's property, on the south bank of the Albert River. Of course, you know all about it as you and Mary were there as well. The bride was Mary Elizabeth Killian, though everyone calls her Elizabeth, for what reason I don't know. She's nine years older than John, but they seem well suited to each other."

"Ah, to be sure, they do at that!" exclaimed John Gavan as he topped up Teddy's and his own glass. "And they've given you four grandsons."

"Yes, even though Elizabeth was thirty-two when they got married. Their first child, Michael Edward, was born back in 1865, although sadly, he died the following year. Then, there was Edward Thomas, James John and, finally, William Killian, who was born in 1871 at their property near the Albert River, Tambourine. Jane, in particular, was over the moon with having the grandchildren and is forever down there helping out; God bless her."

"You have been so lucky to have a woman like Jane to help you and the family through all your troubles and then coming out and setting up down here," ventured John.

"Oh, I tell you, John, if it weren't for Jane, I am not sure how we would have managed. She's small with not much meat on her bones, but she's a feisty one. And she's the practical one. I'm a bit of a dreamer. But Jane brings me down to earth and reality, often with her sharp tongue. I miss Jane so much, even now, John. It was two years ago, come July, that she left us.

"She had been sick for some three weeks with lung problems and the cold here at Tamborine didn't help none. Finally, Dr Doherty said she'd got pleurisy, and that was too much for her. All of us except Andrew and Peter were there when she passed. She was just fifty-four, but her life had been a hard one, giving birth to and caring for eight children, and it was particularly hard after we got evicted from our crofter's plot back in Ireland. It was a wonder how she adapted to the new conditions when we moved to our own place down by the Logan River."

"What about the other children, Teddy? I know that your older daughters have done well for themselves."

"To be sure, to be sure. Our Annie found herself a good man, Michael Yore, from County Meath. They were married at St Stephen's Church in Brisbane in 1866. Michael had come out to Moreton Bay on the *Fiery Star* in 1863 and bought himself some land not far from us the following year. We were all a close lot of farmers down along the Logan and around the new town of Waterford, and it was there that Michael met Annie. Then, he started turning up to help out on our farm, the sly devil; and that gave him and Annie a chance to spend some time together, though Jane was always strict about making sure Maria or Kate, if not herself, were always present."

"Then, in May of the same year, Maria also got married at St Stephen's. She was eighteen and a pretty young colleen. It was no wonder that she caught the eye of Thomas Plunkett, who had come out from County Meath on the *Fiery Star* with Michael Yore. He had also got himself some land that he was farming not far from ours near Waterford, on the south side of the Logan near Dairy Creek. Tom was that keen on Maria, even though he was nine years older than her, that he walked the twenty-odd miles from Waterford, just south of the Logan River, to Brisbane to make the wedding arrangements. Now, would you believe it, he was in so much of a hurry to get married that he forgot to get my permission? So, back he walked to our property, got my permission, in writing, as required, and walked the twenty miles back again to Brisbane the next day!"

"Well, that says something about the lad's resolve as well as his love and dedication for Maria, I would think," said John.

"No doubt about it, John. He was fair smitten by Maria, and I'm not surprised. She is a wonderful person, always helping out, but with a good sense of humour. Anyway, they were married by Father Robert Dunne. You remember, he was that priest who organised us all to come out on the *Erin go Bragh*. He frightened the life out of my mother when he turned up on our doorstep back in Kilclonfert to tell us about getting a passage out here. She thought one of us had died, having a priest suddenly come to her house like that."

"Aye, I remember him well. Having organised for us all to get on the ship, he came out with us as the chaplain on the *Erin go Bragh*. He certainly helped us through some hard times. And that voyage was no picnic with all them people dying, particularly the little ones and some of the parents going out of their minds with grief."

"Well," continued Teddy, "Thomas and Maria first settled on Thomas's property near the Logan River. Then, in October 1869, Thomas purchased a hundred and fifteen acres of land on the banks of the Albert River in Ward County, not far from here. The couple moved there in January 1870, and Tom became the first postmaster for the district.[7] They've now got five children, two boys and three girls, and I suspect there are more to come.

"We have also had some heartbreaks, John, though I guess most families do. Now, could you please put a bit

---

[7] He later became a MLA representing Logan and Albert with Plunkett Road in the area probably named after him.

more of that poteen in my glass here. Dr Doherty says it isn't good for this pain I get in my belly. But it's starting to get chilly, and my bones need warming; and besides, I find a drop of holy water helps cheer me up."

John Gavan obliged. "I heard all about Andrew. That was a tragic accident, Teddy. It was just after you moved here, wasn't it?"

"Aye. Christmas was not a happy occasion in 1867. He was only twenty-five and both Jane and I were heartbroken that another of our children had died before his time. It was a freak accident, it seems. He had ridden his horse from our place on the Logan up to the new racecourse and as he was racing around the track, following some friends, he fell off his horse and was badly injured. They brought him home here and Dr Doherty was caring for him, but there was nothing he could do, and Andrew died three days later, on Christmas Day.

"The following year, though, in June 1868, our dear Catherine (Kate) married William Walsh, in Brisbane. He was another Irishman from County Mallow. They also bought some good land close by us here near the Albert River, where they settled down to raise their children. It was tragic that in May of 1876, Catherine died at her home in Tambourine after giving birth to a daughter. She was only twenty-five. The couple already had three sons[8]. Jane took it particularly badly, and it may even have hastened her end two months later.

"John, it wasn't just myself, but others in our growing family who felt it was good to settle in Tambourine and the Albert River area. By the 1870s, all the Ryan family, including our married daughters with their husbands, had moved and acquired land around here. When they opened up for applications to buy land around Tambourine in 1875, I and a couple of others in the family tried our luck.

---

[8] *The Brisbane Courier 9 May 1876.*

I myself was selected for two hundred and three acres. However, I decided not to take up the land as I had too much to do on the land we had, what with our family moving out. I later picked up eighty acres at Tambourine, at five shillings an acre in 1877, and will use it to graze more cattle."

"What about your youngest daughter, Tessie? I understand she is becoming a woman in her own right."

"Yes, Teresa got herself a lease on two hundred and seventy-three acres of land at Mount Tamborine a couple of years ago but only started paying rent earlier this year. She always had a mind of her own, and I think she's planning on grazing cattle on it. There's a two-room house on the property and it's been partly cleared, with about two hundred acres of it having been ringbarked.

"John also obtained land with a successful application for a hundred acres at Tambourine in 1875[9]; although, that same year, he was unlucky and lost out on a hundred and twenty acres of agricultural land and two hundred acres of pastoral land in a ballot.[10] But then, he has enough going for him anyway, what with his road works and sawmilling."

---

[9] *The Queenslander, 11 September 1875.*
[10] Perhaps the land they gained was wholly or partly available as a result of the *Crown Lands Alienation Act of 1868*. This Act was a serious attempt by the Queensland Government to increase agricultural productivity and, at the same time, reduce the political power of the pastoral fraternity. Achieving these objectives was seen to be through the creation of a rural yeomanry on small farms, with this legislation being the first to use the words 'selector' and 'selection'. In the hands of writers such as Henry Lawson, these words were later firmly implanted into Australia's rural mythology. Among other provisions, the Act split large pastoral holdings in two, one half of which was subdivided into selections varying in extent from forty to one hundred and sixty acres. Theoretically, this made it possible for those with little capital to establish themselves on the land, for selections were procurable at quite low prices or on leases.

"How are you managing, Teddy, with your Jane now gone these last two years?"

"Oh, I'm doing well enough, John. I've got family on all sides and not too far away, and my daughters make sure I get a square meal. And then, John and I have been busy building the hotel at Tambourine this year. It's a grand site, right by the Albert River and near the property where Catherine and William lived, while both Maria and Anne and their husbands have land just down the road. It is the first hotel in the area."

"By the way, did you read in the paper, Teddy, that after its voyage to Moreton Bay, the *Erin go Bragh* sailed down to Sydney where they inspected the hull because of all them leaks? Apparently, they somehow fixed it up enough and it sailed off to some place called Calao in South America with Captain Borlase in command, and his wife and daughter also on board. I figure it might have been lucky to make it there cos even if they patched it up, the ship was that old it was almost falling to pieces, even before it got hit by some of them wild storms. Heaven help the captain and his wife and daughter. I hope they make it home safely, wherever home is."

"Ah, to be sure, it was a wreck when we were sailing on her, so I doubt she will stay afloat for much longer after the voyage out here.

"You know, John, when I left Ireland, I felt I was leaving my birthright and home. But we have done well here and have had more comfort than would have been possible back in Ireland. It was strange and difficult to start with, though with all of us helping, we made ourselves a home. To me, this is home now, although there will always be a place in my heart for Ireland with its green rolling hills and the smell of peat smoke in the air in the late afternoon."

****

Edward (Teddy) Ryan passed away on the 6th of September, 1878, at his home in Tambourine, aged sixty-eight. His death certificate describes him as a grazier. He had been suffering for some ten months with a liver complaint, which was cited as the cause of his death.

Teresa (Tessie) Ryan went on to get freehold title on her two hundred and seventy-three acres at Mount Tamborine in July 1884. She did not get married till 1884, at the age of 28, when she married Charles Alfred Beetham on the 21st of January in the Catholic Church in Tamborine. According to the 1919 Electoral Roles, the couple had moved to Beaudesert, not far from the Tamborine area south of Brisbane. They had four children: John Francis (Frank), Marian Evelyn, Thomas Shepherd, and Teresa Eileen.

William (Will) Ryan married Catherine (Kate) Egan on the 12th of September 1891 in Brisbane. They also moved to Beaudesert. The couple had five children: Andrew Thomas, Theresa Jane, Ethel May, Catherine Elsie, and Isma Philomena.

Author's Notes

How Vast is the Ocean - An Odyssey of Desperation and Hope is based on the travails of the Ryan family as they emigrated to Australia in 1862 aboard the *Erin go Bragh*. As much as possible, I have stuck to the facts I found from various sources, particularly newspaper reports and letters sourced through Trove, the website for the Australian National Library. Other sources were the log, crew and passenger list of the *Erin go Bragh*, plus several communications with other descendants of passengers on the *Erin go Bragh*.

They Came Direct – "Erin-go-Bragh" 1862, compiled by Eileen B. Johnson, was an invaluable source of information about the ship, the passengers, and the regulations relating to such emiorder ships, as well as numerous reports, notices and communications regarding the voyage. Jim Burke's *Gunyah, Grit & Gantry* also provided useful information.

There is much I had to make up as I went along or deduce as best as I could using what related facts or information I had. For example, given that the *Erin go Bragh* was delayed by stormy weather from reaching Queenstown as expected, I surmised that the journey to Cork by train would be a wet and stormy one.

I determined that the Ryan family were not part of the Geashill evictions. However, Griffith's Valuation states they had leased some forty acres of land from Baron Greene in the Parish of Kilclonfert in 1854. Then Edward Ryan was arraigned for stealing bread a few years later. This information, combined with the fact that there were difficult times for farmers in the late 1850s in Ireland, led me to deduce that Edward and his family had been evicted from Baron Greene's estate.

Having records from the ship's log of deaths on board, which also stated the latitude and longitude coordinates on the date of the death, enabled me to plot the ship's course and determine its average speed over the distance between deaths. The appended map is based on this data.

The extended length of the voyage (one hundred and seventy-four days), which normally would have taken about a hundred and forty days, has been put down by press reports at the time to storms and very light winds. Certainly, the average speed of the *Erin go Bragh* over the whole trip was only about four knots or seven and a half kilometres per hour, whereas such ships should have averaged about five knots over the voyage.

There were times when the ship was sailing in the southern Indian Ocean between latitude 40 and 44 degrees south, and taking advantage of the strong westerly winds, that it averaged nearly eight knots. On other occasions, earlier in the voyage, it averaged less than three knots, just a good walking pace. It made slow progress off the coast of South America, with its track suggesting the captain was looking for favourable winds.

As I surmise in the narrative, the discovery of serious leaks in the hull would have necessitated being cautious with speed in rough weather so as not to exacerbate the situation. The holes that were drilled in the hull were reported by the Queensland press. The vessel was quite old and the hull made from pine, which meant that movement of the hull timber and loss of caulking would have been an increasing problem. The fact that the hull had a copper bottom would have helped contain the problem, but the sheets of copper were only nailed on, and water seepage over time would have been inevitable.

The lack of food in the latter stages before the ship called into Hobart was to be expected when as per the certificate signed by Captain Borlase: *Provisions actually laden on board this ship are sufficient, according to the requirements of the Passengers' Act for 387 Statute Adults for a voyage of 140 days.* This referred to the trip from

Queenstown to Brisbane. A 'statute adult' was defined as a passenger of twelve years and upwards or two passengers between the ages of one and twelve. So young children basically were on half rations.

There are several passenger lists, with slight variations in the number of passengers. My best estimate is that there were a total of four hundred and thirty-eight passengers, of whom eighty-eight were children between one and twelve years of age. This means the total number of 'adult' passengers was three hundred and fifty plus forty-four (half of the eighty-eight children) for a total requiring provisions as three hundred and ninety-four. This is already slightly more than the three hundred and eighty-seven for whom rations were provided and for which the ship was registered to carry. Then, in addition, the voyage actually involved one hundred and sixty-four days of sea travel, twenty-four days more than the period for which provisions were supplied.

The ship called into Cape Town to mainly replenish their water supplies, but I am sure the captain would have taken advantage to also add to his food provisions. However, as I imply, there were limits to this, given that the *Erin go Bragh* would have been an unexpected arrival and the need to provision many other ships already in port. So, by the time the *Erin go Bragh* was well on her way across the southern Indian Ocean to Australia, it seemed inevitable that food would have been in short supply. Subsequent reports by passengers in the Queensland press of existing on hard tack and salt pork were probably true. This is further verified by the fact that the ship made an unscheduled call into Hobart Town to take on more food provisions.

I assumed that the Ryan family were able to secure at least some land order assistance to permit them to buy their twenty-two acres in late 1862. There is then documented evidence that two years later, John Ryan purchased fifty-six acres and leased sixty-two acres on the banks of the Logan River, probably some months before marrying Mary Elizabeth Killian in August of 1864.

Paul Ryan
October 2023

Voyage of Erin go Bragh from Queenstown

Date	Distance Travelled (N. miles)	Days Travelled	Average Speed (knots)	Comments
28 Jan				Departs Liverpool
8 Feb				Departs Queenstown
13 Feb	494	5	3.5	First death
25 Feb	550	12	2	
1 Mar	510	4	5.5	
3 Mar	123	2	5.1	
5 Mar	280	2	5.8	
8 Mar	280	3	4	
14 Mar	820	6	5.5	
19 Mar	610	5	4.25	
25 Mar	580	6	4	
26 Mar	53	1	2.2	
27 Mar	53	1	2.2	
28 Mar	81	1	3.4	
30 Mar	304	2	6.3	
1 Apr	194	2	4.4	
2 Apr	84	1	3.5	
12 Apr	830	10	3.5	
14 Apr	280	2	5.8	
19 Apr	363	5	3	
23 Apr	260	4	2.7	
25 Apr	153	2	3.2	
6 May	1088	11	4.1	
7 May	160	1	6.7	
14 May	691	7	4	Arrives in Table Bay, Cape Town
Sub-Totals	8841	95	3.9	
17 May				Departs Table Bay
21 May	330	4	3.4	
30 May	996	9	4.6	
6 June	1344	7	8.0	

7 June	170	1	7.1	
28 June	2050	21	4.1	
3 July	420	5	3.5	
10 July	900	7	5.4	
11 July	45	1	2	Five days in Hobart Town
Sub-Totals	6255	55	4.7	
18 July	40	0.5	3.3	Leaving Hobart
31 July	1100	13	3.5	North of Moreton Island
1 Aug	40	0.5	3.3	Moreton Bay
Sub-Totals	1180	14	3.5	
Total	16376	164	4.1	

Track of the Erin go Bragh, Based on the Ship's Log

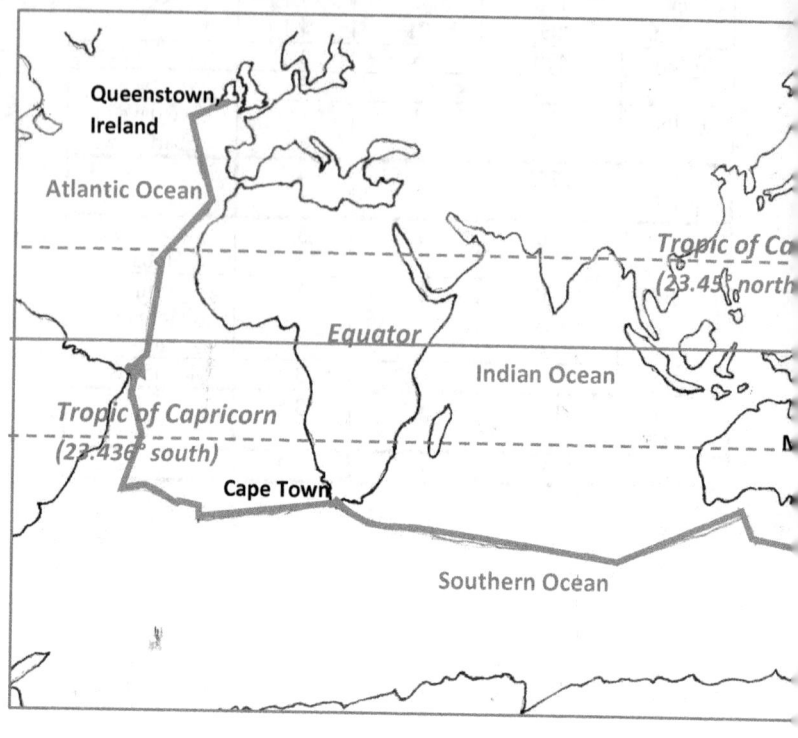

www.ingramcontent.com/pod-product-compliance
Lightning Source LLC
Chambersburg PA
CBHW050306010526
44107CB00055B/2129